# Praise for
## *Beat the Blues Before They Beat You*

"*Beat the Blues Before Th... ...You is a masterful* guide by a masterful clinician. It k... ...out the typical problems of depression and provides clear explanations as to how to solve them. This is a must-read for anyone suffering from depression— and who hasn't at some point in his or her life?"

— **Aaron T. Beck, M.D.**, Emeritus Professor
in the Department of Psychiatry at the University of
Pennsylvania, winner of the Lasker Award in Medicine

"*If you are depressed or vulnerable to depression, this book is for you. Written by one of the world's leading experts in cognitive-behavior therapy, it provides a thoughtful and balanced account of depression and how to overcome it using tried and tested strategies.*"

— **Christopher G. Fairburn, M.D.**, Professor of Psychiatry,
University of Oxford, author of *Overcoming Binge Eating*

"*Dr. Leahy is unique in the mental-health field in his combination of high rigor, accessibility, and readability to consumers and clinicians alike. His new book, **Beat the Blues Before They Beat You**, is the epitome of these qualities and will be of genuine help to those who suffer from depression.*"

— **Thomas Joiner**, distinguished Research Professor and Bright-Burton
Professor of Psychology, author of *Why People Die from Suicide*

"**Beat the Blues Before They Beat You** *gives clear-headed, concise, and practical guidelines for tackling the most common problems in depression. Based on the most current research and clinical work, Leahy once again gives you the tools to help yourself overcome your depression. It's a book that you can pick up and start using today. Empowering, engaging, and enlightening.*"

— **Allison Harvey**, University of California, Berkeley

"*Eminently readable and practical, this state-of-the-art book provides compassionate and user-friendly help for beating depression. I highly recommend it both to practitioners and their patients.*"

— **G. Terence Wilson, Ph.D.**, Oscar K. Buros Professor of Psychology,
... ...w Jersey

# BEAT the
# BLUES
## BEFORE THEY
## BEAT YOU

# ALSO BY ROBERT LEAHY, PH.D.

*Anxiety Free**

*The Worry Cure*

*The Therapeutic Relationship in the
Cognitive Behavioral Psychotherapies*

*Contemporary Cognitive Therapy*

*Psychological Treatment of Bipolar Disorder*

*Roadblocks in Cognitive-Behavioral Therapy*

*Cognitive Therapy Techniques*

*Bipolar Disorder: A Cognitive Therapy Approach*

*Overcoming Resistance in Cognitive Therapy*

*Treatment Plans and Interventions for
Depression and Anxiety Disorders*

*Available from Hay House

Please visit:

Hay House UK: www.hayhouse.co.uk
Hay House USA: www.hayhouse.com®
Hay House Australia: www.hayhouse.com.au
Hay House South Africa: www.hayhouse.co.za
Hay House India: www.hayhouse.co.in

# BEAT the BLUES

## BEFORE THEY BEAT YOU

How to Overcome Depression

## ROBERT L. LEAHY PhD

HAY HOUSE

Australia • Canada • Hong Kong • India
South Africa • United Kingdom • United States

**First published and distributed in the United Kingdom by:**
Hay House UK Ltd, 292B Kensal Rd, London W10 5BE. Tel.: (44) 20 8962 1230;
Fax: (44) 20 8962 1239. www.hayhouse.co.uk

**Published and distributed in the United States of America by:**
Hay House, Inc., PO Box 5100, Carlsbad, CA 92018-5100. Tel.: (1) 760 431 7695 or
(800) 654 5126; Fax: (1) 760 431 6948 or (800) 650 5115. www.hayhouse.com

**Published and distributed in Australia by:**
Hay House Australia Ltd, 18/36 Ralph St, Alexandria NSW 2015. Tel.: (61) 2 9669
4299; Fax: (61) 2 9669 4144. www.hayhouse.com.au

**Published and distributed in the Republic of South Africa by:**
Hay House SA (Pty), Ltd, PO Box 990, Witkoppen 2068. Tel./Fax: (27) 11 467
8904. www.hayhouse.co.za

**Published and distributed in India by:**
Hay House Publishers India, Muskaan Complex, Plot No.3, B-2, Vasant Kunj,
New Delhi – 110 070. Tel.: (91) 11 4176 1620; Fax: (91) 11 4176 1630.
www.hayhouse.co.in

**Distributed in Canada by:**
Raincoast, 9050 Shaughnessy St, Vancouver, BC V6P 6E5. Tel.: (1) 604 323 7100;
Fax: (1) 604 323 2600

Copyright © 2010 by Robert Leahy

The moral rights of the author have been asserted.

*Design:* Tricia Breidenthal

*Page 107:* Excerpt from "The Guest House" by Rumi, translated by Coleman
Barks, from *The Essential Rumi,* © 1997 by Coleman Barks.
Used by permission of the translator.

A catalogue record for this book is available from the British Library.

ISBN 978-1-84850-333-5

Printed and bound in Great Britain by TJ International, Padstow, Cornwall.

To Aaron T. Beck, founder of cognitive therapy,

whose work has saved many lives.

Many thanks to you for inspiring me.

# CONTENTS

# CHAPTER 1

# What Is Depression?

"It all feels so hopeless," Karen said. As she looked into her hands, her tears began to fall. "It's hard to get up in the morning. I set the alarm but don't want to drag myself out of bed. My heart sinks when I think of going to work. I dread the mornings. I don't have anything to look forward to."

Each morning, Karen would awaken in the early hours and feel an overwhelming sadness. She would lay in bed, alone, thinking about how bad her life was. *Why am I like this? I can't seem to get anything right.* These painful, sorrowful thoughts flooded her mind and made her feel as if there was no reason to go on. The dawn had yet to break, and she had begun another day in misery. "I find myself crying for no good reason," she told me. "I just wish I could go back to sleep—forever."

Karen was 32 when she first came to see me. She had been separated from Gary for more than a year, and the divorce would be final in a few months. Their marriage had started off badly four years before—Gary was domineering, dismissive of Karen's feelings, and critical of almost everything she did. She said to me, almost apologetically, "I tried to be a good wife." Then she added, in her defense, "I was working hard at the office and couldn't always get everything done at home the way Gary wanted it done." He would call her irresponsible, lazy, and careless. If she fought back, he would simply put her down more. Nothing was good enough for Gary. He felt superior. And Karen felt beaten down.

At first she had high hopes for the marriage. Gary seemed confident, a take-charge type of guy, someone she felt she could respect. "He was the perfect date," Karen said. "I remember when he would bring me flowers and take me out to nice restaurants and tell me how pretty I was." She looked down. "But that seems like such a long time ago." Karen said that she knew she was making a mistake the week before they got married—Gary was continually critical and even said he wasn't sure he wanted to marry her. But she felt she couldn't call it off. There were too many people coming to the wedding.

Their intimacy dropped off quickly in the first year. There was little warmth, little affection, and very little sex. Gary would come home late, sometimes seeming a little high. He would say he'd been out with business associates—that he had to socialize to keep up with other people at work. Karen eventually began to suspect him of cheating on her, but she had no proof. And in the meantime, they argued about almost everything—who was responsible for the housekeeping, shopping, and planning. After all, Karen argued, "I have a job, too." But Gary wanted things on his terms.

And then, three years in, Gary told Karen that he wanted a separation. He had met a woman through his work—a salesperson in another company. The "other woman" was divorced, with a five-year-old son, and Gary had been seeing her after work for months. "She understands me. She's more my type," he said. "I really want out of this marriage."

Karen felt devastated. She was furious with Gary for cheating and lying. But she also blamed herself. "If I were more attractive and interesting, he wouldn't have cheated on me. I'm not even good enough to keep a man." Now she felt that she had nothing to offer, time was running out for her, and she was all alone. "I've lost contact with my friends," she told me. "I was always sitting at home waiting for Gary. I used to see my friends before we got married. Now I have nothing."

Karen had lost interest in other things, too. "I used to go to the health club and work out. It would energize me and make me feel good about myself. But I haven't gone in over a year." She had been eating junk food—"comfort food"—because it made her feel a little better for a few minutes, but she was losing control of her eating and gaining weight. "Look at me," she said. "Who would want me?"

I asked Karen to give me a visual image, a picture of what her depression looked like. "I see myself in an empty room, lying in bed, the shades drawn closed," she said. "I am all alone, and I am crying." She met my eyes, and then looked away. "That's what my life will be. I will always be alone."

Remembering Karen as I write this, it makes me sad to recollect how bad she felt. I could see the pain, the hopelessness, and the self-criticism that made her suffer. She felt that her divorce proved how unlovable she was and that no one could ever want her. She couldn't see that she had a history of strong connections with people—friends who respected and loved her—and that she was productive and valued at work. She couldn't see that she was smart, kind, and giving. She couldn't understand that her feelings of sadness and self-loathing might not last forever.

But I am fortunate. I know how things ended up for Karen, and that is a happy memory for me. She overcame her depression, and now she has a new man in her life, new self-confidence, and much more realistic self-esteem. How did someone who felt so hopeless, so engulfed in sadness and despair, find a light at the end of the tunnel?

It wasn't finding a new man that rescued Karen. It was Karen who rescued herself from her depression. She learned to take charge of her life—every day. She began to identify and change her negative thinking, which enabled her to feel better and act better. Her relationships grew as she reached out to her friends when she felt isolated and unlovable. And she learned that she could be her own therapist—once she got the tools.

## A MODERN EPIDEMIC

Karen's story may sound like the story of someone you know—or maybe it sounds like your own story. You may say, "I know what it's like to lie in bed flooded with negative thoughts, no energy to do anything. I know what it's like to regret the past and fear the future, to live in a world of darkness where joy never seems to be mine." Like Karen, you may feel that you're unlovable, that your dreams are all behind you, that there is no way out. You may even think that you will spend your entire life friendless and alone—or you may believe that if people really knew you, they could never care for you. Like Karen, you may struggle through the day with a stinging voice in you that tells you that you can't do anything, nothing will work out, and there is no pleasure or meaning left.

If you do, you are not alone. In any given year, about 11 percent of the population of the United States will have a depressive disorder, and 19 percent of us will suffer from depression at some point in our lives—which means that depression will ultimately affect 60 million Americans.[1] I personally don't know anyone well who has not been touched by depression—either they have it or someone close to them does. It's almost a certainty that someone else in your life—a family member, a close friend, a colleague—has been a victim of depression at some point. Depression is a worldwide epidemic that empties lives of meaning and joy and can even kill.

Many people without depression severe enough to qualify for a diagnosis still have depressive symptoms. In fact, over a six-month period, one out of five adults and half of children and adolescents report *some* symptoms of depression.[2] Although depression is not very common with young children, it becomes quite problematic during adolescence, and its prevalence appears to be rising. This is alarming, not just because we'd like youth to be a time of fun and optimism, but also because half of the kids who have depression will go on to become depressed adults. Also the rate of suicide among young people is tragically high.

Why are we more depressed than ever? Psychologist Jean Twenge has found that increases in depression during the last 50 years correspond to a rise in individualism and a loss of social connectedness.[3] In the 19th century, almost no one lived alone; however, today about 26 percent of households are comprised of a single person. We will look more closely later at how loneliness and relationship problems contribute to depression, but other historical and cultural trends play a part, too. Continually changing fashions may make you feel like you are missing out, a steady stream of graphic bad news on television may darken your view of life, and the decline of faith-based communities may give you a cynical outlook. In her recent book *The Narcissism Epidemic: Living in the Age of Entitlement*, Twenge traces the rise of unrealistically high expectations and narcissism and links these trends to an increase in anxiety and depression.[4] The narcissism is reflected in every aspect of the media—in airbrushed photos of women with perfect bodies and perfect skin that don't really exist. The narcissism is reflected in the emphasis on always thinking you are wonderful—no matter what you actually do. And it's reflected in the unrealistic expectations that many young people have when they start working—expecting almost immediate success. Twenge's book traces the rise of a sense of entitlement and unrealistic expectations that has also corresponded to a rise of anxiety and depression. As we expect more, we feel more deprived.

Our culture is marked by less and less of a sense of community. In the 1950s, working-class people would go bowling together, often proud of the team shirts they wore. Now people bowl alone—if they ever bowl. People sit mesmerized in front of television sets while they watch someone else live a "real life" in an endless stream of reality TV. Our connection with one another has dramatically declined—and this is also associated with the increase of anxiety and depression. The continual movement from neighborhood to neighborhood, from job to job, from not keeping the same friends from childhood to adulthood, and to the decline of civic organizations (unions, parent-teacher groups, clubs, churches, volunteer work) has left us more isolated, more lonely, and more depressed.

We have become more and more self-absorbed and less connected with one another.

Maybe there is small comfort in knowing that millions of people know what it's like to dread the day, to walk in sadness through a gloomy world while others walk in sunshine. But the good news is that depression is highly manageable today—*if you get the right treatment*. Like Karen, you may find that there is a way out. You may discover new ways of thinking, acting, and being with others. You may find—much to your surprise—that hidden within you is the courage to open a new door in your life, to walk through it, and to build a life worth living.

## A DOOR IN YOUR LIFE

Over the 27 years I've been a practicing therapist, many people have asked me, "Don't you get depressed working with depressed people?" Ironically, it's just the opposite. I feel great working with depressed people, because I know they can be helped.

Yes, the good news is that, with effective treatment, you can overcome depression—and once you do, you have a good chance of preventing its recurrence. New self-help techniques may be able to help you reverse your negative thinking and your painful sad moods. It's not easy. It requires work on your part. But there are powerful tools—many kinds of tools—that you can learn to use to help yourself.

Most depressed people can be helped with newer forms of cognitive-behavioral therapy (CBT). My colleagues and I have been developing this approach for the past 30 years, and it's now used throughout the world as the psychotherapy treatment of choice for depression and anxiety. This therapy helps you change the way you think (your cognitions) and what you do (your behavior). Once you change the way you think, you will change the way you feel and break the cycle of self-perpetuated pain.

Rather than spending years on the couch of a therapist who strokes his beard and asks tangential questions that make no sense to you, with CBT you can start to change your life *today*. And for many people, CBT has more lasting effects than any other approach. If you treat moderate or severe depression with medication but then discontinue the medication after you have gotten better, the chances are high (76 percent) that you will get depressed again in the next 12 months. But if you've gotten better with cognitive therapy, you have a lower chance (only 30 percent) of relapse after you stop. And, to make things even better, you will learn ways that you can dramatically decrease the likelihood of getting depressed again. Pills don't teach you skills, but CBT does.

If you were one of my patients, I might start our CBT session off by asking you, "What problem do you want to work on today?" In place of passive listening, I would take an active role with you, asking you to evaluate your thoughts, test them against reality, try to find new ways of thinking about things, and consider specific new behaviors that you might try. I would give you self-help homework assignments so that you could be your own therapist in between sessions. We would periodically evaluate your progress, consider why some things weren't working, and experiment with new techniques. We would not give up. And we would push you to work on making changes *today*.

In this book, I want to take this same active, engaging, in-your-face approach with you. In working with depression for nearly three decades, I've learned a lot from my patients and from my own life, and I think that you can learn from the techniques and strategies that my many patients have found useful. This book is your toolbox—it's the place to find the techniques you can use every day to free yourself from the misery of feeling depressed. I'd like you to be able—whenever you feel self-critical, indecisive, or hopeless—to open it up, find the tools you need, and help yourself. The secret is to make you, in effect, your own therapist, your own "life coach," so that you don't need to get reassurance from other people in order to give yourself direction. The ultimate goal is to put you in charge of yourself.

Depending on how severe your depression is, it may be best for you to have some outside help—at least at the start. Chronic, long-lasting, debilitating depression can take an enormous toll on your quality of life; and in many cases, these chronic conditions are the result of inadequate treatment. If your depression has a debilitating effect on you, it's important to take it seriously and treat it aggressively and comprehensively. In addition to the many CBT techniques you'll learn in this book, we can augment everything we do with medication or other biological treatments. The ideal arrangement would be for you to have the assistance of a trained cognitive-behavioral therapist, as well as a physician with whom you can consult about other options, such as medication. You can find listings of certified therapists through the Academy of Cognitive Therapy (www .academyofct.org) and, in the United Kingdom, through the British Association for Behavioural and Cognitive Psychotherapies (www.babcp.com.)

You'll find more resources for exploring your options, as well as information about biological treatments, in the Appendices.

Throughout this book we will work together using techniques that you can put into practice right now. We will also discuss how medication can be part of your self-help. We will examine how you and your partner can have a better relationship and how you can build more rewarding and respectful friendships. Depression can affect every area of your life, so you will need tools that you can use in every area, every day of your life. If I only give you reassurance, you will only feel better for a few minutes. If I give you the tools, you can fix things when I am not around.

Don't wait for someone to rescue you. *You can rescue yourself.*

## THE ANATOMY OF DEPRESSION

Depression is not just one or two symptoms. It's a constellation of different thoughts, feelings, behaviors, and experiences. Psychologists and psychiatrists have come up with a system to evaluate and categorize this elusive, shifting complex of pain. The technical diagnosis that we give is "major depressive disorder," which means that you have been depressed—with a sad mood or loss of interest in activities—for a two-week period and you have at least four of the following symptoms:

- Feelings of worthlessness or guilt

- Difficulty concentrating or making decisions

- Fatigue or low energy

- Insomnia or hypersomnia (increased sleep)

- Loss of appetite, weight loss, or weight gain

- Feelings of agitation or being slowed down in activity

- Thoughts of death or suicide

Before we make this diagnosis, we rule out medical problems that may give rise to the symptoms of depression, such as thyroid imbalance. We also consider what else is going on in your life. For example, we generally don't diagnose someone as depressed who is suffering after the loss of a loved one, unless the depression lasts an unusually long time.

## Different Kinds of Depression

There are lots of ways to be depressed. You can have a major depressive disorder, as we've just described. Or you can have a period of milder depression that lasts for about two years, which we call dysthymic disorder. You can also have dysthymic disorder and a period of major depression concurrently, giving you the diagnosis of "double depression." And many women suffer from postpartum depression after the birth of a child.

One important diagnosis to keep in mind is bipolar disorder. (We used to call this manic-depressive disorder.) People with bipolar disorder alternate between depressed moods and periods of "mania" in which they feel elated, with excessively high self-esteem and lots of energy. They talk rapidly, their ideas are all over the place, they can be extremely silly, and they don't seem to need much sleep. They may take unnecessary risks, or their sex drive may be exceptionally high. People who have some of these manic symptoms, but not in their most severe form are referred to as hypomanic.

If you have had episodes of feeling manic or hypomanic, then you might have bipolar disorder. This is something that your therapist or doctor can determine with you. It's important to tell her or him about the manic symptoms, because if you have bipolar disorder and you're being treated with medication, your doctor may want to consider a specific plan for you.

Relying only on antidepressants can make matters worse if you are bipolar. Many bipolar people will experience a "cycling" into an agitated manic state when they are placed only on antidepressant medications, sending them on a roller coaster of up-and-down moods from depression to agitated mania. However, whether you are unipolar (you've never had a manic episode) or bipolar, the ideas in this book can help you avoid future episodes, which is empowering particularly during periods of depression.

## The Causes of Depression

Depression knows no barriers. Anyone, regardless of income, education, race, gender, success, or beauty, can get depressed. The list of famous people who have suffered from depression could go on for volumes. It includes Bobby Darin, Barbara Bush, Billy Joel, Judy Garland, Buzz Aldrin, Ernest Hemingway, Charles Darwin, John Adams, Harrison Ford, Abraham Lincoln, J. K. Rowling, Tennessee Williams, Winston Churchill, and Mark Twain.

What causes depression? Many people think they have to find the cause of their depression in the way their parents raised them. Indeed, you can spend years on a therapist's couch trying to dig up terrible memories of childhood mistreatment, but it may be pointless: researchers estimate that between one-third and two-thirds of the cause of depression can be traced to your genes.[5] Depression is related to your brain chemistry. Differences in your levels of serotonin, norepinephrine, and other chemicals may make you more prone to being depressed. That said, a number of other factors—from your upbringing to experiences later in life—can put you at higher risk for a depressive episode. For example, your parents may have made you more vulnerable to depression not just by passing on genes that make it more likely but also by communicating with you in ways that led you to feel helpless or self-critical.

Our understanding of the brain chemistry underlying depression has often come from accidental discoveries. Once again this shows that in science you often discover what you are *not* looking for! The first two major classes of antidepressant medications—monoamine oxidase inhibitors (MAOIs) and tricyclic antidepressants (TCAs)—were discovered by accident. Iproniazid, an MAOI, was tried in the 1950s as a treatment for tuberculosis. Much to the surprise of the doctors and patients, it improved patients' moods and made them less depressed. In the late 1950s researchers in Switzerland experimented with TCAs as a treatment for schizophrenia. Again, much to their surprise, the TCAs did nothing to help the schizophrenia, but they did improve the patients' moods. Lithium also was discovered accidentally in 1948 by Australian psychiatrist John Cade, who injected it into guinea pigs. Contrary to his expectations, it produced a calming effect.[6] The discovery of major classes of antidepressants by accident indicates that an observant scientist, finding the unexpected, can open up new possibilities for millions of people.

There are several theories of the causes of depression, suggesting that there may be several different biochemical pathways to depression. And your particular depression may be caused by one or a combination of these varied biochemical models. You should keep this in mind, since it could affect your treatment. You and your doctor may pursue a sequence of trials of medications—if one class of medication does not work, you can always begin a trial of another class. Or you can add a medication from a different class—sometimes a combination of two classes of medication can increase the effectiveness of treatment.

Look at it this way: There are three sets of neurotransmitters that are important in affecting depression: norepinephrine, serotonin, and dopamine. These neurotransmitters are all part of the monoamine class. Think of the brain as consisting of neurons (nerve cells) that communicate with one another across a gap we call a synapse. You have cells that send messages, (presynaptic) and cells that receive those messages (postsynaptic). Tricyclics inhibit the reuptake (or reabsorption) of neurotransmitters; SSRIs (a class of drug called selective serotonin reuptake inhibitors) inhibit reabsorption of serotonin specifically; MAOIs inhibit the metabolism, or breakdown, of molecules stored in the neurons.[7]

Of course, the science behind this is very complex. Recent research indicates that depression may be affected by the communication between neurons activating specific genes. Researchers at Yale University have found that antidepressants stimulate neuronal growth factors by generating new nerve cells.[8] This is why antidepressant medications take some time to become effective—they are generating new cells! The biology of depression is more complex—and more fascinating—than was first thought.

Many parents of depressed kids are also depressed, so they may have a difficult time doing the best job that they could. Parents who are unaffectionate, who don't validate feelings, and who are excessively controlling or critical tend to raise children who grow up to be depressed adults.[9] If your parents gave you mixed messages—"I love you, but don't bother me now"—then you have a greater risk of depression as well. Sexual abuse during childhood is a significant predictor of depression.[10] And if your parents divorced, separated, or died while you were growing up, then you are more likely to be depressed as an adult.[11] An important factor here is how you were cared for afterward: if the loss of a parent brought a decrease in care, warmth, and attention, your risk of depression is much greater.[12] While it's true that your recollection of childhood experiences may be affected by your current mood—you're depressed now, so you're more likely to recall negative events in the past—research suggests that bias in recollection is not the primary reason that depressed adults report such difficult childhood experiences.[13]

In almost all contemporary cultures that have been studied, women are more likely to suffer from depression than men—twice as likely on average, a discrepancy that appears in adolescence and disappears in older age. There may be a number of reasons for this, from the hormonal changes women experience to the fact that they tend to have less power in society than men, place greater emphasis on pleasing others, and perhaps may be more prone to ruminating. However, women and men can get the same benefits from cognitive-behavioral therapy and medication.

What brings on a depressive episode? There are a number of factors that contribute to higher risk. Being widowed, divorced, or separated is a major predictor of depression; so is serious relationship conflict. Women experiencing conflict in their marriages are 25 times more likely to get depressed than women in marriages without conflict.[14] Women who have difficulties with their children are at increased risk, too. Being unemployed is also a factor:[15] for many, unemployment means not only a loss of income but also a loss of identity, contact, and sense of accomplishment. Unemployment need not lead to depression; but if you are depressed, you tend to view it in the most negative light—as a sign of shame, failure, and helplessness.

In one study, 60 percent of depressed people reported a significant stressor in the previous nine months, compared to only 19 percent of non-depressed people. Even daily hassles can accumulate and lead to depression: problems at work, difficult living arrangements, the stress of travel, extraordinary financial pressures, and painful arguments and conflicts with others. And though stressors like these are inevitable in most people's lives, your genes may make you more vulnerable to their effects.[16] If you are genetically predisposed to depression, then stressful events will be 250 percent more likely to make you depressed. But your genes can *protect* you, too. For example, although, as I indicated above, being the victim of abuse increases your chance of being depressed later, it also depends on your *genetics*. If neither one of your parents provides you with a strong *genetic loading* for depression—then you are not very likely to get depressed. Your genes can help you or hurt you—they can even protect you against your own parents!

## The Consequences of Depression

Depression is very costly—on many levels, starting with the most literal. It leads to higher rates of absenteeism from work, lower productivity, and higher rates of disability. About 80 percent of people who are currently depressed say that they are impaired in their daily functioning.[17]

One study found that people with major depression lost 5.6 hours of productive work per week.[18] Take Karen, for example, whom we met earlier. She sometimes couldn't get out of bed to go to work. When she was at work, she would often sit in front of her computer ruminating about how bad her life was. She procrastinated on getting things done. This only made her feel worse, since she feared she would get fired.

Depressed people are more likely to have unhealthy lifestyles that include things like smoking, inactivity, and a poor diet. "I eat ice cream and cookies to try to feel better," Karen told me. "But then afterward I feel awful because I know I've lost control." For some people with depression, this unhealthy lifestyle leads to a greater risk of cardiovascular disease.[19] Depression also places you at greater risk of developing Alzheimer's disease[20] and stroke[21] and even affects the outcome of HIV disease.[22] And elderly people who are depressed are more likely to die earlier.[23]

Depression is not generally a one-time experience. As I mentioned earlier, many people have recurring episodes of depression, some lasting months or even years. Karen had had two earlier periods of depression before she came to me. Depression is one of the leading lifetime burdens in the world, exceeded only by perinatal (or birthing-related) conditions, lower respiratory infections, ischemic heart disease, cerebrovascular disease, HIV/AIDS, and diarrheal diseases.

But depression's most tragic—and unnecessary—consequence is suicide. Depressed people are 30 times more likely to take their own lives than people who are not depressed.[24] My friend Ken was one of depression's tragic victims.

I met Ken years ago when I was in graduate school at Yale. At the time I was interested in working with children, mostly because I thought kids were cute. I wasn't driven by an overwhelming intellectual motivation, but it was fun to work with kids. Ken, who was on the research faculty, was incredibly supportive of me and my work, and he became a friend as well. We would have lunch together; I'd visit him and his family; and we would talk about research, gossip, and whatever came to our minds. He always had a good laugh, a funny comment, or a supportive something to say to me.

Ken never talked about any personal problems. He never seemed sad. He never complained about his work. At lunch, now I recall, he would usually have a martini—sometimes two—but I never saw him drunk. He and Caroline, his wife, would have me over for wonderful home-cooked meals, and we'd sit and talk and laugh. I always felt the quiet warmth of that male friendship—the kind where guys don't have to say how much they care about each other; they just know. Still, I owe so much to Ken that I wish I *had* told him how much he meant to me.

After I got my Ph.D., I left New Haven and pursued my academic career—getting grants for research, editing books, doing all those things you are expected to do. I got more interested in doing child-behavior therapy, and I was thinking about moving in that direction. I sent letters to Ken, and sometimes we'd talk on the phone, but I was away for a few years and had basically lost contact with what was going on in his life.

I was teaching at the University of British Columbia in Vancouver when I got a phone call from a colleague at Yale. "Ken has died. He committed suicide."

I was stunned and bewildered. "I never had a sense that anything was wrong," I said. Suddenly my eyes were filled with tears.

"Apparently he was worried that he was going to get fired," my colleague went on. When his wife and daughter were asleep, Ken went into the garage, turned on the gas, and killed himself.

When I saw Caroline, I could see that part of her soul had been torn to pieces. She was sitting in the kitchen of their old Victorian house outside New Haven, wondering how she could pay the bills. She had turned to her church and her friends, who helped her during this difficult time, but the laughter and softness in her face seemed to have gone away. Her eyes seemed far away as she spoke about Ken. "I feel so angry at him for doing this, leaving us," she said. "He knew I would do anything to support him. But he was just overwhelmed."

As Caroline and I talked, I found out about an entirely different part of Ken—one that I never knew. He was an alcoholic—depressed, lonely, and hopeless. Here he was, a rising star in the field of clinical psychology, who couldn't find the help he needed. He saw no way out. Caroline was pregnant when he died.

A person's death is not a simple statistic. It is the loss of many worlds—his world, his place in the worlds of all of us who loved him. Ken's daughter, Susan, held my hand and said, "Bob-Leahy," as if my name was hyphenated, "Bob-Leahy, you aren't going to go away, are you?" She showed me her dolls, and I hugged her.

I knew I never wanted to "get over" the death of my friend. I wanted to be able to recall how sad I felt at losing him and how glad I was for having known him. And I wanted to build a life large enough with meaning to contain that loss. Although I enjoyed working with kids and their parents, I also thought that working with depression would be more meaningful to me. And it was my good luck that the founder of cognitive therapy, Dr. Aaron Beck, was providing specialized training at the University of Pennsylvania Medical School. I thought, *That's where I will go.* And I did.

I am not afraid of feeling sad thinking about my friend. He gave me the motivation to do what I have been doing ever since. As long as his spirit, his gentleness, and his pain are in my heart and my mind, I know that I can help others find their way out of the dark passages of their lives.

## HOW TO USE THIS BOOK

When I thought about how to write a self-help book on depression, I realized that my patients come to see me with specific concerns. They may say to me, "I feel hopeless about the future," or "I can't get anything done," or "I'm so sad I can't stand it." They don't come in looking for theories about depression or lectures about psychology. They come in asking, "What can I do to help myself?" That's how you probably experience your depression.

That's why I organized this book around specific concerns. You may be feeling lonely or you may be self-critical. You may be indecisive, or you may feel like a burden to others. You may be feeling irritable, or you may have difficulty finding the energy to do things. Whatever your concern, you want solutions. You want to know, "What can I do?"

Each chapter starts with an example of someone who's experiencing a particular aspect of depression. That's how my patients talk to me, and I want to give you the benefit of their experience. You will probably see yourself in many of these examples, but you may not see yourself in all of them. That's okay. No two depressed people are exactly the same. You don't have to have all of the symptoms of depression to benefit from this book. In fact, consider yourself lucky if you don't.

As you read each chapter, you'll find a further explanation of the symptom—how it arises, how it may affect you—and ways to address it by creating effective, positive new habits of thinking and behaving. I've drawn on many different approaches from cognitive-behavioral therapy to gather the techniques and strategies I will show you here. Over the last

30 years, there has been an immense amount of research on what works, and I owe a lot to many people who have contributed their ideas in developing these approaches. But I have learned that no one approach works for everyone. That's why I have tried to use the best of the best.

As I've mentioned, medication, prescribed by your doctor, may also be part of your self-help, so I have included information on medication in Appendix A. But there is so much evidence that cognitive-behavioral therapy is helpful for depression that we now consider it a first-line approach. As you go through each chapter, try to decide for yourself which techniques could be helpful to you. It's always best to have a trained CBT therapist to help you through this, but using some of these proven techniques on your own can give you a head start. This is "news you can use." The tools are here. Your depression may make it hard for you to use these tools. You may feel discouraged. You may feel that you don't have the energy. But like any tools, you won't know if they can fix the problem until you use them. What could you really lose if you tried?

Depression takes the form of self-critical thoughts, indecisiveness, low energy, sadness, hopelessness, withdrawal, sleep disturbance, irritability, and other symptoms. We will approach your self-help by helping you get rid of these symptoms. If you don't have the symptoms, you won't be depressed. It's as simple as that!

## Getting Started

This book is meant to be a resource that you refer to over and over. It's a guide for dealing with your problems and a reminder that you can take action *today* to help solve them. Like any journey, your program of self-help starts where you are right now. So you may want to begin by taking the following simple test to assess your condition and identify the areas where you have the most difficulty—areas you can address as you work your way through this book. There are no right or wrong answers: just describe how you have been feeling in the past week.

Please check the one response to each item that best describes how you have felt for the past seven days.

## The Quick Inventory of Depressive Symptomatology

### 1. Falling Asleep:

☐ 0    I never take longer than 30 minutes to fall asleep.

☐ 1    I take at least 30 minutes to fall asleep, less than half the time.

☐ 2    I take at least 30 minutes to fall asleep, more than half the time.

☐ 3    I take at least 60 minutes to fall asleep, more than half the time.

### 2. Sleep During the Night:

☐ 0    I do not wake up at night.

☐ 1    I have a restless, light sleep with a few brief awakenings each night.

☐ 2    I wake up at least once a night, but I go back to sleep easily.

☐ 3    I awaken more than once a night and stay awake for 20 minutes or more, more than half the time.

### 3. Waking Up Too Early:

☐ 0    Most of the time, I awaken no more than 30 minutes before I need to get up.

☐ 1    More than half the time, I awaken more than 30 minutes before I need to get up.

☐ 2    I almost always awaken at least one hour or so before I need to, but I go back to sleep eventually.

☐ 3    I awaken at least one hour before I need to and can't go back to sleep.

## 4. Sleeping Too Much:

- ☐ 0 I sleep no longer than seven to eight hours per night, without napping during the day.

- ☐ 1 I sleep no longer than ten hours in a 24-hour period, including naps.

- ☐ 2 I sleep no longer than 12 hours in a 24-hour period, including naps.

- ☐ 3 I sleep longer than 12 hours in a 24-hour period, including naps.

## 5. Feeling Sad:

- ☐ 0 I do not feel sad.

- ☐ 1 I feel sad less than half the time.

- ☐ 2 I feel sad more than half the time.

- ☐ 3 I feel sad nearly all the time.

## 6. Decreased Appetite:

- ☐ 0 My usual appetite has not decreased.

- ☐ 1 I eat somewhat less often or lesser amounts of food than usual.

- ☐ 2 I eat much less than usual and only with personal effort.

- ☐ 3 I rarely eat within a 24-hour period and only with extreme personal effort or when others persuade me to eat.

### 7. Increased Appetite:

☐ 0    My usual appetite has not increased.

☐ 1    I feel a need to eat more frequently than usual.

☐ 2    I regularly eat more often and/or greater amounts of food than usual.

☐ 3    I feel driven to overeat both at mealtime and between meals.

### 8. Decreased Weight (Within the Last Two Weeks):

☐ 0    My weight has not decreased.

☐ 1    I feel as if I've had a slight weight loss.

☐ 2    I have lost two pounds or more.

☐ 3    I have lost five pounds or more.

### 9. Increased Weight (Within the Last Two Weeks):

☐ 0    My weight has not increased.

☐ 1    I feel as if I've had a slight weight gain.

☐ 2    I have gained two pounds or more.

☐ 3    I have gained five pounds or more.

### 10. Concentration/Decision Making:

☐ 0    There is no change in my usual capacity to concentrate or make decisions.

☐ 1    I occasionally feel more indecisive or find that my attention wanders more than usual.

☐ 2    Most of the time, I struggle to focus my attention or to make decisions.

☐ 3    I cannot concentrate well enough to read, or I cannot make even minor decisions.

## 11. View of Myself:

☐ 0    I see myself as equally worthwhile and deserving as other people.

☐ 1    I am more self-blaming than usual.

☐ 2    I largely believe that I cause problems for others.

☐ 3    I think almost constantly about major and minor defects in myself.

## 12. Thoughts of Death or Suicide:

☐ 0    I do not think of suicide or death.

☐ 1    I feel that life is empty or wonder if it's worth living.

☐ 2    I think of suicide or death several times a week for several minutes.

☐ 3    I think or suicide or death several times a day in some detail or have actually tried to take my life.

## 13. General Interest:

☐ 0    There is no change from usual in how interested I am in other people or activities.

☐ 1    I notice that I am less interested in people or activities.

☐ 2    I find I have interest in only one or two of my formerly pursued activities.

☐ 3    I have virtually no interest in formerly pursued activities.

### 14. Energy Level:

- ☐  0    There is no change in my usual level of energy.

- ☐  1    I get tired more easily than usual.

- ☐  2    I have to make a big effort to start or finish my usual daily activities (for example, shopping, homework, cooking, or going to work).

- ☐  3    I really cannot carry out most of my usual daily activities because I just don't have the energy.

### 15. Feeling Slowed Down:

- ☐  0    I think, speak, and move at my usual rate of speed.

- ☐  1    I find that my thinking is slowed down or my voice sounds dull or flat.

- ☐  2    It takes me several seconds to respond to most questions, and I'm sure my thinking is slowed.

- ☐  3    I am often unable to respond to questions without extreme effort.

### 16. Feeling Restless:

- ☐  0    I do not feel restless.

- ☐  1    I'm often fidgety, wringing my hands, or need to shift how I am sitting.

- ☐  2    I have impulses to move about and am quite restless.

- ☐  3    At times, I am unable to stay seated and need to pace around.

| Scoring for the Quick Inventory of Depressive Symptomatology | |
|---|---|
| Total scores can range from 0 to 27.[33] Mild Depression (6–10), Moderate (11–15), Severe (16–20), Very Severe (21–27). | |
| Enter the highest score on any one of the four sleep items (items 1 to 4). | |
| Enter score on item 5. | |
| Enter the highest score on any one of the four weight items (items 6 to 9). | |
| Enter the sum of the scores for questions 10 to 14. | |
| Enter the highest score on either of the two psychomotor items (15 and 16). | |
| **Sum the item scores for a total score:** | |

The Quick Inventory of Depressive Symptomatology (QIDS) was used in the largest multisite study of depression ever conducted. You can use it on your own and take it repeatedly over the course of the next couple of months—or anytime—to see how you are doing.

After you take the test, record how you are doing before you start your program of self-help. Then take it again every week. When you have finished this book, give yourself about 12 weeks of working on the techniques you've learned to see how much things change for you. Don't expect a magic bullet or a quick fix. If you were trying to lose 20 pounds, you would give yourself plenty of time. You wouldn't expect to lose all 20 pounds in one week. In the same way, you need time to develop new, productive, positive habits to counter your depression.

The goal in reading and using this book is not only to help you get over the depression afflicting you now but also to give you the tools to prevent future episodes. It's not just about feeling better in the short run—it's about staying better for years. This may sound like a daunting task, but it really isn't. It simply means that you will need to make your new habits of thinking and behaving a part of your life. As one colleague confided to me, "I have to lead a nondepressive lifestyle." It's worked for her, and it can work for you.

## "You Make It Sound Too Easy"

If you are like a lot of people with depression, you've been told that you can help yourself, but nothing has worked. So you may approach this book with a certain skepticism. That is a reasonable position to take. The cognitive-behavioral approach is not meant to be "inspirational"— it's not meant to spark an epiphany that will change your life. Instead, I urge you to hold on to a healthy skepticism. You won't know if these techniques work for you until you have tried them, over and over, for some time. I just ask you to take a skeptical approach to your skepticism.

You will not get better all at once. Getting better is getting better a little bit at a time. It's not always about feeling better right now. You may have to act better before you feel better. It's becoming a little less self-critical, a little more hopeful, doing a little bit more. It's progress but not always steady progress. It's simply moving forward. And the most important step forward for now is practicing positive new ways to think, behave, and interact with people.

"You make it sound too easy," my patients sometimes say. "I can't take these steps, because I'm too depressed. I can't exercise, I can't call my friends, and I can't work. My depression keeps me from doing anything." Then I suggest, "Why not act against your depression? Why not do these things anyway?" Sometimes you need to take action before the motivation can emerge. I ask these patients to think of their self-help as a series of experiments. How will it hurt if they try this? Who knows what could happen if they tried that?

So let's agree to carry out an *experiment,* you and I. Work your way through the chapters of this book, make a note of the different techniques, and try them out for a few months on a regular basis. Consider the medication options described in Appendix A. Be willing to try everything that is available. And then let's see what the outcome reveals.

## Help Is on the Way

The very nature of depression is that you think that it "makes sense" that you are depressed. Your depression may look to you like a reasonable response to the realities of your life. So you may wait a long time to seek help because you don't see that you need it—or because you think it's hopeless anyway. Sadly, most depressed people—76 percent of those with moderate depression and 61 percent of those with severe depression—do not get help at all.[26] And when people do get help, a significant number of them receive inadequate treatment—either insufficient medication for their depression or forms of psychotherapy that are not effective in treating depression.

But knowledge is power. If you know what depression is, what leads to depression, and how your mind works when you are depressed, then you have power over your depression. If you can identify your specific symptoms of depression, you can target them for change. If you know the techniques that you can use to create change—every day—then you can work on making your life better right now.

You don't have to wait to feel better. You don't have to continue suffering. You can build a better life, and this book can be your toolbox. I will give you the tools—tools you can use for the rest of your life.

If you're not convinced that these tools can work for you, let me tell you one more story.

Linda came to see me many years ago for her depression. She felt self-critical, sad, hopeless, and even suicidal at times. She thought there was no hope. But we worked together on her depression, and she got better. After she completed therapy, I didn't hear from her for many years.

Then, a few years ago, I got a letter from her. She told me that in recent years she and her family had gone through some terrible times. Her husband's business almost went bankrupt; her younger daughter was severely disabled; and, to make matters even more horrible, her elder daughter died. Linda wrote that it had taken all of the tools she learned in therapy with me to help her through—but with their help, she made it. She included a photograph of herself, her husband, and her two daughters—one of them in a wheelchair. Linda had to overcome obstacles that few of us will ever face, and she is not depressed today.

If you find yourself stuck in a dark place with no way out, you can open your toolbox and find what you need to make your way out again. When you come out of the darkness, you will find a new world. Remember Karen? After working with me, she said, "I woke up this morning and saw the sun."

## Fact-Check on Depression

### How widespread is depression?

19% of Americans will suffer from depression at some time

50% of children and adolescents and 20% of adults report some symptoms of depression[27]

Kids born after 1960 are significantly more likely to suffer from depression in childhood or adolescence than kids born before 1960[28]

### How long does depression last?

70% recover from their depression on their own within one year[29]

20% percent are still depressed two years after their depression began

11% are depressed five years later

Five years after being diagnosed with depression, 89% are not depressed

People with recurrent depression will have an average of seven episodes during their lifetime[30]

### Is it only depression?

75% of people with depression suffer from another psychological problem

59% also have anxiety disorders

24% also have substance abuse disorders

Depressed individuals are five times more likely to abuse drugs

### How costly is depression?

Depression is the leading cause of medical disability for people aged 14 to 44

Depressed people lose 5.6 hours of productive work every week[31]

80% of depressed people are impaired in their daily functioning[32]

The cost of depression (lost productivity and increased medical expenses) is $83 billion per year[33]

Depressed people are 30 times more likely to kill themselves[34]

# CHAPTER 2

# The Depressed Mind

What does depression sound like?

Let's listen to Eric, who recently lost his job. "I can't do anything right. Nothing works out for me. Everyone is going to think I'm a loser. After all, they're doing great. But now that I don't have a job, my girl-friend will certainly lose interest in me. There are so many other guys out there making a lot of money. I feel so humiliated—I'm really too ashamed to tell my friends I lost my job. I just don't have any energy. What's the use? I know you're going to tell me to start doing more things to help myself, but it's hopeless. Nothing I do works out anyway."

Depression has a mind of its own. When you are depressed, you think in generalizations (*nothing works out*), you don't give yourself credit for anything that you do (*I can't do anything right*), and you label yourself in the most negative terms (*loser, ashamed, humiliated*). You set demand-ing standards that you will never live up to. You may think you need to get everyone's approval, or excel at everything you do, or know for sure something will work out before you try it. Your thinking keeps you trapped in self-criticism, indecisiveness, and inertia—like Eric, effective-ly immobilized.

Where does all this negativity come from? The answer may help us shine a light into the recesses of the depressed mind—and it lies beyond our individual lives, in the far reaches of our human past.

## DEPRESSION AS ADAPTATION

Nearly half the population has a history of a psychiatric disorder, with depression and anxiety topping the list.[1] If depression is so wide-spread and, as we saw in Chapter 1, so much affected by our genes, we may well ask why evolution would select for such a dismal set of char-acteristics. How do sadness, withdrawal, low energy, helplessness, and hopelessness serve the ultimate human goals—the passing on of our genes and the survival of our species? Or, as evolutionary psychologists put it, "What is depression good for?"[2]

There are a couple of important things to remember here. One is that evolution is not about being happy or feeling good: it's the genes that need to survive, even if the individual is sacrificed in the process. The other is that human civilization over the last 10,000 or 20,000 years has changed too fast for human evolutionary biology to keep up. So our hardwiring dates back to the days of primitive hunter-gatherer societies; the abilities and tendencies it left our ancestors with were those necessary for survival in that environment. With that in mind, let's consider the symptoms of depression in terms of how they could have helped our ancestors deal with danger, starvation, and competition within dominance hierarchies. Let's look at how depression makes sense during a time of scarcity and threat.

## A Strategy for Survival

Imagine your ancient ancestors roaming around the forests 100,000 years ago. There have been threats from other tribes, food is scarce, and winter is approaching. What kind of mind-set would make sense? What would make sense is a kind of "strategic pessimism."[3] In the context of scarcity and threat, it is most prudent to assume that resources are few and that energy must be conserved. If winter is approaching and food stores are running low, you don't want to count on more food being available. Running around trying to find more food might be a dangerous waste of energy—you would burn more calories than you would find. Better to lie low, conserve your calories, and wait it out. Even better to turn down your metabolism, slow down your heart rate so you burn fewer calories, and go dormant. Sleep a lot, if you can. If possible, load up on high-calorie foods and carbohydrates so you can store fat and energy to protect you against the long winter of deprivation you are facing.[4]

Protecting yourself against deprivation this way is not unlike what animals do when they hibernate. In Canada and parts of northern Vermont, turtles pile themselves on top of one another at the bottom of a pond during the frozen winter as their metabolism slows to a rate approaching living death. In fact, they seem like they are dead. They cannot be moved. But what they're really doing is surviving the winter by reducing their activity to a standstill, conserving energy and calories, and keeping each other warm. Here in rural Connecticut in the early winter, I can watch the squirrels hurriedly gathering nuts to prepare for the frozen weeks ahead. Nature is using "depressive symptoms" of inactivity and isolation, hiding and conserving, to protect against the deprivation to come.[5] I see this in my patients, too, when they complain of fatigue and low energy. When I ask a patient in this state about going to the health club to exercise, he responds, "But I have no energy." He lies in bed with the shades drawn, half-awake, ruminating about how bad he feels. He may crave comfort foods that are high in calories, fat, and carbohydrates. He reminds me of a sleepy bear getting ready to hibernate—to prepare and protect himself against the lean times to come.

When we take a closer look at some other hallmarks of depressive thought, we see that they, too, form part of this adaptive "strategy" for dealing with deprivation:

- If something bad happens, it means other bad things will happen.

- If something good happens, think of it as unusual; it doesn't predict more good things.

- If you don't succeed, quit.

- Don't pursue sex; you won't be able to support children.

How does this pessimism about "trying harder" make sense? Well, if we think of depression as an evolved strategy to deal with scarcity, then it makes a lot of sense to avoid getting overly optimistic. If you get overly optimistic during a time of scarcity, you end up wasting calories, weakening yourself, and making yourself vulnerable to threat. It also makes sense not to pursue sex—since you can hardly support yourself, why would you want to risk having more mouths to feed? And in fact, sex drive decreases substantially when you are depressed. From an evolutionary point of view, it's even adaptive to think you are not sexually attractive, because this reduces your inclination to pursue sex. By reducing sex drive and sexual behavior, your ancient ancestors, during times of deprivation, were able to conserve their resources and wait for a better day—a day, perhaps, when food was in greater supply and when there was less threat from outsiders.

This is why I view depression as a strategy to avoid further losses.[6] The depressed mind works this way: *You have suffered some setbacks. You have very little left. Better to be very, very cautious. Don't take any more chances—after all, if you lose any more, you may end up with nothing, and then you will die. If you try, just try a little—test the waters, but don't get in too deep. You might not be able to rescue yourself. You might lose everything. You might drown. Wait for certain information that things will work out. Keep collecting information to find out if there is any danger. Protect yourself—at all costs.* Depression is a defense against the risks of being overly optimistic. For many depressed people, optimism carries the risk of losing even more—getting rejected, failing, losing resources that are scarce to begin with.

If you see yourself in this portrait of "strategic pessimism," then you are not alone. Our ancient ancestors who were wise enough to know when to be pessimistic were the ones who survived. The ancient ancestor with "happy feet," who danced around nonstop during times of deprivation and threat, wasted calories and resources and finally fell victim to predators or enemies. That ancestor never lived long enough to pass down those overly optimistic genes, so they died with him or her—while the cautious, pessimistic, risk-averse genes continued on their way down to you and me.

## Depression and Submission

Another evolutionary theory of depression is called "social ranking theory" or "rank theory."[7] According to this theory, depression helps you realize you are defeated so that you can adjust to your lower ranking in the group. It's an instruction to give up while you still have a chance. When you feel depressed, your voice may be softer, your eyes may be downcast, and you may fear rejection. You think, *I have nothing to offer, so I will lay low.* When you are around other people, you may be the quietest of all as you stand back, both admiring and feeling threatened by the more confident members of your group who smile, speak more loudly, initiate conversations, and make plans. You reluctantly but quietly follow along; even if you think that the leader's ideas are wrong, you don't want to risk an argument. You don't want to make others dislike you. You feel you have very little going for you, people think badly of you, and rejection would be devastating. Like the smaller dog intimidated by a larger, more aggressive dog, you lower yourself, showing that you are not a threat.

How do this inhibition, shyness, and submission to others make sense from an evolutionary point of view? Go to a zoo and watch the baboons or the chimps. Within a few minutes you will notice who the dominant ones are and which ones are lower in the hierarchy. The dominant monkeys get the best food and access to the females. The submissive monkeys lower themselves, don't challenge the dominant monkeys, and don't pursue reproduction.

This aspect of evolutionary theory gives us a revealing guide to some factors that trigger depression. It is not surprising that the triggers for depression are losses in relationships (such as conflicts, rejection, or break-ups) and loss of social status (such as losing a job, losing money, or losing rank). Feelings of humiliation and being trapped are key factors in this model. You lose social rank when you feel humiliated, and you cannot control events if you feel trapped.[8]

## How Depressed People Think

What strikes me about the way my depressed patients think is that they are relentlessly negative, even when the facts are positive. Karen thought that she had nothing to offer—she thought she was unattractive, boring, and a burden to other people. From my perspective, she was good-looking, intelligent, conscientious, and kind. She didn't give herself credit for anything she did at work—she focused on a few negatives and blew them up in her mind as catastrophes—but her boss thought she was doing a good job, even if she wasn't perfect. Cognitive therapists have found that when we are depressed we tend to have a negative view of ourselves, our experiences, and our future. We call this "the negative triad."[9]

When you take this negative view of yourself, anything you do looks like a failure or a flop to you. Even when someone points out your positives, you discount them as irrelevant: "That's no big deal—anyone could do that." You can't seem to enjoy anything; you think that your exercise is a waste of time, your vacation was a waste of money, and your relationships are boring and demanding. You take a dim view of the future, too, anticipating that you will never get better, you will fail the exam, you will get fired from your job, and you will end up alone for the rest of your life. Which comes first—the thought or the depression? It's really everything—these negative thoughts lead to depression, maintain it and prolong it, and are often the result of depression. The important thing is to catch them, test them out, and change them.

This overriding negativity is expressed in specific biases in your thinking. In cognitive therapy we call these biases "automatic thoughts." These are thoughts that come to you quite spontaneously; they seem plausible and true to you, and they are associated with feeling down. Look at Table 2.1, and see if any of these biases seem familiar.

| Table 2.1<br>Automatic Thought Distortions |
|---|
| **Mind reading:** You assume that you know what people think without having sufficient evidence of their thoughts. *He thinks I'm a loser.* |
| **Fortune-telling:** You predict the future negatively: things will get worse or there is danger ahead. *I'll fail the exam. I won't get that job.* |
| **Catastrophizing:** You believe that what will happen will be so awful that you won't be able to stand it. *It would be unbearable if I failed.* |
| **Labeling:** You broadly assign negative traits to yourself and others. *I'm undesirable. He's a rotten person.* |
| **Discounting positives:** You write off the positive things you or others do as trivial. *That's what wives are supposed to do, so it doesn't count when she's nice to me. Those successes were easy, so they don't matter.* |
| **Negative filtering:** You focus almost exclusively on the negatives and seldom notice the positives. *Look at all of the people who don't like me.* |
| **Overgeneralizing:** You perceive a global pattern of negatives on the basis of a single incident. You go beyond one experience and generalize to a pattern that characterizes your life. *This always happens to me. I seem to fail at a lot of things.* |
| **Dichotomous thinking:** You view events or people in all-or-nothing terms. You are either a "winner" or a "loser"—not in between. *I get rejected by everyone. It was a complete waste of time.* |
| **Shoulds:** You interpret events in terms of expectations and demands rather than simply focusing on what is. *I should do well. If I don't, then I'm a failure.* |
| **Personalizing:** You claim a disproportionate amount of the blame when bad things happen, and you don't see that certain events are also caused by others. *The marriage ended because I failed.* |
| **Blaming:** You focus on another person as the *source of* your negative feelings, so you refuse to take responsibility for changing yourself. *I'm lonely because of her. My parents caused all my problems.* |

**Unfair comparisons:** You interpret events by standards that are unrealistic—for example, you focus primarily on others who do better than you. Ironically, you seldom compare yourself to people who are worse off. *She's more successful than I am.*

**Regret orientation:** You focus on the idea that you could have done better in the past, rather than on what you can do better now. *I shouldn't have said that. I could have had a better job if I had tried.*

**What if?:** You keep asking questions about "what if" something happens, and you refuse to be satisfied with any of the answers. *Yeah, but what if I get anxious? What if I can't catch my breath?*

**Emotional reasoning:** You let your feelings guide your interpretation of reality. *I feel depressed; therefore, my marriage is not working out.*

**Inability to disconfirm:** You reject any evidence or arguments that might contradict your negative thoughts. For example, when you have the thought, *I'm unlovable,* you reject as *irrelevant* any evidence that people like you. Consequently, your thought cannot be refuted. It's impossible to prove that your negative thinking is wrong, so you hold onto it. *That's not the real issue. There are other factors.*

**Judgment focus:** You evaluate yourself, others, and events as good/bad or superior/inferior, rather than simply describing, accepting, or understanding. You are continually measuring things according to arbitrary standards and finding that they fall short. *I didn't perform well in college. If I take up tennis, I won't do well. Look how successful she is. I'm not successful.*[10]

Your negative automatic thoughts can be true or false—or have a grain of truth to them. You might think, *She doesn't like me.* We categorize this as mind reading, because you probably don't really know what she thinks. Later, you find out she actually doesn't like you. That's when you get upset. But why do you get upset? It's because you have a very demanding set of rules. Some of your rules may be "I must get everyone to like me," and "If someone doesn't like me, then there is something wrong with me." Or let's say you have the automatic thought that you will do poorly on an exam. So we might say that you are fortune-telling. But it turns out that you get a B, and now you think, *I must be an idiot.* This is where your rule book comes into play. Your rule is that anything less than perfection is a failure.

## ASSESSING YOUR ATTITUDES

To combat your depression effectively, we need to evaluate your underlying rule book, the assumptions that make you more likely to get depressed. The test that we use is called the Dysfunctional Attitudes Scale (DAS). Take some time to fill out the questionnaire in Table 2.2. Then we'll see how vulnerable you are to thinking in ways that will make you more depressed.

This inventory lists different attitudes or beliefs that people sometimes hold. Read each statement carefully and decide how much you agree or disagree with the statement.

For each of the attitudes, show your answer by placing a check mark in the column that best describes what you think. Be sure to choose only one answer for each attitude. Because people are different, there are no right or wrong answers.

To decide whether a given attitude is typical of your way of looking at things, simply keep in mind what you are like most of the time.

### Table 2.2
### Dysfunctional Attitudes Scale (DAS)

| Attitude |
| --- |
| 1. It is difficult to be happy unless one is good-looking, intelligent, rich, and creative. |
| 2. Happiness is more a matter of my attitude toward myself than the way other people feel about me. |
| 3. People will probably think less of me if I make a mistake. |
| 4. If I do not do well all the time, people will not respect me. |
| 5. Taking even a small risk is foolish because the loss is likely to be a disaster. |
| 6. It is possible to gain another person's respect without being especially talented at anything. |
| 7. I cannot be happy unless most people I know admire me. |
| 8. If a person asks for help, it is a sign of weakness. |
| 9. If I do not do as well as other people, it means I am an inferior human being. |
| 10. If I fail at my work, then I am a failure as a person. |
| 11. If you cannot do something well, there is little point in doing it at all. |

## Your DAS Score

Every item on the DAS is scored from 1 to 7. Depending on the content, either "totally agree" or "totally disagree" will be the anchor point of 1 and each answer from that point will score one higher. That is, if "totally agree" scores 1, then the next category, "agree very much," will score 2, and so on, up to "totally disagree," which will score 7.

There are 30 "dysfunctional" and 10 "functional" items in the scale. The following functional questions are scored in ascending order ("totally agree" = 1; "totally disagree" = 7): questions 2, 6, 12, 17, 24, 29, 30, 35, 37, and 40. The remaining questions are scored in descending order ("totally agree" = 7; "totally disagree" = 1).

The total score is obtained by adding up the sum of the scores. Your total score thus reflects the overall intensity of your dysfunctional beliefs.

Write your total score here: _____

| Totally Agree | Agree Very Much | Agree Slightly | Neutral | Disagree Slightly | Disagree Very Much | Totally Disagree |
|---|---|---|---|---|---|---|
| | | | | | | |
| | | | | | | |
| | | | | | | |
| | | | | | | |
| | | | | | | |
| | | | | | | |
| | | | | | | |
| | | | | | | |
| | | | | | | |
| | | | | | | |

| Attitude |
| --- |
| 12. Making mistakes is fine because I can learn from them. |
| 13. If someone disagrees with me, it probably indicates that he does not like me. |
| 14. If I fail partly, it is as bad as being a complete failure. |
| 15. If other people know what you are really like, they will think less of you. |
| 16. I am nothing if a person I love does not love me. |
| 17. One can get pleasure from an activity regardless of the result. |
| 18. People should have a reasonable likelihood of success before undertaking anything. |
| 19. My value as a person depends greatly on what others think of me. |
| 20. If I don't set the highest standards for myself, I am likely to end up a second-rate person. |
| 21. If I am to be a worthwhile person, I must be truly outstanding in at least one major respect. |
| 22. People who have good ideas are more worthy than those who do not. |
| 23. I should be upset if I make a mistake. |
| 24. My own opinions of myself are more important than others' opinions of me. |
| 25. To be a good, moral, worthwhile person, I must help everyone who needs it. |
| 26. If I ask a question, it makes me look inferior. |
| 27. It is awful to be disapproved of by other people important to you. |
| 28. If you don't have other people to lean on, you are bound to be sad. |
| 29. I can reach important goals without slave-driving myself. |
| 30. It is possible for a person to be scolded and not get upset. |
| 31. I cannot trust other people because they might be cruel to me. |
| 32. If others dislike you, you cannot be happy. |
| 33. It is best to give up your own interests in order to please other people. |
| 34. My happiness depends more on other people than it does on me. |
| 35. I do not need the approval of other people in order to be happy. |
| 36. If a person avoids problems, the problems tend to go away. |
| 37. I can be happy even if I miss out on many of the good things in life. |
| 38. What other people think about me is very important. |
| 39. Being isolated from other people is bound to lead to unhappiness. |
| 40. I can find happiness without being loved by another person. |

| Totally Agree | Agree Very Much | Agree Slightly | Neutral | Disagree Slightly | Disagree Very Much | Totally Disagree |
|---|---|---|---|---|---|---|
| | | | | | | |
| | | | | | | |
| | | | | | | |
| | | | | | | |
| | | | | | | |
| | | | | | | |
| | | | | | | |
| | | | | | | |
| | | | | | | |
| | | | | | | |
| | | | | | | |
| | | | | | | |
| | | | | | | |
| | | | | | | |
| | | | | | | |
| | | | | | | |
| | | | | | | |
| | | | | | | |
| | | | | | | |
| | | | | | | |
| | | | | | | |
| | | | | | | |
| | | | | | | |
| | | | | | | |
| | | | | | | |
| | | | | | | |
| | | | | | | |
| | | | | | | |
| | | | | | | |

## What the DAS Tells You

We know that people who score higher on the DAS are more likely to be depressed and to have future episodes of depression.[11] They are more likely to be perfectionistic, have eating disorders, feel anxious, and have other problems.[12] They are also more likely to recall negative experiences. For example, when Karen was depressed she seemed to recall only the really bad things in her life.

Your dysfunctional, or maladaptive, attitudes may go underground when you are *not* depressed. You may not even be conscious of them. It's as if they are waiting to be activated or primed by a setback in your life. It may be that when you are not depressed, your responses to the DAS questions seem no different from those of someone who has never been depressed. But when you have an experience that sets off an unhappy mood, your negative beliefs and values are activated. This makes it more likely that you will spin into a deeper depression.

As you go over your DAS results, take a look at the items on which you scored highest. This will tell you a lot about whether you are focused on pleasing others, getting approval, or trying to be perfect, as well as how you evaluate yourself. Your extreme responses are the attitudes that make you more likely to get depressed and stay depressed. These are the areas you'll want to keep in mind and work on as you go through the book.

### CHALLENGING YOUR NEGATIVE THINKING

Although cognitive therapy and medication are both effective for treating depression, it's interesting that dysfunctional attitudes change more as a result of cognitive therapy than they do in response to medication.[13] In some cases, patients experience sudden improvement in their depression, sometimes in just one or two sessions of therapy. Patients with sudden improvement are even more likely than patients who gradually improve to maintain their improvement a year later.[14] Researchers have found that changes in negative thinking precede this improvement—*so changing the way you think changes the way you feel.*

Throughout this book you'll learn a lot of techniques for modifying your negative thinking. One way to start is by getting perspective on it—breaking it down so you can take a close look at specific thoughts and the feelings that accompany them.

We have already seen that we can classify your negative thinking into several categories of automatic thought distortion—mind reading, fortune-telling, labeling, catastrophizing, discounting positives, and so on. You can also note how your emotions vary with what you are thinking in different situations. As an example, let's take Lisa, who was thinking of calling her friend Lindsay and feeling bad at the prospect. I asked Lisa to simply state her situation: "thinking of calling Lindsay." Then I asked her to identify the specific emotions that she experienced as she anticipated making the phone call and the degree to which she felt each emotion, from 0 to 100 percent. Lisa's emotions as she anticipated calling her friend were: anxious (90 percent), guilty (90 percent), and sad (75 percent). Finally, I asked Lisa to identify the automatic thoughts that underlay those emotions, the degree to which she believed each thought, and the type of distortion at work. Her automatic thoughts were:

- Lindsay will be angry with me (95 percent)—fortune-telling, mind reading

- I'm an idiot for not calling her earlier (75 percent)—labeling, all-or-nothing thinking

- I never do anything right (50 percent)—all-or-nothing thinking

By breaking down your moods and thinking in this way, you can see whether you tend to use the same automatic thought distortions over and over. Are you constantly mind reading? Do you tend to overgeneralize? You can also address the thoughts themselves and find practical ways to challenge them. One of the first things to do is to evaluate the advantages and disadvantages of having a particular thought; this may help you get motivated to change it.

Table 2.3 on the following page shows four questions to ask of any negative thought that you have. Let's look at an example using one of Lisa's thoughts about her phone call.

| Table 2.3<br>Testing Your Negative Thoughts | |
| --- | --- |
| **Thought: *I'm an idiot for not calling Lindsay earlier.*** | |
| 1. What are the advantages and disadvantages of this thought for me? | **Advantages:** Maybe I'm being realistic. Maybe I can motivate myself by criticizing myself.<br><br>**Disadvantages:** This thought makes me anxious and depressed and makes me more likely to avoid calling Lindsay.<br><br>**Conclusion:** I'd be much better off without this thought. |
| 2. What thinking distortion am I using? | I am labeling myself, and I am also thinking in an all-or-nothing way. |
| 3. What is the evidence for and against my thought? | **For:** I haven't called Lindsay yet. I feel depressed.<br><br>**Against:** I am not an idiot. I work productively, I'm a good friend, and I am educated. Being depressed is an illness, not a sign of being an idiot. |
| 4. What advice would I give a friend who is having this thought? | I'd tell my friend to be kinder to herself—and to give herself a break. Try to be compassionate toward herself. I'd tell her to challenge her negative thinking, and call Lindsay. |

Going further, Lisa and I then worked together to come up with some alternative ways of thinking about each of her thoughts on the phone call. We challenged the first thought (*Lindsay will be angry with me*) with *I don't know how Lindsay will feel. We often have gone a few weeks without talking. I've known her a long time and she's been understanding of me. Everyone gets busy and forgets to call.* We challenged the second thought (*I'm an idiot for not calling earlier*) with *I'm not an idiot. I have an excellent education. I've been a good friend to Lindsay in the past. Everyone makes mistakes, and no one is perfect*. And we challenged the third thought (*I never do anything right*) with *I do a lot of things right. I've gotten good feedback at work. I have a lot of abilities that I can be proud of. I even do things right as a friend of Lindsay; I was there for her when she had some problems with Don*. Then Lisa rated her belief in these positive responses—these ranged from 50 percent to 100 percent. Finally, she gauged her emotions again. By challenging her negative thoughts with helpful responses, she had reduced her anxiety from 90 percent to 40 percent, her guilt from 90 percent to 30 percent, and her sadness from 75 percent to 40 percent. Note that she still had some negative feelings—this is what it's like in the real world. It takes time to chip away at your negativity. But being able to modify your feelings in a few minutes is a powerful tool. Keep at it. The more you challenge your negative thinking, the better you will feel in the long run.

## HABITS OF THE MIND

The negative automatic thoughts we've been discussing are probably all too familiar to you. That's because they figure into nearly every facet of depression. So one of the most important steps in your self-help will be to develop and practice new patterns of thinking.

In the chapters ahead, we'll see how negative automatic thoughts contribute to specific symptoms of depression by distorting the way you think about yourself and your experiences. For now, let's take a closer look at a few of the mental habits that can powerfully prime you for depression—and take a first look at some ways to counteract them.

## How Do You Explain What Happens?

Let's say you take a test. You've studied for it, but not as much as you could have, and you are concerned about how you will do. You finally get your grade back, and it's poor—a C+. Understandably, you are disappointed. But how do you explain the outcome?

People who are depressed tend to attribute a negative outcome such as this to their own lack of ability. People who are not depressed tend to attribute it either to lack of effort or simply to bad luck (for example, the questions they studied for were not on the test). What's more, people who are prone to being depressed may overgeneralize the outcome (*I won't do well on any other tests*) rather than look at it as a specific event (*I didn't do well on this organic chemistry exam*). We refer to these styles of describing outcomes as "explanatory style."

You can think of causes for events as categorized in two different ways—two dimensions. They are either internal (qualities within you and actions you control) or external (factors outside your control), and they are either stable (qualities that don't change) or variable (qualities that do). If you attribute your C+ to lack of ability, that's a stable, internal trait—a quality intrinsic to you that cannot change. If you attribute it to bad luck, that's a variable, external trait—your luck is out of your control, and it can change. There's also a third dimension—how general or pervasive the cause is: "This is how I will do on other tasks" versus "This only applies to the current task."

For example, if something doesn't go well for you, which of the following are you likely to tell yourself?

- I didn't try hard enough (Internal/Variable)

- I'm just not that smart (Internal/Stable)

- I was unlucky (External/Variable)

- It's really a difficult task (External/Stable)

- I won't do well on other things either (General)

- I didn't do well on this task, but that means nothing about other tasks I'll take on (Specific)

Conversely, when something does go well, how do you explain your success? Is it because of your ability or effort, because it was an easy task, or because you were just lucky?

Thinking back to Karen's story from Chapter 1, we can see that her explanatory style was a negative style. She blamed herself for her marriage not working out, and she generalized this failure to other relationships—even to her work. She didn't give herself credit for the good work that she did or the good relationships that she had in her life. As a result, Karen felt helpless about doing anything to make things better and hopeless about the future. Her style of explaining things led to both pessimism and self-criticism.

Once you see how you explain things to yourself, you can experiment with a different style of thinking about causes. For example, let's say that something doesn't work out for you. Instead of chalking it up to a fault of yours that there's no hope of changing (*I'm just not that smart*), what if you said to yourself, *Maybe I can try harder next time* or *I was just unlucky?* Or what if you said, *Maybe that didn't work out, but other things can work out?* For example, Karen was able to see that the reason things didn't work out with Gary was that he was critical, self-centered, and uncommitted to the relationship. Rather than blaming herself, she could see that the task was too difficult—how do you work things out with someone who's not working on things? She could also see that her problem was specific to Gary; it wasn't generalized. She had other friends, she got along with people at work, and she had other potentially rewarding experiences in her life. This change in explanations was helpful in lifting her mood and letting her see that she had very little reason to blame herself and feel hopeless about other things.

Try these helpful hints for changing your own explanatory style. When something bad happens, ask yourself if it makes sense to think the following: *This is only one example. I do well at other things. Maybe the next time I can try harder. Maybe this is a challenge, and I can learn from this. Other people also might find it hard.* And when you do well at something, try this kind of thinking, and see how it feels to you: *I am good at this. I worked hard and I'm smart. I also do well at other things. I should give myself credit. Maybe I can try some other challenging things and see how I do.*

## Overgeneral Memory

People who are prone to depression often remember events in vague and overly general terms. Rather than recalling specific details of an event or a period of time, they may say, "It was kind of depressing and difficult. Things weren't going well." A more specifically detailed memory would sound quite different: "I was having some problems with my husband, Ted, at the time, mostly focused on how to deal with the kids. He wanted to discipline them more and have curfews, but I thought it was okay for them to be out as long as they called and let me know where they were."

People less prone to depression recall details and specifics. Why is this important? If your experience is framed in vague and overly general terms, then you're going to have a hard time specifying how to solve a problem. For example, the wife who recalls specific disagreements can then suggest specific solutions—for example, making sure that the kids call after 9:00 P.M. or touching base with an adult who knows where the kids are, like a coach or a neighbor. But it's hard to solve a problem when the problem is that things are "depressing and difficult" or "not going well."

Focusing on specifics rather than generalities is something we'll discuss throughout this book. I will periodically ask you to describe *exactly* what happened—what was said, who did what, and what specific outcome occurred—and then we will examine alternative ways of thinking and reacting and look at problem-solving skills that you can use. You can apply specific problem-solving techniques if you can specify the problem. When you do, you'll feel more empowered and less helpless.

## Rumination—Going Over It Again and Again

When Karen gets depressed, her mind lands on something unpleasant and just gets stuck. "I sit at home and think about how unhappy I am. My mind keeps going over bad things that have happened. I keep thinking, *What's wrong with me?*" This style of thinking is a major factor in making you more vulnerable to getting depressed and staying depressed.[15] (Unfortunately, it's a style that is more common among women and may be a main reason why women are more likely to get depressed.[16]) You get stuck on a negative thought or feeling and just keep spinning your wheels.

Why would rumination be associated with depression? Well, when you ruminate, you are focusing on negative experiences. When your mind is stuck in negative, you feel bad. And when you ruminate you are passive, isolated, and ineffective. Like Karen, you may be stuck at home, stuck in your rumination, and stuck in feeling down. When you are not ruminating, you are able to make plans, get things done, and feel effective, which feels good.

But if rumination makes us feel so bad, why do we do it? First, some people believe that they can ruminate their way to a solution. "If I keep thinking about how bad I feel, maybe I will come up with some way to feel better," Karen might say. Second, people who ruminate often don't realize that they have a choice: "I generally feel that when these negative thoughts come into my head, I can't let them go." Third, people who ruminate can't stand uncertainty, unfairness, or not being in control. They imagine that if they keep thinking about a problem, they will finally get closure, figure out the "real reason," and gain some control. Of course, this doesn't work, which makes them think they need to ruminate some more. And, fourth, rumination can be a strategy to avoid unpleasant experiences. Rather than just feeling sad, angry, confused, or anxious, you can try to think your way out of it.[17] When you are thinking, you are not feeling, acting, or communicating. You are stuck in your head.

In a later chapter we will examine some powerful techniques to let go of rumination and get on with your life. For now, I'd like you to pay attention over the next couple of days and try to notice if you are getting stuck on some negative thought—over and over. See if your mind is spinning its wheels in mud.

## Mindful Awareness

From what I've said so far about the way you think when you're depressed, one thing should be obvious: much of the suffering depression causes is created in the mind. Since this is true, it may be worth asking: Is there a way to change the way our minds work? Could there be some technique that would allow our minds to see more clearly what's happening outside them, without the distortions that cause us so much pain? Can we stand back and simply "observe" our mind—as if we are watching a movie? The answer to all of these questions is yes. It is what we call mindful awareness, and we will be discussing it throughout this book.

People from many traditions all over the world—spiritual teachers, psychologists, religious figures, medical authorities—have insisted that it *is* possible to train our awareness in this way, using a practice called mindfulness. This practice is at the heart of many forms of Eastern meditation, especially Buddhist forms, but you don't need to be a Buddhist, or even know the first thing about Buddhism, in order to practice it. Mindfulness is simply a way of experiencing the world—including your inner world—in which you are fully aware, *in the present moment,* of what is happening. You are not thinking, judging, or trying to control what is going on—all these are departures from awareness.

In mindfulness, you change your relationship to your thoughts. You don't try to change or eliminate the thoughts, and at the same time, you don't obey them—you just observe them. For example, you can have the thought, *I need to get more done,* but simply observe the thought without jumping up and doing something. When you are depressed, you tend to confuse your thoughts with reality. In mindfulness, you practice standing back and being aware of your thoughts *as thoughts,* noticing how they arise and then pass away with no apparent effort on your part. In our everyday life, we are often trying to *do* things—controlling, making things happen, keeping busy. Mindfulness lets you move from *doing mode* into *being mode*—experiencing and noticing, standing back and observing, watching and then letting go.

Research shows that mindfulness training can help you recover from depression and prevent future episodes. In the chapters ahead, I'll show you some specific ways you can use mindful awareness to step back from your negative thinking in any given moment. Then, in Chapter 12, about preventing relapse, I'll explain in more detail how to develop a mindfulness practice that can help you stay well.

## Pleasure, Effectiveness, and Rewards

Recall how Karen was spending a lot of time at home alone, ruminating and isolating herself. She was no longer going to the health club, no longer seeing her friends, and avoiding getting things done at work. She had stopped doing things that were pleasurable and rewarding, and this may be an important aspect of your depression, too. It may be that you have "lost" some rewards (for example, a relationship ended), or that some rewards have become less rewarding (your partner is not as attentive and affectionate), or that you are not doing the things you need to do to get rewards (you've become passive and withdrawn). Such a decrease in rewarding behavior is a hallmark of the depressed mind—but fortunately it's something that you can change almost immediately.

## Your Reward Menu

I often ask my depressed patients to make a list of rewarding experiences they've enjoyed in the past—a reward "menu." Think about this. What kinds of things did you enjoy doing before you were depressed? Make a list of things that you did, big and small. For example, Karen listed seeing friends, going bike riding, exercising, watching movies, taking classes, going to museums, and traveling. I asked her for some very simple examples as well, and she came up with taking a bubble bath, listening to music, baking, talking with friends on the phone, and writing poetry. Her reward menu was growing.

The next step for Karen was to begin sampling from the reward menu, assigning herself some pleasurable and rewarding activities every day. Planning ahead, one day at a time, she would have rewarding experiences to look forward to. Rather than focusing on her ex-husband as her only source of rewards, she now had a growing reward menu that was in her control. This was an important boost to her mood.

You can also link some rewards to positive activities that otherwise challenge you. For example, let's say you find it particularly hard to get to the health club and exercise. You may want to build in a "payoff" for this activity—a reward such as taking a nice bubble bath when you get home, sitting and reading something you enjoy, or listening to music for 20 minutes. Keep rewarding yourself on a regular basis—daily—for things that you do to help yourself. For example, you can give yourself a reward for reading this book!

## Gauging Your Pleasure and Effectiveness

Pleasure is simply a measure of how much you enjoy an activity. Unfortunately, depression can reduce your pleasure in activities you used to enjoy. For example, Karen found that her exercise at the gym was less pleasurable than it was before she got depressed. This is a natural consequence of depression. The important thing to remember is that the more you do these activities, the more the pleasure will accumulate and grow. It's like investing a little bit every day to get a bigger payoff later. It's hard to feel depressed when you think, act, and feel a different way.

Another source of depression is due to unpleasant life events. These may be frequent conflicts with your partner, difficulties at work, problems in traveling to and from work, extra long hours at work, or anything that seems unpleasant. I realized that I found it unpleasant to take the subway or bus to my office—it was crowded, and it was hard to relax. So I decided to start walking; it's about 35 minutes. I put on my iPod and listen to music, and I arrive at work energized and upbeat. I'm never late and never worried about how long it will take. Or let's say that you find that there are people in your life who are simply a burden—someone who is critical, negative, and undermines you. You might try being assertive and telling them to treat you better. Or, if that doesn't work, you might give yourself a break from interacting with them. You have a right to take care of yourself by limiting your contact with unpleasant people.

Another factor that affects your depression is the degree to which you feel effective or competent in doing something. This is different from feeling pleasure. For example, it may be difficult to get a job done, but you may have a feeling of being effective when you do. And feeling effective is a powerful antidote to depression.

A good way to find out how your pleasure and effectiveness change (according to what you are doing and who you are with) is to keep track of your moods for several days. This may seem a bit of a burden, but it can reveal some important (and perhaps surprising) trends.

Once you've kept this log for a week or so, you can review it to see which activities are pleasurable, which are associated with feeling effective, and which are "downers." Make a list of the up and down activities, and increase the former as you decrease the latter. As you go through the book, you'll find that we come back to the concepts of increasing rewarding behavior and boosting your pleasure and effectiveness as powerful antidotes to many aspects of depression.

## CONCLUSION

Throughout this book we will delve into the depressed mind and see what you can do today, right now, to begin changing the way you think so that you can change the way you feel. Once you see how your mind keeps you trapped in your negative feelings and self-defeating habits, you can begin developing strategies to change things. In the chapters that follow, you will practice new ways of thinking, behaving, feeling, and communicating so you don't become a victim of your own mind.

Let's see what this looks like. Figure 2.1, shows the various modes of thinking we've looked at in this chapter. See if you can identify your particular depressive mind-set. You have an evolutionary history that has primed you to avoid risk, conserve resources, and essentially shut down in times of scarcity and threat. Your depression is supported by—and in turn reinforces—dysfunctional attitudes such as pessimism, negative thinking, and a tendency to blame yourself for failure. You are also prone to ruminating, remembering experiences in vague and overgeneral terms, and slipping into inactivity and isolation. Your depression "makes sense"—and now we are ready to change it.

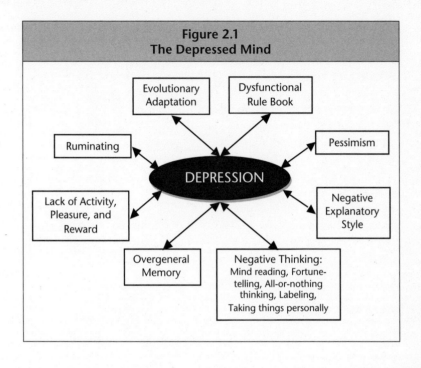

**Figure 2.1**
**The Depressed Mind**

# CHAPTER 3

# "Nothing Works Out": How to Overcome Your Hopelessness

Jenny and Bill had broken up a month before Jenny came to see me. During our meeting, she was telling me that she was so sad and depressed, so overwhelmed by the breakup, that she thought she could never be happy again. "Nothing seems to work out for me," she said. "I thought that Bill and I had a chance, but he just lost interest. And I'm getting older. My chances are less and less." Jenny was 29 years old.

Hopelessness is one of the most serious symptoms of depression. You feel that the future looks bleak, nothing will work out for you, and the cards are stacked against you. You may think you're cursed by the fates, your luck is bad, or you just don't have what it takes to be happy. You may look back on your life as a string of failures that predict a future of failure and sadness. In your desperate state of mind, you can't believe you will ever feel good again.

## HOPELESSNESS AND DEPRESSION

As painful as it is, hopelessness is just that—a symptom. It's part of your depression, not an accurate reflection of your reality. It's like a fever is a symptom of an infection—it doesn't mean that the temperature in the room is 102°F. When your depression takes over, your mind focuses almost exclusively on the negative. So, it's natural that you will feel negative about the future.

You may believe that things are hopeless *because* you feel depressed. This is what we call *emotional reasoning*. You are basing your prediction about the future on your emotions, not on the facts. We don't know what the facts will be in the future. Imagine if someone said, "I feel happy right now, so I am absolutely convinced that I will be happy for the rest of my life. In fact, I will become so happy that I will be ecstatic. I will be the happiest person in the world." Well, if you are like me, you would think that this person is far too optimistic. Life has its ups and downs. Of course he will have some sad—even terrible—experiences. That's what it means to be human.

Your predictions about your awful future are no more reliable than that person's predictions of perfect bliss. They are simply part of your depression. Most of my depressed patients over the last 25 years have had feelings of discouragement and hopelessness. In fact, I'll share with you a little secret. I like to get patients to predict that they will always be depressed and never have a happy experience. I like to get these all-or-nothing predictions—"I will never be happy again!" Here's why: it's so easy to prove them wrong and to help them recognize that hopelessness is the biggest distortion that you can have. In this chapter, we'll take a closer look at the ways hopelessness takes hold and the things you can do to overcome it.

## How Does Hopelessness Help You?

As with many negative thoughts, hopelessness is often accompanied by a hidden "strategy" to avoid disappointment. You have been hurt, rejected, and frustrated in your life, and now your mind kicks in to tell you that the future is hopeless—that nothing will work out—so you may as well give up. It's cutting your losses so you don't keep up an effort that is doomed or get your hopes up again only to be disappointed.

Sometimes we even fear having hope. If you have hope, you might get excited about the future, try new things, take some risks—only to find out that none of these things works, and you have been wasting your time. But even worse than wasting your time, you will feel disappointed and shamed: *What a fool I am to believe it could work out.* You don't want to be a "fool," so you opt for hopelessness.[1] Hopelessness is your way of saying, "I'm smarter than that. I've learned my lesson."

You may even find it annoying if someone tries to tell you that things *aren't* hopeless. You may feel that they don't understand what you have been through, how real this pain and despair are for you. They don't understand what it's like to be you—to have to live with your regrets, sadness, and sense of isolation from others. Even when you are not alone, you feel alone with your feelings, because no one understands as well as you how hopeless it really is.

You may get angry when people say, "But maybe things will work out." They are invalidating how bad it feels to you, but even worse, they are asking you to take some new risks—to get your hopes up again.[2] They are encouraging you to put yourself out there, set some goals, get on with your life—which just means you will face more frustration, more disappointment, more regrets. All you want is to be left alone—just you and your hopelessness. No one can understand that; no one can really appreciate that your hopelessness not only makes sense but also protects you from the future: *If I give up, I can't get hurt again.* There is solace, there is peace, and there is comfort—at times—in this hopelessness. In fact, your hopelessness may be the only thing you can really count on.

To see whether hopelessness is serving such a purpose for you, try this experiment. Make a list of the advantages and disadvantages of believing that things are hopeless. Don't try to be overly rational. Recognize that you may get some hidden gain from believing that things are hopeless. Then examine what you've written.

For example, if your fear of disappointment keeps you stuck in hopelessness, that may seem like an advantage: being hopeless protects you from being let down when things don't work out. But think about the logic of that statement. Since you can't prevent setbacks from happening, you are in effect saying, "I will be better at handling setbacks if I am depressed." I doubt it. I think it's *harder* to handle disappointment if you are sad and self-critical and indecisive. Hopelessness doesn't prepare you; it defeats you.

Once you realize why and how you think hopelessness protects you, we can examine how to let your guard down.

## What Are Your Reasons for Feeling Hopeless?

You probably believe that you have a lot of good reasons for your hopelessness. If I asked you, "Why do you think the future is so bleak?" you might come back to me immediately with a laundry list of misery: "Nothing will ever work out for me," "There aren't any good men (women) left," "I'm too old (not attractive enough, not rich enough, not interesting enough, too much of a burden, damaged goods)," "I can't compete," "I'm cursed," and "My opportunities are all behind me." Think, for a moment, about your *reasons* for why the future is so bleak. Write them down. We'll examine them.

Let's take your list of personal "deficits" that make you think no one will want a relationship with you. You might think that you have to look like Angelina Jolie or Brad Pitt to find someone, but you would be wrong. Here's an assignment for you. Go to city hall and walk into the room where people are getting marriage licenses. Ask yourself, *Is this place filled with movie stars?* It's probably not. Or go to any mall in the United States, and look around at the people—with their kids and their spouses—enjoying themselves and living their lives, and ask yourself, *Are these people perfect?* Your views about yourself may be negatively distorted—but even if they were true, there are millions of people willing to love someone who is imperfect. You just have to give them a chance—and be willing to love someone who isn't perfect either.

Or think about your idea that you will never be wealthy or famous. First, you don't know if that's true. Second—and much more important—*it makes no difference anyway.* You can get stuck believing that you can never be happy unless you have money and fame, but there are millions of very happy people who are not wealthy or famous. And there are lots of wealthy and famous people who are miserable. Pick up *People* or any of the gossip magazines, or count the number of divorces among the rich and famous, and my point will be proven.

Maybe you simply say, "The reason I'll be depressed in the future is that I feel depressed now." In fact, about 50 percent of people overcome their depression without any therapy or medication. And most people who do have therapy or medication get better. But you might say, "With my luck, I'll be among the few who never get better." But isn't that partly up to you? If you simply assume that you will be depressed forever, then you might make your nightmare come true.

## Is Your Hopelessness a Self-Fulfilling Prophecy?

Right now you may truly believe that things are hopeless. You are sure that nothing will work out. But what is the consequence of this belief? Hopelessness is a *self-fulfilling prophecy*, because you don't try things that could make you feel better, you quit if anything is frustrating, and you don't stick with positive behavior long enough to see a payoff. You are counting on hopelessness, so you are not willing to invest any time and energy or initiate any actions to make things different. You have built your future on hopelessness, so your hopelessness may well prove true.

But what if you did two things—as an experiment? First, what if you decided to doubt your hopelessness? Then, what if you decided to act against your hopelessness? What could happen? Let's try it and see. Doubting your hopelessness simply means recognizing that you can't be completely sure about the future. You don't know for sure that you will never be happy. You don't know for sure that you will never have the relationship that you want, the job that makes you feel great, high self-esteem, or enjoyment of your life. You may be depressed, but you are not a fortune-teller. Isn't it *possible* that you could be wrong about hopelessness? I ask you only to entertain a slight doubt—to admit that you may be wrong about how bad the future will be. That slight doubt could be a big step—enough to open a new door to the future.

Now, what would you do *differently* if you felt less hopeless? Would you be more active or more outgoing, make plans, or try some new activities? What if you decided, as an experiment, to act that way anyway—to act the opposite of the way your hopelessness dictates?

Let's imagine that you feel hopeless about finding that relationship that you think will make your life more complete. Try an experiment. Make believe that it is not hopeless. Tell yourself that it's certain you will eventually find that relationship. What would you do right now? Karen, whom you met in Chapter 1, decided to try this experiment. She said to herself, *Well, if I believed I would eventually find someone, I would probably enjoy my life more right now. I'd probably go out more, take classes, learn some new things. I'd take more chances.* So, Karen was on to a new experiment: to act as if things would work out. I suggested that since she would be on her own until things changed, this was the time to have adventures. And that's what she did. She signed up for a film class, she took up Indian dancing, she got involved in a political organization, and she began working out and feeling better about herself. As a result of making believe that things weren't hopeless, she felt better about her life, more hopeful about the future, and less needy of a relationship. When she finally met a guy she really liked, she was a more positive, more interesting, more attractive woman—one who didn't actually need a relationship but might be open to it.

The results of Karen's experiment could be yours, too. By putting hopelessness up on the shelf, by saying, "I'll act as if things are hopeful," you may find that you can make things feel better not only right now but also in the future.

## ACT AGAINST YOUR HOPELESSNESS

Let me tell you about Andy, my "Yankee Ticket" patient. Andy was 29 years old when he came to see me. He was depressed, defiant, and completely uncooperative. He lived at home with his parents—whom he was driving crazy with his complaints about how they didn't understand him, how they didn't prepare him for the real world, and how they expected too much of him. He refused to do anything to help himself. Our sessions together were an exercise in frustration for both of us—he felt depressed no matter what we did, and I felt frustrated that he rejected everything I said. After a couple of months, I said to him, "You know, Andy, you seem to take the position that you will do nothing to help yourself: you won't take medication, you won't do any self-help homework, and you just complain. How do you think I'm going to be able to help you?"

He responded immediately. "You can't."

"Well, I guess the only alternative is to get used to being depressed."

He looked at me, confused and a little annoyed. "What are you saying?"

"Well, you are telling me that it's hopeless and you won't do anything to change, so maybe it *is* hopeless."

He told me right then that he was going to quit therapy.

And he did quit. But he called me back two weeks later and said, "Maybe you're right. Maybe I need to do something to help myself."

I said, "On the depression inventory you took, you scored a 45. That's very high. I'm not guaranteeing anything, but I'll make a bet with you. I'll bet that we can reduce your depression by 50 percent in 12 weeks if you do everything I tell you to do. Here's the bet: if your depression drops to a score of 22 or below, you have to buy me two tickets to a Yankees game."

"Okay, it's a deal," Andy said. "But what do I get if my depression doesn't fall to 22?"

I chuckled a little. "I wouldn't be concerned. I intend to win."

And so it began. We worked at changing his relationship with his parents. I suggested that he apologize to them for complaining and blaming them for everything and ask them for ideas about how he could be helpful at home. We also worked on setting goals every day, challenging his self-critical thinking, and doing whatever we could to hook him to being more active and rewarding to other people. He got a part-time job. When the 12 weeks were over, Andy's depression score had dropped to 14, and he got me the tickets.

I said, "Want to see the Yankees with me?"

So the two of us went to the ball game.

Years later, I was walking down the sidewalk in New York, and he came up to me. He was smiling, he looked absolutely terrific, and he said, "You saved my life." I asked him what he was doing, and he told me he was working in a day-care center. He was really a kind, loving guy who had gotten trapped in his depression. But together we had gotten him to act against his hopelessness.

Incidentally, I can't remember if the Yankees won. But both of us won the bet.

## What Would You Have to Change to Feel Better?

You may feel stuck and hopeless about the future because you really do need to change some things in your life. Andy was a clear example of that. He was feeling hopeless partly because he didn't have a job, he had lost contact with his friends, and he didn't have a plan. So one way to approach your hopelessness is to begin by asking, *Where do I want to be?* or *What do I want to happen in my life?* Andy told me that he wanted to feel more productive, he wanted to get out of the house, he wanted to have friends again, and he wanted to get a job. He also wanted money of his own so he wouldn't have to go to his mother and father for support. Those all seemed like good goals. But there were things that would have to change in order for him to get from point A to point B.

If I have to drive from my house to a place I've never been, I plan my trip using MapQuest. I start with where I am and type in where I want to go. You can do that for your life, too. MapQuest your life. Where are you with friends, relationships, health, fitness, money, work, leisure, spirituality, learning, and feeling effective? Okay. Where do you want to end up?

As part of his treatment, Andy and I focused on friends. He had lost touch with people. In some ways this might be a good thing, since some of his old friends were alcoholics and drug abusers. He had a chance to focus on the more rewarding, more empowering friends—the people who could be a positive influence. And maybe he could aim at making some new friends. But we had to look at what is involved in building friendships. We identified two problems that Andy had in this area: he didn't return phone calls; and when he saw people, he just complained. So the first step was to initiate some phone calls, apologize for being out of touch, and make some plans. The second step was to stop complaining, focus on describing some of the positive things he was doing, and be a good listener to the people he wanted in his life.

At a deeper level, Andy realized that he would have to change his tendency to blame everyone else for his problems. That wasn't going to solve the problem. It would only alienate other people and make him more angry. Anger and blaming are a form of helplessness, and this sense of helplessness may lead you to feel hopeless about anything ever improving. It's better to share the responsibility so you don't feel hopeless about changing things. Also, anger and blaming don't accomplish anything. No one builds a successful business or a rewarding marriage by blaming and being angry. Blaming yourself won't change things for the better, either. Andy finally realized that blaming others or himself left him with the same problems. And he discovered that some of the things he had felt hopeless about were actually in his power to change.

## What Is Not Hopeless?

Some people say, "Everything is hopeless," which is very depressing indeed. But how could *everything* in the world be hopeless? Even if your relationship is hopeless, you still get dressed, still have lunch, still go to work, and still see your friends. So hopelessness may feel global and universal—as if nothing is all right—but this is a distortion and exaggeration. If you identify things in your life that *aren't* hopeless, you can regain perspective and redirect your energy.

Let's take Betty, who was going through her second divorce. She felt hopeless about ever reconciling with her husband, Carl, and hopeless about the rest of her life, too. She kept ruminating, *If only we could get back together I could be happy again.* But that seemed like an impossibility. It really *was* hopeless—with him—but Betty generalized this hopelessness to her entire life.

I asked Betty to think about what her life had been like before Carl. What did she enjoy? She made a list with me of the many things that gave her pleasure. This included seeing friends, working, learning, listening to music, traveling, exercising, interacting with animals, exploring the city, hiking, sailing, and meeting new people. Then I asked her, if she had been able to enjoy her life before Carl, why wouldn't she be able to enjoy her life without him now? So we took her list and began making a plan to combat hopelessness, setting specific goals for every day, every week, every month, and the next year.

On her first day, Betty made her list of goals and then called a friend and put her planned activities into her schedule. In her first week, she went back to the health club, made dinner plans, and focused more on her work. Her longer-term plans included traveling, taking some courses (she wanted to sharpen her knowledge about business), and meeting new friends. In place of her one truly hopeless situation—her marriage to Carl and the sadness it caused her—she began focusing outward on goals that were not hopeless. Her mood began to lift, and she began to feel better about herself. Although Betty still had symptoms of depression, her hopelessness had lessened. "I realize that by doing something today, I'm making a little progress a little bit at a time," she said. "There's something that I can aim for—and that gives me hope."

## No One Thing Is Necessary for Your Happiness

You can see that Betty's plan for overcoming hopelessness did not include Carl. This is a very important point to keep in mind. We often feel hopeless about one thing that we think is absolutely necessary to our happiness. It's not. Your happiness does not depend on a specific person, a specific job, a specific accomplishment, or a specific amount of money in the bank. Look at it this way. If your marriage were necessary for you to be happy, then you could never have been happy before you met your spouse. If your job were necessary, then you would never have been happy before you got that job. But the world isn't like that. There are literally billions of alternatives.

Imagine a little girl is born. Her parents love her. Other people love her. She grows up, and she does well in school and has friends and accomplishes a number of things. But every moment of her life, someone is telling her, "You can't be happy until you meet a guy named Carl and get married. Only then are you a worthwhile person, and only then can you be happy." Now, this would be an outrageous thing to do to a child, depriving her of every other source of happiness—making her believe that everything depends on someone named Carl whom this little girl may never meet. If it weren't such nonsense, we might even consider it a form of child abuse.

But you may be doing the same thing to yourself. If you think that your future is hopeless because you tell yourself this one thing is necessary for your happiness, aren't you depriving and abusing yourself in the same irrational way?

## Have You Been Here Before?

Another way to put your hopelessness in perspective is to recognize that you have felt that things were hopeless before—and you have been wrong. Look back at your life, and ask yourself if you have ever had the following thoughts:

- I will never get over my depression.

- I will never feel happy again.

- I will never have another relationship.

- I will always be alone.

- I will never have any success.

Now look back at your life, and check out the facts. Let's say that you said to yourself, *I will never feel happy again*—but that was five years ago. Have you smiled or laughed since then?

Betty had had a number of hopeless thoughts and hopeless periods in her life. She had tried to commit suicide five years earlier, been hospitalized twice, and been divorced before—all very serious experiences. But the reality was that after her first divorce, she was depressed for a while and then got over it, met Carl, fell in love, and married again. She was reasonably okay for some time. She had some success in her job, and she got good feedback on her work. So her experiences after periods of hopelessness were more positive than she remembered.

Perhaps you believe that things are hopeless because you think the obstacles you face now are just too big to overcome. But all of us have overcome difficulties at some point in our lives. You may be focused on how bad things are right now and how bad they will be in the future, but what about the obstacles you have overcome in the past?

Betty had overcome a number of obstacles. Her mother was critical, her father was distant—and then he died when Betty was only 11. She had difficulties with other kids at school. But she still managed to survive. She made friends, did well in school, got into college, dealt with freshman loneliness, and made friends who are still in her life today. She weathered several bouts of depression and each one had been resolved. I'm willing to bet that you can come up with a similar list of challenges that you've faced and overcome.

Think about it—and as you do, keep in mind that hopelessness may be *temporary*. You've been wrong in the past, and you may be wrong again. We won't know if it's hopeless until you've tried everything you can.

## Have You Tried Everything?

You might say, "Look, I've been depressed for over a year, and there is no end in sight. I've had therapy. I've tried medications. Why should I feel optimistic about the future?" I'm not telling you to feel optimistic. All I can do is ask you to hold open a doubt about the hopelessness in your future.

You can't decide for sure that things are hopeless unless you have tried literally every way possible to resolve your depression—and I can guarantee that you haven't tried every last therapeutic technique out there. (I wrote a book for clinicians called *Cognitive Therapy Techniques*—there are about 100 techniques in there. I'm positive you haven't tried them *all*.) I am confident that you have not exhausted all the medications and combinations of medications that are available, either. And I doubt you have tried all of the more intensive treatments that can be very effective for treatment-resistant depression, such as electroconvulsive (shock) treatment, or ECT, and other interventions. I suspect that the more dramatic options will be completely unnecessary for you; my point is that there are many ways of beating depression, and I can assure you that you have not tried all of them. For one thing, there are new interventions, new medications, and new forms of therapy being developed all the time. There is hope.

Here is an example of hopelessness that was turned around.

Ellen had been in and out of psychiatric hospitals for years. She had seen therapists, taken medications, and had good support from her loving family. But nothing worked. When I spoke with her, it became clear to me that her depression was really bipolar disorder. But she had been misdiagnosed, and as a result her treatment was not targeted to her real problem. Using this information she finally convinced her psychiatrist that she was bipolar and needed to take lithium, a medication that helps stabilize mood. This helped immensely, but she still had some mood swings, though not as bad as before. Her psychiatrist suggested ECT, and her mood improved dramatically after several sessions. But things slipped back after a couple of months. Finally they decided to try

her on maintenance ECT, which involved monthly sessions of brief electrical stimulation. She has been vastly improved now for several years.
Ellen is 67 years old—she didn't get the effective treatment until she had
been going through depressive cycles for almost 40 years. She probably
thought she *had* tried everything, but there was still hope.

## THE END OF HOPE

The greatest tragedy of depression is suicide—the ultimate expression of hopelessness. And when a patient is at risk, preventing it is treatment's most pressing task.

Many people who are depressed have thoughts of suicide but say
they would never act on them. Your therapist can help you decide if suicide is a risk for you. Important predictors of risk include having made a
prior attempt, the wish to die during a prior attempt (sometimes attempts
are not "meant" to be lethal), self-mutilating behavior such as cutting or
hitting yourself, access to a firearm, hoarding pills, writing a suicide note,
threatening to commit suicide, abusing drugs or alcohol, lacking social
support, feelings of hopelessness, and lacking reasons to live.

People with thoughts of suicide may talk about reasons to die—such
as to escape pain, because life is too hard, or to stop being a "burden" to
others. But I ask my patients to consider their reasons to live, and I ask
you to do the same. Their reasons sometimes include guilt about hurting loved ones, hope that therapy and medication can help, hope that
the situation may change, the possibility that their depressed thinking
is not realistic, fear of the afterlife, moral scruples, fear of botching their
suicide attempt, and missing out on the opportunities they might have
had if the depression lifted. If your depression makes it hard for you to do
this exercise, try asking yourself, *If I were not depressed, what would be some
reasons to live?* This is important, since your reasons to live may improve
substantially once your depression lifts.

Taking your life is the most important decision that you will make.
Does it make sense to decide at a time when your thinking may be dramatically distorted in the negative? Does it make sense to decide when
you have not pursued every option available? You will read about people
in this book whose lives seemed completely hopeless. It makes me feel
wonderful today to know that they are alive and well—and happy. You
can't get better unless you are alive to work on these problems.

However, if your depression is so overwhelming that you become a danger to yourself, it is an important time for you to turn to family members, friends, and your therapist for the support you need. It might be helpful to consider a brief "time-out" in a hospital setting where you can be protected, receive medication, and have a break from the pressures of everyday life.

Sam had previously attempted suicide and was beginning to feel hopeless and suicidal again. We arranged for him to go into the hospital for a couple of weeks where more aggressive treatments could be administered. In his case, a combination of a more powerful medication and ECT turned him around. When I saw him after his discharge from the hospital, it was like meeting an entirely different person. He treated his depression at that point like the emergency that it was, and he is alive today. I know that his wife, his two children, and his many friends are happy that he made that decision.

Take your thoughts of suicide seriously and discuss them with your therapist or someone close to you. This is a decision that you need to think through, get the best advice on, and find positive ways to address. Many of my patients who have overcome their depression once had thoughts of suicide. We sometimes look back together to those dire moments of hopelessness and appreciate our relief that they chose treatment rather than ending their lives.

Hope is not always easy. It requires work, it involves frustration, and it is about a future that you do not yet know. But hope is real—it's not a fantasy—and I can tell you that I have seen many examples of hope made true by perseverance and openness to help.

As the saying goes, "You save the world one man at a time." I believe that. And I believe that you can save yourself. But you have to give yourself the chance to do it.


## IS THE PRESENT MOMENT HOPELESS?

Hopelessness is always about the future: "I'll never be happy," "I'll never have the relationship I want," or "I'll always be a failure." You are predicting the future, so by definition you are not living in the present moment.

The question for you right now is, "Is the present moment hopeless?"

What are you aware of in the present moment? Perhaps you are sitting in your room reading this, and you are alone. But as you read my words on this page, you and I are focusing on what you are thinking and experiencing at this moment. So let's see what we can do with this present moment. First, focus on your breath. Notice that it flows like waves of air, in and out. Stand back and observe your breath as if you were watching it from afar. Don't try to control your breath, don't judge it, don't try to make it slower or deeper, better or worse. Simply observe your breath going in and out. Stay with your breath now for a few minutes. When other thoughts come into your mind, just let them go and gently return your attention to your breath.

Now I want you to take something that smells good—an orange, a pine cone, or perfume. If it is an orange, peel the skin off, and smell the orange. Notice the subtlety of the fragrance of the orange. Perhaps you have never taken a moment like this to simply notice how it smells. How does the smell enhance your enjoyment of eating the orange? If you're holding a pinecone, run your fingertips over it. Touch the individual scales. Is there sap on it? If you choose perfume, put some on your wrist or neck. Now smell it gently. Try to notice the different layers of fragrance. Stay in the moment with this. Notice how the fragrance seems to come and go.

Now set this aside for a while. We're going to try something else.

I want you to close your eyes, and imagine the woods in the moonlight. There is snow on the ground. Snow is gently falling, one flake at a time. You notice each flake in slow motion, caressing the night as it falls ever so gently to the drifting snow beneath. As the snow falls, you feel the cool air and the snow. You notice the shape of a flake in slow motion falling to the ground.

Imagine now that you are the snow that falls. You are falling as a flake, repeating yourself over and over. You are a snowflake falling in the night air. You are snow that is falling, one small piece of snow in each moment, over and over again. You are falling in the night as the light of the moon shines down and it is silent, quiet, and peaceful all around you. You and the snow keep falling, over and over again.

Stay in this moment. Silent, gentle, natural, in the light where the snow is falling. At peace.

If you have been able to do these three exercises—observing your breath, smelling the fragrance, and watching the snow fall in your imagination—you have stepped away from hopelessness, into the present moment, and have lived completely in this moment in time.

There is no hopelessness in the present moment. It just is. It is not the future—it is now, in the present, one moment in time. In this moment, you simply are. Moment after moment, snowflake after snowflake, breath after breath. Repeating and returning. Stay here and then let go and another moment happens.

And you are born all over again.

As you live in the present moment—experiencing, hearing, feeling, tasting, sensing—you recognize that you can find something right now that makes you feel alive. Being alive is being conscious. It is being fully aware. Give up your judgment, give up your need to control, let go of the future, and stay here in the present moment. Here in the present moment there is no hopelessness—and there is no such thing as hope. There is only the experience of now.

## CONCLUSION

One of the hardest things to do is to feel hopeless—*and still go on.* The fact that you are reading this book means that you feel there is some hope. You hope to get hope in these pages. Every day I talk with patients who feel hopeless about their depression or anxiety, but it's not discouraging to me because I have great confidence that in working together we will turn things around. We need to keep in mind that predictions are not facts; it's not over until you've tried *everything;* you can do something positive each day; and if you can make positives happen, then it's not hopeless. You need to repeat the positive to get the rewards; and even if some things don't work out, other things can work out. Think of this as being flexible enough to make progress.

Throughout this book I will suggest countless techniques and viewpoints that you can try—over and over again—to change the way you feel. After you are feeling better, go back and examine your negative predictions—so you can keep in mind that you've made the changes you never thought you could make.

## Challenging Your Hopelessness

- Realize that hopelessness is not a realistic response to your reality—it's a symptom of your depression.

- Ask yourself if there is an advantage to feeling hopeless. Is your hopelessness protecting you against disappointment or helping you in some other way?

- Why do you think things are hopeless? Write down your reasons, and then examine them.

- Is your hopelessness a self-fulfilling prophecy? See if you can entertain a little doubt that things are hopeless. Then imagine what would happen if you acted as if they weren't.

- Ask yourself what would have to change in order for you to feel better. Maybe it's an achievable goal.

- What goals are *not* hopeless in your life? Focus on those instead of the ones you can't hope to achieve.

- Realize that no one specific person or experience is necessary to your happiness.

- Ask yourself if you have felt hopeless before. Did things change?

- Maybe you think the obstacles you face now are just too big. But what obstacles have you overcome in the past?

- Are there techniques and medications that you have not tried to combat your depression? It's not hopeless until you've tried *everything.*

- Try an exercise in mindful awareness. You'll see that you cannot be hopeless about the present moment—and you can come back to the present moment anytime.

# CHAPTER 4

# "I'm a Loser":
# How to Handle Your
# Self-criticism

Tom had been unemployed for two months and had been feeling down ever since he lost his job. He'd been working at a bank, doing fairly well, but the bank needed to downsize because of losses it incurred. In fact, about 15 percent of the people at the bank were let go. But Tom felt that he had failed. "After all, they kept 85 percent of the employees," he said. "How do I face my friends? I mean, they're going to feel sorry for me—but that just makes me pathetic."

Tom told me that he sat in his apartment by himself at night thinking that he was a loser, no one would want him, and he had failed in every area of his life. Dejected, self-loathing, and feeling like a pariah no one would ever care for, Tom found it hard to go on. Although Tom was a good-looking young man, since he got depressed he'd also felt unattractive.

## SELF-CRITICISM AND DEPRESSION

Self-criticism is a core feature of depression for many people. It takes the form of blaming yourself (*It's all my fault*), labeling yourself (*I can't believe how stupid I am*), hating yourself (*I can't stand myself at times*), doubting yourself (*I just can't make the right decisions*), and discounting your positives (*Oh, anyone could do that—it's not hard*). And, when you are self-critical, the smallest mistake or slightest imperfection becomes a target for your self-loathing. If you spill a cup of coffee, you are an oaf.

The problem with self-criticism is that it ties in with many other symptoms of your depression. For example, your rumination may focus on self-critical thoughts about something you've done wrong or something that's wrong with you. Take a look at the list below to see if self-criticism is making any of these connections for you.

- *Rumination:* I keep thinking over and over about how I have messed things up.

- *Unfair comparisons:* I keep comparing myself to people who do better, and I don't measure up.

- *Can't enjoy activities:* When I do something I can't enjoy myself because I am constantly thinking how poorly I am doing.

- *Indecisiveness:* I can't make decisions because I have no confidence in myself.

- *Fear of regret:* I can't make changes in my life because if they don't work out I will suffer regret.

- *Helplessness:* It's hard for me to do anything because I just don't think anything I do will change things.

- *Isolation:* I have a hard time being around people because I feel I have nothing to offer.

- *Fear of intimacy:* I am afraid of getting involved in a relationship because once people know the real me, they will reject me.

- *Sadness:* I am sad and dejected because I don't feel good about myself.

There's another side to that coin, though: getting over your self-criticism can affect almost every other symptom of your depression, too. If we beat self-criticism, we can defeat hopelessness, indecision, isolation, and rumination, so it's a good target for you to aim at. Let's get started.

## Voicing Your Criticism

It was fairly simple to get Tom to identify his negative thoughts about himself. "I feel like a loser. I worked hard to get this job, and I thought I was doing well, but they axed me. Here I am at 28 without a job. Everyone else I know is doing well. But look at me. No job. Nothing."

Your negative thoughts about yourself can take many forms. For example, you might label yourself as boring, stupid, ugly, inferior, or unlovable. You might find yourself criticizing almost everything you do: *I can't believe how stupid I am. There I go again!*

One way of recognizing how your self-criticism affects your depression is to keep track of any self-critical thought you have. You can take a piece of paper and simply write down examples of your negative thoughts as they occur. You might find that you criticize yourself from the moment you get up in the morning to the moment you go to bed at night. Or you might find that you do it more frequently in certain situations— for example, when you meet new people, or when you're interacting with someone at work, or when you don't get something right the very first time. One woman who kept track of her self-critical thoughts decided to note them by saying to every negative thought, "There I go again."

## Defining Your Terms

Before you condemn yourself forever with your self-criticism, it might be useful to define what you're really saying about yourself. What do you mean by a "loser" or a "failure"? I asked Tom to tell me what these terms meant to him. He replied, "A loser is someone who never wins. It's someone who can't do anything right. The same thing with being a failure. You can't succeed at anything. Nothing works out for you."

"What is the opposite of a loser?" I asked.

"Someone who can actually get something done—get it right. Someone who feels confident in himself. Someone different from me."

"Okay, Tom. You actually gave two very different definitions of the *opposite* of a loser—the first definition was someone who can get things right, and the second definition was someone who feels confident."

"Yeah, that's right."

"Is it possible to get something right but not feel confident about other things?"

"I guess it is."

"If you base your self-criticism on not feeling confident, then you are locked in a vicious circle. You're saying to yourself, *I'm self-critical because I don't feel confident, and I don't have confidence because I'm self-critical*. It's like you are criticizing yourself because you don't have confidence. Doesn't that sound like you are actually criticizing yourself for criticizing yourself?"

"Now that you put it that way, I guess it does."

So, we now had Tom's definitions:

- *Loser* = Someone who never wins. Someone who can't do anything right.

- *Failure* = Can't succeed at anything. Nothing works out.

- *Opposite of loser* = Someone who can get something done and get it right.

## Examining the Evidence

I decided to bring Tom back to the issue of confidence that we'd touched on when we defined his terms. "You know, when you base your self-worth on 'feeling confident,' you are using a thought distortion that we call *emotional reasoning*," I explained. "It's like saying I feel bad because I feel bad. There's no way out. You can feel bad, but you can still do some worthwhile things. Isn't that possible?"

Tom agreed. "But how do I change the way I feel?"

I replied, "Well, it may take some work, but the first thing that we have to do is examine whether you are looking at the facts. When we look at the facts, we may see that you have done a lot of positive things, but it is also a fact that you are not giving yourself credit for them. Perhaps we can look at why that is."

We decided to look at the evidence that Tom was a loser. He came up with the following: "I'm depressed, I lost my job, I don't have a lot of money, and I'm not married." We then looked at the evidence that he was not a loser (that he was "someone who can get something done and get it right"): "I got into college, I graduated, I have a number of friends, I actually did a good job on my job, I've traveled and studied and done some spiritual work, and I'm reasonably okay-looking."

So, what do you think about the evidence that Tom is a loser and a failure? Is it convincing to you? Do you think that Tom would be able to convince a jury that he is a loser and a failure? When you are depressed you focus on one example of a negative—"I lost my job"—but you don't consider all of the positives about yourself. Your view is biased. And you don't consider how valid the evidence is. For example, would you consider everyone who loses a job to be a loser? Aren't there many people who lose their jobs because of changes in market conditions, downsizing, and management changes? Don't these people find new jobs? Are they losers in between jobs and winners when they get new ones?

## What Is Self-Criticism Good For?

In the last chapter, we looked at how hopelessness might be helping you just as earlier in the book, we examined what depression itself might be good for. So it makes sense to ask if there are advantages to self-criticism. What might you gain from criticizing yourself?

We may think that if we criticize ourselves it will help motivate us. We won't get lazy. We will try harder. I asked Tom what he thought the advantage was of criticizing himself. Trying to give me the answer he thought I wanted to hear, he said, "Oh, I know. It's irrational. There's no advantage."

"Whether it's irrational or not, we usually think that our beliefs will help us in some way," I said. "What do you think you might hope to gain from criticizing yourself?"

"I guess I think that this will motivate me. Maybe I'll be able to scare myself into trying harder. If I feel bad enough, maybe I'll go out and get another job."

"So you think that self-criticism is a good way to build motivation?"

"I know it sounds crazy, but yes, sometimes."

"Can you imagine a self-help book with the title *Ten Things to Hate about Yourself to Become Successful*?"

Tom laughed. "No, but you could probably get on late-night TV with that one."

"Or how about a motivational book entitled *How Thinking I Was a Loser Helped Me Win*?"

"Okay, okay. I get the point."

"What's the point?"

"The point is that there is no real advantage in criticizing myself."

But you might think there is. You might think your self-criticism will light a fire under you and get you up and going. Sometimes a criticism might motivate you to try harder—some sports coaches think so. But unless you think you have the mettle to make it to the Superbowl (and since you are depressed anyway), self-criticism will only defeat you. Rather than becoming the screaming critical coach, you might try becoming your own best cheerleader.

Or you might think that you are simply being realistic: "But I really *am* a loser." But checking out all the facts, weighing the pros and the cons, asking yourself the advice you would give a friend with a similar problem are not ways of being unrealistic. You need to look at *all* the facts, not simply the negative ones. In fact, you might even conclude that your self-criticism is unrealistic.

Or you might be afraid that if you don't keep yourself in check with criticism, you will let your guard down, become too self-confident, and make an even bigger fool of yourself. These beliefs about self-criticism can keep you depressed. If they were working so well, then you would be feeling great, wouldn't you? If your criticism is so helpful, then why do you feel so bad?

## SETTING YOUR STANDARDS

The fact is, there is a grain of truth in these beliefs. You don't want to become so complacent that simply breathing becomes your standard of excellence. But what would be a reasonable standard for you? Here are some criteria to consider.

### Set Achievable Goals

When you set a standard for yourself, the goals should be things you can achieve every day. You want to have opportunities for success every day. For example, when I have a deadline hanging over my head, I will say to myself, *Do some writing for one hour.* That's a goal that I can usually achieve. I don't say, *Write a book today.* That's not realistic.

### Replace Self-criticism with Self-reward

When you are feeling good, it's not difficult to say positive things to yourself, such as *That was a good job* or *I'm glad I put the effort in.* But when you are depressed, this self-rewarding behavior can drop out, leaving only your self-critical thinking. So when you achieve your goal for the day—or for the moment—make it a point to say something positive to yourself. Make a mental list of self-reward statements that you can pull out at any moment when you need them. Here are some good examples: *Good for me. I tried. I'm making progress. I got something done. I am moving toward my goals. I'm doing better than before. I put a lot of effort in, and that's good.* One of my patients imagined himself giving himself a high five, another imagined himself spiking a football in the end zone, and another imagined herself bowing before a loving audience.

You can also build in some concrete self-rewards. For example, say to yourself, *If I finish writing these letters, then I can go for a walk.* List some activities that you really enjoy, and make them rewards for doing things that are less enjoyable.

## Use Self-correction

Tom wanted to turn off his harsh self-criticism, but we knew it wouldn't work if he just tried to tell himself that everything he did was wonderful instead. Imagine sitting in front of a mirror telling yourself that everything is great, you are the best in the world, and no one can stop you. You might feel better for a few minutes, but you won't believe a word of your pep talk unless it is really based on facts. You can't fool yourself.

So we decided to try an alternative—self-correction. This means simply being honest about your mistakes. For example, Tom realized that he was making a mistake to think that a job with a bank lasted forever. Rather than isolate himself by staying in his apartment, filled with shame and ruminating about "being a failure," he could be proactive and plan how to network to look for another job. We discussed some people he could contact to let them know that he was on the job market. He could put his name out to some recruiters. He could call friends, have lunch, talk about prospects. He could work to correct the passivity and isolation that his self-criticism was feeding.

As another example, let's take Sally, who was going through a breakup. When she looked at what went wrong, two things occurred to her— one, the man wasn't really right for her, and two, she complained a lot. Rather than label herself a failure, I suggested that she could learn from her mistakes and ask herself how she could choose better in the future. Sally realized that the man she had broken up with had problems with commitment and anger, and he had a difficult time dealing with her emotions. This was information that she could use next time.

Sally could also learn that continual complaining can be a problem—and, rather than judging herself harshly for it, explore some alternatives. We discussed reasonable assertion ("Say what makes you feel better, and reward the other person when he does it"), mutual problem solving in a relationship ("Present a problem as something both of you can solve—and then generate possible solutions together"), and knowing when to quit ("Sometimes it's better to accept a loss than to persist in finding a solution").

Here's why self-correction works better than self-criticism. When you are learning how to play tennis, your instructor will correct your swing and show you how to hit the ball correctly. But what if your instructor hit you over the head with the racket and called you an idiot? How well would you learn tennis?

Rather than criticize yourself, ask yourself the following:

- Is there a better way to do this?

- What can I learn?

- Who does a better job at this—and how can I learn?

## Use the Double-Standard Technique

Try listening to yourself and imagine being this critical of others. Would you be as tough on them as you are on yourself?

The double-standard technique asks you to apply the same demanding standards to others as you would to yourself or to be as lenient with yourself as you would be with others. This is one of my favorite techniques because it really asks you to be fair to yourself. I like using role-plays with my patients so they can hear what they sound like.

"Tom, I want you to make believe that I am your friend who has lost his job. I want you to be as critical as you can be with me—call me a loser, failure, and all the terrible things that you call yourself. I'd like you to hear what it sounds like. I'll stay in the role of being a person you are criticizing. So just go after me. Let's start with me saying, 'Tom, I just lost my job.'"

TOM, *skeptical*. Okay, you must have done something wrong to lose your job.

BOB. Like what?

TOM. Oh, you weren't as smart as the other people there. The boss didn't like you.

BOB. It sounds like you are pretty critical of me.

TOM. Yeah. You can't do anything right. You're a loser.

BOB. That makes me feel really bad to hear that. I was counting on you for support.

TOM. How can I support you? You can't do anything right.

Stepping outside of the role-play, I asked, "How would you feel telling someone that they are a loser because they lost their job?"

"I can't ever imagine telling anyone that," Tom replied. "It's so cruel."

"But isn't that how you sound to yourself every day?" I asked.

What is your rationale for being kinder to others than you are to yourself? You may think that being tough on yourself will motivate you, but it will very likely paralyze you and depress you. You may think that you are "superior" to other people—as one man said, "I don't compare myself to the average; I compare myself to the best." But this is a real problem, because now you think that you can only be kind to yourself if you win a gold medal. Why do you *have to be the best?* A lot of our demands on ourselves come from this kind of perfectionism. What is the consequence for demanding more from yourself than you do from others? Does it make you miserable?

What if you decided to be as lenient with yourself as you are with others? "I know a lot of people who have been laid off," Tom said. "It's tough on them, and they need all the support that they can get from their friends. The last thing I would ever do is criticize them." So, what if Tom decided to be his own best friend at this time? What would he say to himself? He realized that he would feel a lot better about himself and his life.

## Evaluate Your Evaluating

As far as we know, we humans are the only animals to stand back and evaluate ourselves—to try to figure out how we measure up. Moose don't stand around comparing themselves to other moose. But we often evaluate ourselves by comparing ourselves with other people—and, if we are prone to depression, we compare ourselves to people who are doing better than we are. We evaluate ourselves using impossible standards of perfection.

But why do we have to evaluate ourselves at all?

Let's imagine that I am completely in the moment—say, in the experience of observing a butterfly. I appreciate the beauty of its multicolored wings, I am in awe of its delicacy, and I love watching it hover above the lilies. I am experiencing the butterfly in the present moment. I am out of my head and into the butterfly. In this present moment, I am not evaluating myself, nor am I comparing the butterfly with all of the other butterflies. I am observing, letting go, appreciating, in the moment. I feel great.

Imagine that I am sitting in my chair, and I decide to try some mindful breathing. In this exercise, I simply observe my breath—in and out. I feel the flow of air into my chest and then out of it. But soon I begin to notice myself evaluating how I am doing: *Am I breathing too rapidly? Am I doing this right?* Now I'm even evaluating my breathing. There is no end to this self-evaluation.

So I can try the breathing exercise again and watch for any thoughts that might get in the way of simply breathing and observing. As I notice the evaluation thought appearing, I can observe that thought and decide that I will let it go. I can form an image of this thought on a stream of air floating away. It may come back; I can let it go again. The flow of thoughts comes and goes. As another thought comes, it rides the wave of air that comes in and then rides the air going out. I don't need to answer those thoughts, just watch them come and go. I am feeling more relaxed as my evaluation thoughts come and go. They, too, will pass.

Tom was evaluating himself constantly. He caught evaluation thoughts the minute he woke up—*I'll probably screw up today, too.* Even the suggestion that he could catch himself and observe his evaluation thoughts became an occasion to evaluate himself—*I'm not sure if I will do this the right way,* and *I'm so messed up I am probably evaluating myself all the time.*

Try to catch yourself evaluating yourself. Don't be concerned with how well you catch yourself. Just be aware of how often you slip into self-evaluation.

Now, let's see what you can do with the thoughts you catch.


## Observing and Accepting

If you go outside and look at the sky, you may observe some clouds floating gently, slowly, in the distance. Stand back and observe them. Notice their shapes and motions. Notice how they float at different speeds, depending on the wind. Some are darker, some lighter, some larger. Imagine that you are trying to paint the clouds, so you are trying to observe, at this moment, the various shades of white and gray.

Now imagine that you are part of the clouds, lighter than air. You have become a cloud for this moment, and you are floating along with the other clouds. You see yourself, a cloud, from above Earth. You are floating with the clouds, gently, slowly, across the atmosphere of Earth to become part of the mass of clouds that comes and goes throughout the day.

You may close your eyes for a few minutes in silence and imagine the floating of the clouds, the Earth, and the coming and going of this experience.

You have just practiced mindful awareness, simply being present with the clouds and the moment. You did not have to evaluate yourself or the clouds. You did not have to control anything. You simply observed things as they were in the moment—and you accepted them as they were.

You can do this every day whenever you notice that you are evaluating yourself. Let's say you are walking along, and you begin thinking, *I don't feel very attractive.* You notice that your mind is now shifting to your appearance and how other people might see you. You are evaluating yourself again.

You can now shift into observing and accepting.

What will you observe and accept?

You can start with simply observing that you have a negative thought. It's there for this moment. Rather than try to get rid of this thought—or get angry at it—you might say, "Here you are again." You can welcome the thought. You can ask the thought to come along for a walk.

Let's imagine that your negative thought comes along with you.

As you walk along, with the negative thought chattering away and criticizing you, you can decide to accept that it is there. You can even ask it to join you in observing. You can say, "Let's look around at what is in front of us on this walk." You notice that you are walking along, and there is a mother pushing a baby carriage. The baby is bundled in a light blue outfit. The mother smiles at you as you are looking at the baby. You observe that she seems happy.

Your negative thought may still be with you, but you are walking along in the present moment, observing and accepting the reality in front of you.

Perhaps you don't feel that you are looking your best. Perhaps you think that you are not doing the best job at work. Perhaps you are sure that your life could be better. Rather than criticize yourself because things aren't where you want them to be, you can simply observe that that's the way it is right now. *Things aren't the way they could be. They could be better.* But you recognize that you have a choice right now. *I can either criticize myself or observe and accept things the way they are.*

If you accept yourself the way you are, you may eventually be able to turn in a new direction. But if you criticize and hate yourself, you are stopping yourself in your tracks. Rather than measure yourself against any standard, say to yourself, *I am who I am.*

## A New Rule Book

A lot of us have certain rules about how we *should be and should think.* These rule books can make us worried, regretful, self-critical, anxious, and depressed. Your rule book may include some of the maladaptive attitudes you endorsed on the Dysfunctional Attitudes Scale in Chapter 2. See if the maladaptive rule book on the following page sounds like the one you're living by.

Tom had several of these rules in his head, which fed his self-criticism. He was following these rules diligently, which guaranteed that he would stay depressed. But what if you replaced these self-critical rules with self-affirming rules—rules that allowed you to feel better about yourself? What if you had new rules that allowed you to be human, learn from experience, grow from your mistakes and setbacks, feel compassion toward yourself, and live a life of successful imperfection? What if you had a rule book that was based not on punishing yourself, but on loving yourself? What would these new rules look like? Let's take a look:

- If I make a mistake, I realize it's because I am human.

- I can learn from mistakes.

- I should treat myself as well as I treat others.

- I should give myself credit for anything positive that I do.

If you followed these new rules, what do you think would change for you? Take some time to think about what rules you are using and what effect they're having on you.

| |
|---|
| **Table 4.1**<br>**Maladaptive Rule Book** |
| • I should be successful at everything I try.<br><br>• If I am not successful, I am a failure.<br><br>• If I fail, then I'm worthless (I'm unlovable; life isn't worth living).<br><br>• Failure is intolerable and unacceptable.<br><br>• I should get the approval of everyone.<br><br>• If I am not approved of, I am unlovable (ugly, worthless, hopeless, alone).<br><br>• I should be certain before I try something.<br><br>• If I am not certain, the outcome will be negative.<br><br>• I should never be anxious (depressed, selfish, confused, uncertain, unhappy with my partner).<br><br>• I should always keep my eye out for any anxiety.<br><br>• If I let my guard down, something bad will happen.<br><br>• If I make a mistake, I should criticize myself.<br><br>• I should hold myself to the highest standards all the time.<br><br>• I shouldn't praise myself unless I am perfect.<br><br>• I should go over my mistakes so I can avoid repeating them.<br><br>• If people see that I'm anxious, they will think less of me (reject me, humiliate me).<br><br>• My sex life (feelings, behaviors, relationships, etc.) should be wonderful and easy at all times. |

## How Is Your Thinking Distorted?

In cognitive therapy, we ask patients to write down their negative thoughts and see if there is a pattern to the way they see themselves and their lives. We call these thought distortions "negative automatic thoughts" because they are associated with feeling depressed or anxious, and they pop up in your mind without your control. They fall into several categories, which we looked at in Chapter 2. Those that link most directly to your self-criticism are discounting the positives (your tendency to think that good things don't count), negative filter (you focus on one negative and don't see the positives), all-or-nothing thinking (you're at 0 or 100 percent, no in-between), labeling (you label yourself based on limited information), and overgeneralizing (you take one incident and extrapolate from it to your whole life).

Sometimes, of course, your negative thoughts can be true—for example, you might think, *She doesn't like me,* and indeed she might not. But if you are distorting your view of life on a consistent basis, you can take steps to change your thinking.

## What Is Your Core Belief about Yourself?

Each of us has a core or central belief about ourselves. When you are depressed, your core belief is excessively negative. This belief may be that you are unattractive, boring, incompetent, helpless, or unlovable, or that you have some other undesirable trait. Your core belief is a like a shaded lens through which you see the world. And your core belief leads you to use specific thinking distortions that support your negative outlook.

In addition to your core belief and your negative thinking distortions, you also have a set of demanding and negative rules for yourself, which we discussed in the maladaptive rule book a couple pages back. Your negative core beliefs, thinking distortions, and maladaptive rules work together to support and reinforce your depressive outlook about yourself. For example, if your belief is that you are incompetent, you might find yourself thinking that you mess up on everything, and anything you do that is positive is trivial. You are even more likely to think this way if you're going by rules that require perfection and self-punishment.

Look at Figure 4.1 and note the relationship of your core beliefs, negative distorted thoughts, and maladaptive rules. It's immediately clear how your depression is reinforced by your belief system and how it reinforces those beliefs—a vicious cycle indeed. By the same token, we can break the cycle by changing your beliefs at any level—but the most important level is your core beliefs. Here's why. Let's imagine that you actually believe that you are competent and desirable. This core belief will direct you to think in more positive and realistic ways. So, rather than thinking, *I can't do anything right,* when you make a mistake, your core belief that you are competent allows you to support a more positive view of yourself, which translates into more positive and realistic thoughts to replace the negative distortions. As a result, you might gather more personal strength by thinking, *Even though I didn't do well on that one thing, there are a lot of other things I do well. After all, I am basically competent.* Or you think, *The breakup was all my fault,* but then you call on your positive self-image and realize that you have a lot going for you. You're lovable. You have friends. And it takes two to cause a breakup. And, after all, you might be better off in the long run.

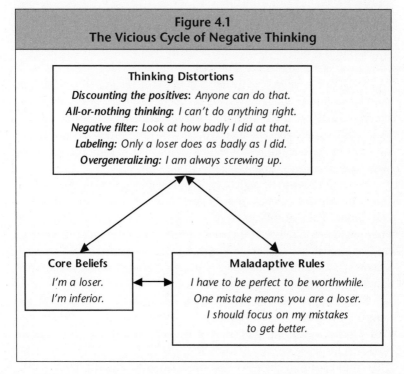

### Figure 4.1
### The Vicious Cycle of Negative Thinking

**Thinking Distortions**
*Discounting the positives:* Anyone can do that.
*All-or-nothing thinking:* I can't do anything right.
*Negative filter:* Look at how badly I did at that.
*Labeling:* Only a loser does as badly as I did.
*Overgeneralizing:* I am always screwing up.

**Core Beliefs**
*I'm a loser.*
*I'm inferior.*

**Maladaptive Rules**
*I have to be perfect to be worthwhile.*
*One mistake means you are a loser.*
*I should focus on my mistakes
to get better.*

Now, you might say, "But that's just the problem. My core belief about myself is that I am a loser. How do I change *that*?" One way to change it is to do a mental experiment. Simply assume—for the sake of the experiment—that you *are* worthwhile and competent. Then imagine how someone with this positive core belief would respond. This way, you can try on a different "head." Experiment with being positive about yourself. You might be surprised that you can change your own negative distorted thoughts, beliefs, and rules along the way.

## Look at Yourself along a Continuum

When we put ourselves down, we are usually using the very highest standards to judge ourselves. We think that unless we are perfect, we are losers. I remember when I was nine years old, and my teacher got angry at me because I didn't get 100 percent on a test. "You can do better!" she said. Though I felt intimidated, I said, "I'm trying to do the best I can." And she slapped me. I can still remember my shock at this—a little kid getting slapped for not being perfect.

Imagine if you did that to yourself—if every time you did less than perfect you slapped yourself in the face. Imagine how terrible you'd feel. If perfection is one of the requirements in your rule book, you *are* punishing yourself in much the same way.

I was lucky when I was nine. I didn't criticize myself, because my mother was strong enough to go to the school, and that teacher got fired. I didn't have the chance to turn the painful experience into a self-criticism or a negative core belief about myself, because my mother's action showed me that the teacher, not I, was out of line. Maybe you can fire the critic in your head who keeps demanding perfection from you.

You don't have to be perfect to be good enough. One helpful alternative is to think of yourself along a continuum that runs from 0 to 100. Now, none of us is at 100, and no one who is a 0 could read this book. You are somewhere in between these endpoints. If you were placing yourself on this scale in terms of achievement, wealth, looks, personality, values, kindness, or acceptance of others—and you thought of the average person as a 50—where would you be?

Let's take Tom. Here's how he compared himself to the average person: achievement (85), wealth (75), looks (80), personality (80), values (90), kindness (90), acceptance of others (95). Before we began deconstructing his negative view of himself, Tom was thinking, *I'm a total loser.* That would put him close to 0. But when we break it down into the various qualities that he has, he's up in the top 20 percent.

## Don't Take Yourself Personally

We all tend to think of ourselves as the center of the universe. So when you criticize yourself, you think, *I did it* and *It was my fault*. It's as if the outcome depends entirely on your doing or failing to do something.

Tom is a good example of this—thinking that the loss of his job was completely up to him. It's as if the bank was downsizing because he had failed. In fact, it wasn't "up to" Tom at all, because the downsizing of the bank was the result of a lot of other factors that didn't involve him.

The same can be said for breakups in relationships. You may blame yourself: *If I were more desirable, we would still be together.* But that may not be the real reason. In fact, there may be lots of reasons why the relationship broke up. It could be that your former partner has a different set of values, or he had a childhood that led him to have certain preferences, or that the timing isn't right, or that he is actually doing you a favor. It might be that the two of you are mismatched—and wouldn't it be better to know that now rather than later?

## Humanize Your Mistakes

It was the great English poet Alexander Pope who said, "To err is human, to forgive divine."

Imagine if you applied that to yourself.

All of us make mistakes, and we'll continue to make mistakes in the future. We make mistakes because we are not gods. We are human. We are still learning. But when you criticize yourself for making mistakes, you are acting as if you should be greater and better than all the rest of us. You are saying that you, among the billions of the rest of us, should never make a mistake.

Who do you think you are?

If all of us make mistakes, then you should join with the rest of us and make some mistakes, too.

## Use a Learning Curve

Sometimes we fail. Sometimes we make the wrong decision, do something that's really stupid, or say something that other people feel is inappropriate. I know I have—and I suspect that you have made similar mistakes. But what do you do with this information? We seem to think that making a mistake is a complete waste of time. But every time we make a mistake, we have learned something. We have learned what doesn't work.

Henry Petroski is a professor of engineering and history at Duke University. His book *Success through Failure: The Paradox of Design* is a fascinating history and review of "proactive failure analysis" (how will this design fail?) and how failure in design paves the way for innovation. In 2000, a comprehensive analysis of failures in medical care led to the publication of *To Err Is Human: Building a Safer Health System*.[1] This honest and detailed appraisal has been helpful in reducing mistakes and infections in hospital care throughout the United States.

I'll give you an example from my own experience. Years ago, when I was first doing cognitive therapy, I noticed that some of my patients just didn't respond well—some would even get angry. I would get frustrated and wonder, *What's wrong with them?* or *What's wrong with me?* Of course, blaming them or blaming myself only made matters worse. Then it occurred to me that maybe I was stuck in my techniques—maybe I could learn from my patients. So I got interested in how their resistance to change actually made sense. I began taking notes, writing some papers, giving some lectures. Eventually I wrote a book on the topic, *Overcoming Resistance in Cognitive Therapy*. I dedicated the book to my patients. They taught me the value of learning from the areas where I had failed.

Let's imagine that you thought of mistakes as information and opportunities. Mistakes are information because they tell you that something doesn't work. That's worth knowing. For example, getting involved with someone who doesn't want what you want is a mistake. It's great to learn from that. Or not studying for your exam and getting a bad grade—well, that's a mistake. Learn from that. Study next time. The real issue is not whether you are making mistakes; it's whether you learn from them.

And mistakes are opportunities. They tell you when to give up on a losing cause. For example, give up on drinking too much, give up on being with someone who is not supportive, and give up on banging your head against the wall. Mistakes create opportunities because they help you close one door—the mistaken door—to open new doors to new goals and new behavior.

Table 4.2 shows some common self-critical thought distortions, along with examples of more realistic thinking to put your inner critic in its place.

| Table 4.2 Correcting the Critic | |
|---|---|
| **Distorted Thinking** | **More Realistic Thinking** |
| **Discounting your positives:** Anyone can do that | Really? But not everyone is doing the positive things you can do. If you count the negatives, you should also count the positives. Isn't that fair? Wouldn't you give someone else credit for their positives? |
| **All-or-nothing thinking:** I can't do anything right | Anything? Of course you've done lots of things right. You don't have to be perfect to give yourself credit for your positives. |
| **Negative filter:** Look how badly I did at that | Maybe you didn't do well at that one thing, but you did get some things right, and you did learn something. |
| **Labeling:** Only a loser does as badly as I did | All of us make mistakes, which means—in your thinking—we are all losers. Very smart, successful, worthwhile people make a lot of mistakes. Ask around about the successful people you admire. I bet you'll find that they have made mistakes. The difference is that they learn from their mistakes, while you are busy criticizing yourself. |
| **Overgeneralizing:** I am always screwing up | Again, you are going far beyond the truth. You may or may not have made a mistake here, but that hardly means that you are always screwing up. Haven't you ever done anything that is positive? What would your best friend say on your behalf? |

## CONCLUSION

Many depressed people get caught in a vicious cycle of self-criticism. In fact, some people criticize themselves for being depressed in the first place and then feel depressed because they have criticized themselves.

In this chapter, we've reviewed a number of techniques that you can start using today to reverse your self-criticism. Much of your self-critical thinking is based on distorted negative thinking about yourself. I don't mean to imply that you should tell yourself that everything you do is fantastic. You know that would be nonsense. But it's likely you are looking at a few negatives (if any are there) and blowing them up until they are the only things you see.

You can begin putting yourself in perspective by weighing the positives and the negatives, giving yourself credit for things that you do, and thinking of yourself as you would think of a friend. You are probably much kinder to a total stranger than you are to yourself. Try putting yourself on your own side for a change, and see if you can feel better. Try taking a compassionate view of your mistakes.

## Challenging Your Self-criticism

- Identify your negative thoughts. For example, is your self-criticism linked with rumination or indecisiveness?

- Define your terms. If you're telling yourself you're a failure, what constitutes a "failure" for you?

- Examine the evidence. Is your self-criticism founded on facts?

- Ask yourself what the advantage of criticizing yourself is. What do you hope to gain?

- Set goals you can achieve. Instead of aiming to write a book today, plan to write for one hour.

- Reward yourself when you achieve a goal.

- Instead of criticizing yourself, correct your mistakes.

- Use the double-standard technique. Would you be as tough on anyone else as you are on yourself?

- Catch yourself evaluating yourself. Do you really need to?

- Replace evaluation with observing and accepting.

- A lot of us have rules about how we should think and how we should be. Do you have a self-critical rule book?

- How is your thinking distorted? Are you labeling or overgeneralizing? How could you counter those automatic thoughts?

- What is your core belief about yourself? Imagine it is different. How would your thinking change?

- Look at yourself along a continuum. You don't have to be perfect to be good enough.

- Don't take yourself too personally. Most things don't depend entirely on you.

- Humanize your errors. Every one of us makes mistakes, including you.

- Use a learning curve. See mistakes as information and opportunities.

# CHAPTER 5

# "I Can't Stand Making Mistakes": How to Feel "Good Enough"

Allen was having real difficulty getting things done at work. He was afraid he would make a mistake and then regret it. "I either spend an incredible amount of time working on something to get it just right," he told me, "or I avoid it entirely. There's no in-between for me." Working for a marketing firm, Allen had to write up reports on a regular basis. Allen's fear of making mistakes led him to research every angle before completing a report, asking anyone he could for advice and reassurance. Rather than spending eight hours at work, he would stay at the office until late in the evening, and then take home more work that would fill up his nights and weekends. When he wasn't absorbed in trying to get things just right, he was worrying that he had made a mistake in a report and that it would come back to haunt him.

Allen lived in constant dread. He pressured himself about saying the right thing, writing the right thing, and always appearing to be "on top of things." Ironically, this desire to get everything right made him seem insecure to his colleagues. He would say to Lisa, his coworker, "I'm not sure if I've covered everything on this report. Do you think I should go over these figures again? What if the boss doesn't like it? Do you think she's in a bad mood today?" Lisa would turn away wondering why Allen was so insecure. She might have been thinking, *Maybe he's right. Maybe he isn't doing a good enough job.*

Allen mistakenly believed that acting like a perfectionist was a sign of his merit and his professional seriousness—not his insecurity. But his continual search for reassurance became annoying to his coworkers. "How many times do I have to tell you that it will be fine? Stop driving me nuts with these constant questions," Lisa finally said. "I have my own work to worry about."

## Perfectionism and Depression

When you are depressed, you personalize mistakes. You think that if you make a mistake, it's entirely your fault—no one else is to blame. You think you should know the future before it happens. And you think that a mistake is not an inconvenience or a bump in the road, it's a catastrophe. When you make a mistake, you label yourself in the harshest terms: *I'm an idiot. I'm dumb. I can't do anything right.*

Your fear of making mistakes—and the self-criticism, rumination, and regret that follow—makes you miserable. It makes you indecisive, isolates you, and holds you back from taking risks. How can you try something new? You might make a mistake. You are trapped by your fear.

But it doesn't have to be that way. We'll see in this chapter that mistakes come with the territory. It's part of playing the game. It's part of living a life. The goal is not to eliminate mistakes; it's to learn to live with them, accept them, even use them to grow. The ability to make mistakes—and move on—liberates us to make decisions and learn from our experiences. Good decision makers understand that mistakes are part of the "game," and they are quick to accept a mistake, cut their losses, and move on to the next decision. You have to pay to play, they say.

When we make a mistake we may focus exclusively on that one outcome, filtering out all the other positives in our lives. This is the same negative-filter thought distortion that we learned about in Chapter 4. You are so focused on one mistake that you don't realize that there are hundreds of things that are going right. All that you can see is that one mistake. It stands out because you see nothing else.

And you think that if you make a mistake, you have to regret it, mull it over and over, and criticize yourself endlessly (and we saw in the last chapter how harmful that can be). No wonder you want to avoid mistakes at all costs. You think that you can't stand regretting a mistake. You don't realize that regret is universal (all of us have regrets) and that regrets can be temporary. We don't have to dwell on our regrets, just recognize them and move on to the next positive at hand. But for you, regrets are a permanent condition. No wonder you feel stuck.

## Are You a Perfectionist?

Many of us have high standards and work hard to make sure that we do a good job. Being conscientious can be rewarding. But when your high standards become unrealistic, they can drive you to the ends of the Earth trying to live up to your own expectations or what you think others expect of you. The self-test in Table 5.1 can help you gauge whether your standards for yourself are reasonable or off the charts. Take a few minutes to take the test and then we'll look at what your answers might mean.

| Table 5.1 | | | | | |
|---|---|---|---|---|---|
| **Multidimensional Perfectionism Scale** | | | | | |
| Please circle the number that best corresponds to your agreement with each statement below. 1 = Strongly disagree; 5 = Strongly agree | | | | | |
| 1. My parents set very high standards for me. | 1 | 2 | 3 | 4 | 5 |
| 2. Organization is very important to me. | 1 | 2 | 3 | 4 | 5 |
| 3. As a child, I was punished for doing things less than perfectly. | 1 | 2 | 3 | 4 | 5 |
| 4. If I do not set the highest standards for myself, I am likely to end up a second-rate person. | 1 | 2 | 3 | 4 | 5 |
| 5. My parents never tried to understand my mistakes. | 1 | 2 | 3 | 4 | 5 |
| 6. It is important to me that I be thoroughly competent in everything I do. | 1 | 2 | 3 | 4 | 5 |
| 7. I am a neat person. | 1 | 2 | 3 | 4 | 5 |
| 8. I try to be an organized person. | 1 | 2 | 3 | 4 | 5 |
| 9. If I fail at work/school, I am a failure as a person. | 1 | 2 | 3 | 4 | 5 |
| 10. I should be upset if I make a mistake. | 1 | 2 | 3 | 4 | 5 |
| 11. My parents wanted me to be the best at everything. | 1 | 2 | 3 | 4 | 5 |
| 12. I set higher goals for myself than most people do for themselves. | 1 | 2 | 3 | 4 | 5 |
| 13. If someone does a task at work/school better than I do, then I feel like I've failed. | 1 | 2 | 3 | 4 | 5 |
| 14. If I fail partly, it is as bad as being a complete failure. | 1 | 2 | 3 | 4 | 5 |
| 15. Only outstanding performance is good enough in my family. | 1 | 2 | 3 | 4 | 5 |

| | | | | | |
|---|---|---|---|---|---|
| 16. I am very good at focusing my efforts on attaining a goal. | 1 | 2 | 3 | 4 | 5 |
| 17. Even when I do something very carefully, I often feel that it is not done quite right. | 1 | 2 | 3 | 4 | 5 |
| 18. I hate being less than the best at things. | 1 | 2 | 3 | 4 | 5 |
| 19. I have extremely high goals. | 1 | 2 | 3 | 4 | 5 |
| 20. My parents have expected excellence from me. | 1 | 2 | 3 | 4 | 5 |
| 21. People will probably think less of me if I make a mistake. | 1 | 2 | 3 | 4 | 5 |
| 22. I never felt like I could meet my parents' expectations. | 1 | 2 | 3 | 4 | 5 |
| 23. If I do not do as well as other people, it means I am an inferior human being. | 1 | 2 | 3 | 4 | 5 |
| 24. Other people seem to accept lower standards from themselves than I do of myself. | 1 | 2 | 3 | 4 | 5 |
| 25. If I do not do well all the time, people will not respect me. | 1 | 2 | 3 | 4 | 5 |
| 26. My parents have always had higher expectations for my future than I have. | 1 | 2 | 3 | 4 | 5 |
| 27. I try to be a neat person. | 1 | 2 | 3 | 4 | 5 |
| 28. I usually have doubts about the simple everyday things I do. | 1 | 2 | 3 | 4 | 5 |
| 29. Neatness is very important to me. | 1 | 2 | 3 | 4 | 5 |
| 30. I expect higher performance in my daily tasks than most people. | 1 | 2 | 3 | 4 | 5 |
| 31. I am an organized person. | 1 | 2 | 3 | 4 | 5 |
| 32. I tend to get behind in my work because I repeat things over and over. | 1 | 2 | 3 | 4 | 5 |
| 33. It takes me a long time to do something "right." | 1 | 2 | 3 | 4 | 5 |
| 34. The fewer mistakes I make, the more people will like me. | 1 | 2 | 3 | 4 | 5 |
| 35. I never felt like I could meet my parents' standards. | 1 | 2 | 3 | 4 | 5 |

Now, without being a perfectionist in evaluating your response to the test, look at how strongly you have endorsed certain items. You may be concerned about making mistakes, or focused on personal standards of excellence, or trying to live up to your parents' expectations. Or you may be someone who is always doubting what you do—or someone overly focused on organization. Seeing how you structure your standards may help you understand how your perfectionism gets in the way of accepting yourself.

The Multidimensional Perfectionism Scale has several subscales, which are located in Appendix B.

## What Kind of Perfectionist Are You?

Psychologists used to think that perfectionism was always bad. We are all familiar with the self-destructive kind of perfectionism—the kind where your standards are totally unrealistic, you can't stand making any mistakes, and you criticize yourself all the time. But there are adaptive qualities to some perfectionism, too.[1] For example, you can set high standards for yourself, work very hard, and derive a lot of satisfaction from your achievements.[2] Adaptive perfectionism can help you persist, help you take pride in what you do, and help you achieve valued goals. You don't need to criticize yourself or achieve the impossible if you have this kind of healthy, proactive perfectionism. For example, let's look at Bill, who works hard at his job and puts in extra hours. He tries to do the best he can, but he accepts that he won't be perfect. When he does well on something, he gives himself a pat on the back. But when he doesn't do well, he doesn't think, *I'm worthless and incompetent.* He thinks, *I need to put more effort into this* or *This is going to be a challenge.*

Bill has healthy high standards and is a bit of a perfectionist—but it's adaptive for him. He's able to get things done, and he feels generally good about his work. Your perfectionism becomes maladaptive when your standards are unrealistically high, you are excessively concerned about being negatively evaluated, and you can't get much satisfaction from what you do. In this maladaptive perfectionism, you focus on your "flaws" and blow them up in your mind to be absolutely unbearable.[3] This kind of perfectionism makes you anxious, worried, depressed—and it may even lead to procrastination because you just don't think you'll do a good enough job.

Linda, who we met in Chapter 1, has maladaptive perfectionism. She won't accept anything less than 100 percent from herself (and sometimes from others). She drives herself so hard that she doesn't get enough sleep. She can't take "good enough" for an answer, and she continually worries that her boss will think she's a slacker if she doesn't do a perfect job. She doesn't even enjoy getting positive feedback, because she thinks that it's gratuitous and even condescending. *I know I could do better than this. Who is she kidding with these compliments?* As you can imagine, Linda is under constant stress from her perfectionism.

Take a look at the table below and see which kind of perfectionism you have.

| Table 5.2 Maladaptive vs. Adaptive Perfectionism | |
|---|---|
| **Maladaptive** | **Adaptive** |
| 1. My goals are so high I can almost never achieve them. | 1. My goals are high—but realistic. |
| 2. I can't stand making mistakes. | 2. I don't like mistakes, but I can accept them. |
| 3. I focus on my negatives rather than my positives. | 3. I balance my negatives against my positives. |
| 4. Nothing I do ever feels good enough. | 4. I can get satisfaction from my work. |

We can fine-tune our understanding of your perfectionism even further by looking at where it's focused—on how (you think) others evaluate you or on how you evaluate yourself. We call these two types "social" and "personal" perfectionism.[4] Personal perfectionism reflects how you evaluate yourself—your excessively high standards for yourself, your doubts, your focus on mistakes, and your obsessive preoccupation with making sure that things are organized.[5] Your "social perfectionism" is focused on the standards that you think others have for you—what your parents might think, what friends might say—and your fear of any criticism. You try to be perfect to avoid these evaluations from others. Of course, you can have both personal and social perfectionism—which will only make matters worse, since there is no escape for you.

There is a third dimension of perfectionism—your standards for how others should behave. You are judgmental of others, intolerant of their mistakes, and generally frustrated and angry with other people. So, if your coworker or your partner doesn't do exactly what he or she "should" do, you get very upset. This leads to more arguments, more dissatisfaction—and, for you, more depression.

So, your perfectionism can be adaptive or maladaptive. It can be social, personal, or other-oriented. It is not always bad—and not always good. Think for a moment about your own perfectionism. Are you generally more concerned about your own standards or about how others think of you? Do you aim for realistic goals, or are you trying to achieve the impossible? Do you demand perfection from others, or are you willing to accept that others are human and fallible?

## The Consequences of Perfectionism

If your perfectionism is maladaptive, then you are at risk for a lot of problems. The research shows that perfectionism is related to depression, anxiety, eating disorders, procrastination, and thoughts about suicide.[6] Perfectionists have lower self-esteem and more psychological stress, they worry more, and they have fewer pleasant experiences in their lives.[7] Your perfectionism can also have an effect on how you deal with your emotions. In one study, researchers found that perfectionists had a more difficult time labeling their emotions and remembering them.[8] This may be because perfectionists have a fear of feeling negative emotions and rely on their perfectionism to avoid ever feeling badly. The research shows that worriers—who are also perfectionistic—have difficulty labeling their emotions and tolerating difficult feelings. People worry to avoid emotions, and perfectionists try to excel to avoid feeling disappointed. One way to think of perfectionism is that you are always trying to get the very best—what psychologists call "maximizing." Other people who are not perfectionists are more willing to be satisfied. Various studies have shown that maximizers are more prone to depression and regret, they feel less happy, they are less satisfied with things they buy, and they continually compare themselves to people who have more or do better.[9]

Your perfectionism can also affect your intimate life. For example, perfectionists report lower sexual satisfaction in their relationships.[10] They are less likely to improve in therapy because they often are unwilling to "lower their standards" to accept their limitations.[11] Perfectionism adds to your general stress level in every area because you can never be satisfied with anything that you do. You evaluate almost any task as insurmountable, and you lose confidence in your ability to cope. Your self-esteem plummets.[12]

Since perfectionists put themselves under constant pressure to accomplish the impossible, they render themselves helpless—no matter what they do, it's not good enough. As a result, they feel hopeless—nothing will ever get better, because they are their own worst enemies. And perfectionists are much more likely to criticize and label themselves in all-or-nothing terms: *I am a complete failure.* Finally, they often believe that others won't tolerate anything less than perfect—that they have to live up to the highest expectations that other people (supposedly) have of them. These unhappy perfectionists are filled with shame and humiliation. Not surprisingly, maladaptive perfectionism has a special role in making people more vulnerable to suicide.[13]

## OVERCOMING YOUR FEAR OF MISTAKES

We know that to err is human. We all make mistakes. Now, let's look at why. First, we don't always have the information that we need to make the "right" decision, so we have to make decisions based on imperfect information. When you get involved with someone, you don't know how he will really turn out to be. When you buy something, you won't know if you will like it next week. But you buy it anyway. We get more information *later*—and then we find out if it was a mistake or not. We don't know the future until it happens.

Second, we may make decisions based on our emotions—say we're eager to "make a killing" in the stock market, so we take an unnecessary risk. Sometimes it works out and sometimes it doesn't. Or we get involved with someone because she is pretty or he is cool, and then we find out that our emotions are sometimes a poor guide to what is good for us. But you can't live without emotions, instincts, or intuition. They allow you to make decisions and find meaning in life. And, yes, they can sometimes lead to mistakes. I have a compass on my hiking watch. Sometimes I head north because I think that's the right direction. Sometimes it's not.

Third, we often have a choice between two undesirable alternatives—so we choose one. But the other could have been *worse*. You buy a car, and it turns out to have some problems—but the model that you rejected might have been worse. Or you take a job, and it turns out to be rather unpleasant—but if you didn't take the job you might have been unemployed for a really long time. Who knows?

I don't know about you, but I've made lots of mistakes, and I plan to make more. The reason I "plan" to make more is that I intend to live my life fully. I might make a decision, and it might turn out badly. But at least I'll be able to make decisions and live a life. I'll be part of the human race.

## What's the Worst Thing about a Mistake?

Allen would worry so much about making any mistakes on his reports at work that it seemed anything less than perfection was intolerable. "I can't stand making mistakes," he strongly asserted to me. I've always wondered what it means to say "I can't stand" something. After all, if Allen acknowledged making mistakes—and he was still around to tell me—he apparently *could* "stand" it. It's like saying, "I can't stand this cold water," while you are swimming around in it for hours. Perhaps "I can't stand it" really should be "I don't like it." But so what if you don't "like" making mistakes? You certainly have been able to live with them.

Having dispelled the misconception that he couldn't "stand" mistakes, we looked deeper at what it meant to Allen if he made one. "Okay, Allen," I said. "Let's say that you make a mistake at work. That bothers you because it makes you think what?"

Allen looked at me and said, "It means that my boss will see it, she'll get angry, and she might fire me."

"Okay, that sounds pretty bad. What else does it mean to you if you make a mistake?"

He continued, without missing a beat, "It means I'm irresponsible. It means that I'm not doing my job."

But maybe his boss is like a lot of bosses. Maybe she doesn't use a standard of perfection to decide whether to keep an employee. Maybe she will complain about a mistake and then get back to work. Here's the evidence: Everyone working in Allen's office has made mistakes. They are still there. The boss has made mistakes. She's still there.

And making a mistake doesn't mean you are irresponsible. Of course, it depends on what you mean by irresponsible, but I would say that someone who is lazy, doesn't come to work, lies, cheats, steals, and doesn't care at all about other people on the job would qualify as a definition. I doubt that this describes you. The fact that you are reading a book on how to make your life better suggests some responsibility. Mistakes are a sign of trying and not always succeeding. They're not a sign of being dishonest, lazy, or careless.

## Everyone Makes Mistakes

So, now we had Allen's equations for mistakes. Mistakes equal getting fired, being irresponsible, and not doing your job. Let's see. In 2008, the best hitter in major-league baseball was Chipper Jones of the Atlanta Braves. Jones hit for a .364 average, which means that two out of three times he was "out." Let's count the outs as "mistakes." Was Chipper Jones not doing his job? Was he irresponsible?

Mistakes come with being a player—in any game. If you are in the game, if you are working, participating, relating, living a life—then why would an occasional mistake be so terrible? Don't responsible people make mistakes sometimes?

Here's how to find out about responsibility and mistakes. Think about the three most responsible people you know. Perhaps your list consists of a parent, perhaps a colleague, or maybe a friend. Now, what makes them responsible? You'll say, "They try their best to be reliable. They're honest. They try hard." Okay. I'm with you so far. Now, is it possible to be reliable and honest and try hard and still make mistakes? Well, go out and ask these people if they have ever made a mistake.

Most of my patients won't bother asking their friends or colleagues—they know that the question will sound like it has an obvious answer. "Of course I make mistakes. I'm human." That's the response you will get almost every time. You actually know this. But try asking friends or colleagues whom you respect. Responsible people make mistakes. In fact, really smart people sometimes do really stupid things. If they are honest, they will reveal some great stories. People make serious mistakes—like getting involved with the wrong person, buying stocks that plunge in value, or taking a job that is not the right fit. And everyone has made smaller mistakes, such as buying coats they never wear, forgetting their driving directions, saying things they regret, or wearing ties that don't match their shirts. I purposefully want you to recognize that we all make big, medium, and small mistakes. We are human.

I'll tell you about a mistake I made more than 20 years ago. I bought Microsoft stock. Then, feeling content with a 25 percent increase in the value of my stock, I proudly sold it. This was 1989, and I had about $10,000 worth of stock. It would be worth almost $1 million today. But that's the nature of investing. You make a decision based on the information available at the time. Looking back, it was an incredible mistake. A mistake I can live with.

But that's just it. It's a mistake *looking back*. I wasn't all-knowing and all-powerful in 1989 (not that I am today). How could anyone know that over the next 20 years Microsoft stock would increase to 83 times its original price? Who has a crystal ball?

I wish I had. But I don't. And, last time you looked, you didn't have a crystal ball either.

## A Mistake Is Not the End of the World

Some of us treat every mistake like the end of life as we know it. *I can't believe I missed that deadline. My boss will never trust me again. What if I take the job and I don't like it? I'd regret it for the rest of my life.* Ellen, who we met in Chapter 2, had a beautiful apartment, but she just couldn't make a decision to decorate or furnish it. She went several years with bare walls and a few pieces of furniture. "What if I buy something and I don't like it? I just couldn't stand it," she said.

"Why wouldn't you be able to stand it?" I asked dubiously.

"Because it makes me feel awful," she said, wondering why I had a hard time understanding the obvious.

It sounds like Ellen is facing a catastrophe. But this is how you think when you are afraid of tolerating a mistake. You make it into a drama. It's awful, terrible, unbearable—you *can't stand it.*

Sounds very dramatic. But is it true?

Ellen and I looked at some decisions she had made in the past that included some mistakes. These included her job, some courses she'd taken in college, some people she'd become friends with—even the apartment itself. None of these choices was perfectly right for her; she could have done better. If only she had taken more practical courses in college, or chose the other apartment she looked at, things would be different. But her mistakes were not 100 percent negative, either. There were *some* good things about her apartment—it was in a nice neighborhood, for instance—but it could have had better lighting. The same for her job— things could have been better. Her salary wasn't great, but she was able to be creative in her work and there was a possibility of advancement. Her life still went on. Nothing was essential, nothing was really terrible, the drama wasn't as horrendous as she thought. "I adjusted," she confessed when I asked her how she'd managed to live with these mistakes. "I got used to it." Hmmm. I wondered if she could do that with her apartment.

Once Ellen realized that mistakes were not the end of the world, she began buying a few items—here and there. She protested, thought it could be better, got a bit annoyed—and then she got used to it. It turned out that waiting years to get her apartment "together" was the only real mistake. "I missed out on having things more finished. But I guess I'll have to live with that."

What mistakes have *you* learned to live with?

## You Don't Have to Regret Mistakes

One of the reasons why it's hard for you to make decisions—and one of the reasons you criticize yourself so harshly—is that you think you *have to regret* a mistake. "I know that I would just regret it if I chose the wrong thing," Ellen said. But why would you have to regret a mistake? Think about it. Maybe you could simply say, "I guess that was a mistake"—and then move on. "How could I just move on if I know I've made a mistake?" Ellen said emphatically. Well, why not? Why couldn't she say, "I did make a mistake, I guess I regret it, but I've regretted it enough, and I am moving on. I want to focus on the positive things that I can experience now."

Let's imagine you are driving along. You take a wrong turn. Your car gets stuck in mud, and you start spinning your wheels. You get out of the car, look at the mud, sit down, and say, "I really regret taking the wrong turn." A panel of experts comes along and they say, "You really shouldn't have taken that turn. What got into you? How could you make such a *stupid mistake?*"

A divine creature comes down—an angel of misery—and he confirms that this was, indeed, a stupid mistake. In fact, it was a mistake you had been warned about. The angel beats his wings in furious agitation and says, "How could someone who is as smart as you make such a stupid mistake? I tell you, I have a hard time believing it. Your wheels are really spinning in that mud. It didn't have to be this way. You could have taken the dry road. But *nooo*, you always have to do things your way. You're really not as smart as you think you are."

Okay. I'm with you so far. Dumb mistake, could have seen it coming, I was warned, and my wheels are spinning. And, damn it, I have mud all over me.

But—here's the catch—what are my options now?

I have two options. I can sit down by the side of the road and spend a lot of time—let's say six months—regretting this. Or I can get a tow truck to pull me out. But, to make life interesting, *I can't do both.* I can either continue regretting things, or I can make my life better by pulling myself out of this ditch, dusting the dirt off my nice new jacket, and driving on.

So I decide that a few minutes of regret has taught me the lesson I needed to learn. *I got the point. I made a mistake.* Now I'm moving down the road and leaving the mistake in the ditch.

It's your decision.

## LET "GOOD ENOUGH" BE GOOD ENOUGH

I hope I've convinced you that mistakes are a part of life you can live with—and that holding yourself to impossible standards is bad for your health. Now you may want to consider an alternative to your perfectionism. I call this alternative "successful imperfection."[14] When you first hear this term you might have a gut feeling that I'm contradicting myself. "How can you be successful and imperfect?" That's exactly the point. You can. Here's how I know.

I know a lot of successful people: in academics, business, finance, sports, theater—and people with successful marriages. Every one of them is imperfect. Every one of them has made mistakes, every one of them is able to persist even when they fail at something. They all have high standards—but achievable standards. They know they are not perfect—but they don't buy into the idea that you're either a hero or a zero.

Successful imperfection means that you have given up on 100 percent, and you are willing to settle for less. Maybe it's 90 percent or 80 percent. Maybe you are willing to settle for simply doing better than you did before. Maybe you are even willing to settle for simply trying.

Let's take Charlene, who is working on her term paper. She keeps thinking, *I could do a better job, but I just won't have the time.* She worries about getting it done. She thinks it won't get an A+, and she has a hard time tolerating anything less than perfect. We look at the advantages of aiming for a very good—but less than perfect—paper. "Well, if I aim for very good, then I guess I could actually have a chance of achieving that," she says.

"And could you feel okay with yourself doing something that is very good, but not perfect?"

"Yeah, that's the hard thing. It could always be better."

But anything you do could always be better. You could write a better paper, do a better job, look better, compete better, be better at being better, be the best, and then beat that. You could drive yourself crazy with this demand for better and better until the best becomes the only thing you settle for. Or you could aim—every day—for successful imperfection.

For example, today I am working at a level of successful imperfection on this book. I will go out and do some cross-country skiing, and I can absolutely guarantee you that this will be imperfect—but successful, because I know I'll have a good time. I can make dinner—and though I'm a fairly good cook, it will pale in comparison to a serious chef's cooking. But it will taste good enough, and I will be satisfied. In fact, come to think of it, any success that I have had has been due to my willingness to do things that are imperfect.

The key to successful imperfectionism is to have reasonably high standards, push yourself forward to make progress, give yourself credit for trying—and for improving—and persist. Successful imperfectionism works better than absolute perfectionism. It *is* better; it's almost the "best."

Ask yourself, right now: *What can I do today that will be imperfect, but will move me forward?*

## Aren't Standards Arbitrary?

Many of my friends in academics try to achieve the highest standards. They think that there are absolute standards of excellence. But is it true?

A professor at Yale, years ago, sent an article to a journal. He got a review back from the editor, who thought it was a mediocre and useless paper. Without changing a single word in the paper he sent it off to another journal, and that editor wrote back, "This will be a classic in the field." Highly educated experts in the field couldn't agree. What standard were they using?

Or let's take the standard of physical beauty. I've noticed that people have a wide range of standards—some people find one guy attractive, some don't. Some men like a particular look, some do not. And, much to our amazement, we find that women or men whom most of us would consider attractive (whatever that is) seem to be the ones who focus on their slightest "imperfections." The standard of beauty is in the eye—or the head—of the beholder.

I'm not saying there is no reality out there. Just try to challenge the law of gravity. But many of the standards that we use are quite arbitrary. Many of them are social conventions: "That tie looks ridiculous" or "I thought that was the best movie ever made." You take your out-of-town friends to a great ethnic restaurant—one that you cherish—and they want to throw up after they eat. The old Latin phrase *De gustibus non est disputandum* means "There is no disputing taste."

In your perfectionist mind, there is an absolute standard for your appearance, your work, your lifestyle, your sex life, and your cooking. But many of our standards are completely arbitrary. My European friends hold a fork differently than my American friends do. Some people like rather turgid, rigid prose; others like a more informal style of writing. Some people enjoy funky clothing; others are more businesslike. Some people like my cooking, some don't. Go figure.

But if standards are arbitrary, then how is perfection even possible? Isn't the real goal to have a happier life? How would perfectionism fit into that goal? I don't think it does.

## Don't Be Proud of Perfection

A lot of perfectionists seem to be proud of their high standards and their unwillingness to compromise on what they believe is right. Allen was no exception to this hidden pride in perfectionism. "Other people don't know as much as I do, so they might not see that what they are doing is a problem," Allen confided, with a little pride in his "superior" knowledge. When I asked him to compare himself with the average person when it came to making mistakes, he protested, "I'm not average. I hold myself to a higher standard." This was a major obstacle for Allen—his fear of being "ordinary," and hence his rejection of "average."

Here's the paradox of the fear of the ordinary. All of us are special in some sense. After all, we are generally most interested in our own welfare and our own feelings. I feel confident in saying that you spend more time thinking about yourself—your thoughts, feelings, appetites, discomforts, and frustrations—then about anyone else. So you are special to yourself. And you are special to other people as well.

But if each of us is special in some sense, we are all ordinary in another sense. We all have our share of those universal feelings and needs. We want love, acceptance, growth, comfort, security, a sense of accomplishment, and recognition. We have all failed at something, we have all made mistakes that we regret, and we are all mortal. What is ordinary about us unites us.

Being proud of trying to be perfect makes it hard for you to accept your inevitable limitations and then learn from them. If you dread mistakes, you will limit your growth. You won't learn from mistakes because you will hate yourself for them. It's better to use mistakes as a step up on a ladder to something better. I suggested to Allen that he try the "two-step" approach to mistakes: "Make one step to recognize that you are human and a second step to aim for progress."

When Allen was able to accept that we all are universally ordinary human beings, himself included, he was able to use a mistake as a step toward progress—toward learning how to make things better. It's a dance in life—one step back, another forward.

## Develop Your Bill of Rights

If you have been living your life trying to obey your rules of perfection, you have lost any freedom you ever had. It's time for you to stand up, rebel, and write your own Bill of Rights so that you can exercise your freedom to be a human being rather than live as a slave to perfection. You begin with your Declaration of Independence: "I hold this truth to be self-evident—that all men and women are created equal, that they are endowed by the Creator with certain inalienable rights, and that among these are the right to make mistakes, be imperfect, and be happy."

Allen could begin his Bill of Rights with the following:

1.  I have the right to pursue happiness and self-acceptance.

2.  I have the right to make mistakes.

3.  I have the right not to get everyone's approval.

4.  I have the right to be good enough.

I suggested to Allen that his Bill of Rights could be universal—it could be applied to everyone, including himself. Everyone can pursue happiness (as he or she saw it), everyone can make mistakes, everyone can live a life that others might or might not approve of, and everyone can feel good enough. Exercising your right to being good enough is a first step in being assertive about the life you want to live. One way of looking at "rights" is to ask, "Wouldn't people be better off if they thought this way?" So, wouldn't we be better off if we tolerated and accepted and forgave mistakes that others make? And, wouldn't this be a good "universal" rule to apply to ourselves? After all, aren't we human, too?

## Make Your Perfectionism Look Dumb

There's that voice in your mind that keeps telling you, "You're just not good enough. You're always making mistakes. How stupid can you be?" You've been listening to this voice, obeying it, fearing it, and thinking that you have to live your life a captive of your own mind. But maybe your perfectionism isn't so smart, after all. It's been taking this superior position with you, talking down to you as if you are a moron and you can't think for yourself. Your perfectionist voice hasn't been on your side; even when you do well, it doesn't tell you that you are good enough. It just sets higher goals, or it discounts what you do, saying, "Anyone could do that," or "That's what we expected, anyway." This voice makes you feel bad about yourself, makes you feel ashamed, makes you avoid trying new things.

Let's strike back.

"Okay, Allen, we've been talking about your perfectionism, so now let's do a role-play. You can be a rational human being, and I can be that terrible perfectionistic voice that has been beating you over the head with shame and guilt. Now, I want you to really go at me, make me—the perfectionist—realize how dumb I really am."

BOB. You never do anything right. You are always making mistakes.

ALLEN. That's not true. That's your all-or-nothing thinking. I've done a lot of things right. I graduated from college, I have a job, I've gotten some good feedback. I don't have to be perfect.

BOB. Yes, you do have to be perfect. That's what life is about—always being the best.

ALLEN. Why do I have to be perfect?

BOB. Because that's the only way to feel good about yourself—to feel good enough.

ALLEN. Well, that's not working for me. I've been trying to be perfect all my life, and now I realize it never makes me feel good enough or good about myself. It's failing.

BOB. Are you calling me a failure? After all the hard work I've done to make you better?

ALLEN. Yes, you've failed me. You've made me feel like I'm inferior—and I'm not.

BOB. But if you don't try to be perfect, you'll end up mediocre.

ALLEN. I don't even know what that means. I could end up accepting myself as a human being rather than listening to you all the time.

When you criticize your perfectionist voice, you are not criticizing yourself—you are criticizing your critic. You are standing up for yourself. You are defeating what defeats you. As I listened to Allen arguing against his perfectionism, I realized that he was getting distance from it, he was able to fight against it, and he was realizing that perfectionism is really dumb. It masquerades as a superior, condescending voice—but it fails in many ways. It fails to make you feel good, it fails in your relationships, it fails your self-esteem, and it fails to give you any satisfaction.

Is it time to fire your perfectionist voice?

## Make Peace with "Good Enough"

Valerie was an intelligent, conscientious woman who really wanted to do the best she could. But she was afraid of making mistakes. She ruminated about past mistakes, regretted them, and criticized herself. She was stuck in her past mistakes and afraid to try anything that would risk any more. Her parents had fed into this fear. They gave her two conflicting, impossible messages when she was growing up: "Valerie, you are so smart. So much smarter than the other kids. We expect great things from you," and "Valerie, how could you not do well in that course? You will never get anywhere if you keep this up." They had her coming and going. When she did do well, they would say, "That's what we expected of you."

No matter what she did, her mother never said that it was "good enough." It could always be better. Her mom was always raising the bar, always setting some new goal that was out of reach. And, if Valerie failed to reach that higher goal, then all emotional support was withdrawn, and she was viewed as lazy, not making the grade, and at the risk of failing in life.

Looked at this way, Valerie's depression made sense. Since she could never be good enough, she might as well give up. Hopelessness was a logical conclusion. "You don't understand. I have to be the best," she told me while the tears came down her face. "I must be a failure in the eyes of my parents."

But just think about the two assumptions that Valerie was making. What were they? She thought that she had to be the best (rather than simply "good enough"). And she thought that she had to live up to her parents' irrational, unreasonable, and unfair expectations. But we decided to examine these assumptions—and change them.

"Why do you have to be the best?" I asked her. She thought for a while and then said, "Because that's what they always told me."

"Are your parents really great models of loving and healthy parenting? Or would you say that they are well-meaning but quite neurotic?"

Valerie had to admit that they were neurotic. "I'd never raise my kids that way."

"So you are living your life for someone else's neurotic beliefs. And these are the beliefs that you would never in a million years use with your own kids. Do I have this right?"

"Yes," she admitted. "I know it sounds crazy."

"How can you be happy if you want to please people who are intolerant, judgmental, and self-contradictory? You can't. But you can choose to accept that these other people have neurotic beliefs and that they can live alone with them. You don't have to march in step to their drummer." Valerie agreed that if she could accept being good enough, then she would be more accepting of herself, less depressed, more willing to try new things, and more likely to go back to school to finish her course of study. *Good enough* would be quite helpful. But she also realized that she resisted this. "Settling for good enough is the same as being mediocre," she said. "I don't want to be mediocre."

But is "good enough" just mediocre? Let's imagine we have a scale that goes from left to right, with 0 on the far left and 100 on the far right. Where would most people put "good enough"? Valerie suggested that most people might accept 85 percent as good enough. (I actually think most people would accept 50 percent—but what do I know?) More important, she realized that she only had two points on the scale, 0 and 100. She was doing all-or-nothing thinking. Recognizing that a range a little below 100 qualified as "good enough" would help her break free.

Another way of challenging your perfectionism is to ask, "Good enough for what?" Think about what you are trying to accomplish. For example, Valerie would obsess about her appearance not being good enough—she'd spend an inordinate amount of time getting ready in the morning. But she was a teacher, and her students were 12 years old. It's unlikely that these kids would expect her to wear Prada. She would ob-sess about getting her report cards in, making sure that they were impec-cable. But I wonder how carefully anyone reads the reports, anyway. If her goal was to be perfect, that meant that good enough was—well, not good enough. But if her goal had been something practical, then all she needed was to meet a reasonable standard.

You've been equating "good enough" with being a mediocre, care-less failure. It's not the same thing. Good enough is not failing, it's not mediocre, it's not being a fool. It's simply *good enough*.

Valerie came in one day and said she had been talking with two friends of hers about her perfectionism. She said, with a smile—with re-lief—"I don't have to be perfect. I just have to be good enough."

That was good enough for me.

## Develop an Accepting Voice

You've been marching around to the sound of your perfectionist voice. It's been chanting, "You've got to be perfect," and "You're never good enough." It's made you miserable.

But let's call on another voice that is within you—the voice of accep-tance, love, and kindness. Let's imagine that this voice is soft, a whisper in your ear. Imagine it puts an arm around your shoulder and tells you, whenever you worry about making a mistake, "I'm with you. Just keep at it if you can." This voice is your friend, one who is loyal, who cares about what is best for you. "Yes," it says, "I know it's hard sometimes. But I love you the way you are, with any imperfections that you have, with your wonderful heart and your wonderful mind. I am on your side."

When I try to use this voice, I imagine my grandmother speaking to me. She was gentle and warm. She would hold my hand. She would tell me that she loved me, she smiled at my attempts at humor, and she made me my favorite dish. When I think about her today, I realize that she wasn't "perfect" according to any absolute standard. But I loved her and she loved me—and that was always good enough.

## Make Room for Mistakes

You have been organizing your life around the idea that you have to keep mistakes out. They are the unwelcome visitor who, you think, will destroy your peace of mind. You peer out of the windows of your mind, afraid that the mistake will barge through the door and disrupt your life. You have been standing with weapons in hand, ready to defend yourself.

What if you opened the door instead?

Imagine that you live in a cabin, alone with your thoughts. Imagine yourself in the poem "The Guest House" by the Sufi writer Rumi:

> This being human is a guest house.
> Every morning a new arrival.
>
> A joy, a depression, a meanness,
> some momentary awareness comes
> as an unexpected visitor.
>
> Welcome and entertain them all!
> ......
> Be grateful for whoever comes,
> because each has been sent
> as a guide from beyond.

It's not difficult to think of mistakes as guides—we already know we can learn from them. They can guide us to self-acceptance, to new self-knowledge, and to compassionate acceptance of others who make mistakes, too.

And just as you occasionally entertain someone who is not exactly "your kind of person," you may think of extending your kindness and hospitality to your mistakes. As a host, you greet the mistake at the door, welcome it in, and say, "I have been expecting you." You ask the mistake to come in and warm himself by the fire that beats in your heart.

You and the mistake sit down and have an imaginary conversation. Here's what it might sound like.

YOU. Has it been a long journey for you to find my home here in the mountains?

MISTAKE. Yes, I got lost many times. I am always getting it wrong. I don't know what's wrong with me.

YOU. We all make mistakes. But the important thing is that you are here with me. And I have made your favorite dish. I hope you will find it to your satisfaction.

MISTAKE. Ah, but that's the problem for me. Nothing ever satisfies me.

YOU. If you stay long enough and relax, you might be here when Satisfaction arrives. You never know when he might show up. I often find that he shows up when I never expect him.

MISTAKE. All my life people have been criticizing me, making fun of me. People are ashamed to be seen with me.

YOU. In my home, there is always room for you. You don't have to worry about me. I never feel ashamed of you. You are part of my family—you have always been with me—always my companion.

MISTAKE. But don't you feel that I am a burden to you? Don't I remind you of your imperfection?

YOU. You remind me that I am human. You keep my humility in my mind and in my heart. I need you to keep me connected with the family of men and women that I love so dearly.

MISTAKE. I feel at peace now. Would you mind if I lay my head down on this bed and rest? I have been traveling so long, and I have finally found someone who accepts me.

YOU. My home is your home. Peace be with you.


## CONCLUSION

You've been making yourself depressed and anxious because you fear mistakes, and you criticize yourself whenever you make them. Underlying your fear is your perfectionism, the demand that you live up to absolute standards so you will never regret anything. You may fear the judgment of others—or, more likely, your own judgment. But you do have a choice. You can choose successful imperfection.

We have seen that whatever standards you have are really subjective and arbitrary. Your perfectionism hasn't really helped you—it's made you more vulnerable to depression, more self-critical, and less satisfied with life. You now have the choice to continue criticizing yourself for your imperfection or to accept yourself as good enough. Mistakes are sometimes information, sometimes a sign of progress, the cost of doing business, the evidence that you are a player. There is no escape from them—and no need to escape. Welcome your mistakes into your life as visitors, and make room for yourself as a human being. Being good enough can help you live a better life.

## Challenging Your Fear of Mistakes

- Are you a perfectionist?

- What kind of perfectionist are you?

- What are the consequences of perfectionism in your life?

- Ask yourself, *What's the worst thing about a mistake?*

- Realize that everyone makes mistakes. If you're not convinced, ask around.

- A mistake is not the end of the world. What mistakes have you learned to live with?

- You don't have to regret mistakes. You can simply acknowledge them and move on.

- If absolute perfectionism isn't working for you, practice successful imperfection.

- Ask yourself what standard you are using to judge yourself. Aren't standards arbitrary?

- Ask yourself if you are secretly proud of your perfectionism.

- Declare your independence from perfectionism. Develop your own Bill of Rights.

- Does your perfectionism tell you that you're not good enough—even that you're dumb? Try making your perfectionism look dumb.

- Accept that being "good enough" is good enough.

- Develop another voice to counter your perfectionism— an inner voice of kindness, acceptance, and love.

- Make room for mistakes in your life. Welcome them for the gifts they bring.

# CHAPTER 6

# "I Can't Get Myself to Do Anything": How to Build Your Motivation

Jennifer sat at home alone and couldn't seem to get herself motivated to do anything. Since she'd become depressed, she had been spending more and more time in her apartment, often lying in bed for a couple of hours after she woke up. She didn't have any energy. When she got home from work, she just wanted to hibernate, stay at home, and munch on junk food. Nothing seemed like it was worth doing. Before she got depressed, she had been more active; she would go to the health club three times a week, see her friends during the week, go out to movies, and even ride her bicycle along the river. But none of that seemed appealing anymore.

As Jennifer sat in my office and told me how low she felt, even her voice seemed subdued. "I can't get myself to do anything," she said. "I don't have any motivation." She looked down at the floor, sad and defeated.

When you are depressed, you have a hard time initiating action. You wait for the motivation, which seems never to come. You're like a hibernating bear conserving energy, sitting in your "cave," waiting for better times. You think of different things to do, but none of them seems all that exciting. *Too much work*, you think. Your feeling that you cannot do anything leads you to withdraw even more from friends and activities, and your inactivity translates into fewer rewarding experiences. You begin feeling more helpless, like you can't do anything at all. Eventually you start to criticize yourself because you aren't doing anything. This makes you even more depressed. It's a vicious cycle.

It's time to break out of it.

Okay. Let's get to work. We'll start by taking a closer look at this idea of being motivated.

## THE MYTH OF MOTIVATION

Jennifer thought she couldn't do anything unless she felt motivated to do it. When she felt down, she would isolate herself, become less active, and dwell on how bad she felt. She was waiting for her motivation to return—waiting for her mood to change, waiting for her life to get better.

That could turn out to be a pretty long wait.

I decided to suggest an alternative. I said, "What if you saw me walking outside on 57th Street; and I was pacing up and down the block, acting like I was looking for someone. And you came up to me and said, 'Bob, what are you looking for?' And I said, 'I'm waiting for my motivation to show up. I thought it would be here by now.' What would you think?"

Jennifer said, "I'd think you were crazy."

"Let's imagine that you stopped waiting for your motivation to show up. Say you decided to go to the health club and work out even though you didn't feel motivated. You just made a decision and went. What would happen?"

Jennifer looked at me and said, "I'd probably feel better because I was actually doing something to help myself."

"Well, maybe getting better is exactly that. You can do productive things even if you are not motivated—even if you feel tired, discouraged, or bored. You can do it anyway."

"You're right," she admitted. "I've gone to the health club sometimes even when I haven't felt motivated."

"And maybe the motivation comes later. Maybe you feel more interested in doing things after you've done other things. Maybe action creates motivation. Have you ever noticed that?"

"I guess so," Jennifer said. "Sometimes after I work out, I've noticed I have more energy for other things."

"Let's turn motivation on its head—upside down. Imagine if you decided right now—today—that you were going to do things that you weren't motivated to do. You would make up a list of activities that used to make you feel better and do them anyway, even though you had no motivation. You wouldn't wait until you felt like doing them, you'd just choose to do them. Let's see what happens to your overall level of motivation after you've done this for one week. Every day you'll do something you aren't motivated to do."

If you're like Jennifer, you've been saying to yourself, "I have to feel like doing it in order to do it." But that's a myth. You can change yourself from someone whose behavior is "caused" by "motivation" to someone whose behavior *creates* motivation—someone who chooses to do what needs to be done and who gets the motivation later.

## Be Willing to Do What You Don't Want to Do

When we say we're not motivated to do something, we're really just saying, "I don't want to do that." We may phrase it differently, saying to ourselves, *It's too hard,* or *I'm not ready,* but the underlying meaning is the same: we don't *want* to do it. And we think that it's impossible to do what we don't want to do.

But haven't you done a lot of things in the past that you didn't really want to do? Like study for exams, go to work, take out the garbage, or put up with someone else's behavior? The reality is that you don't have to feel like doing something in order to do it. You just have to be *willing* to do it. And that's different from being motivated, comfortable, or ready.

So how do you make the leap from *wanting* to *willing?*

I decided to explore this with Jennifer. "Have you ever thought, *That might be a good thing to do, but I really don't want to do it?*"

"Yeah," she said. "Like exercise, dieting, calling friends, getting my work done. . ."

"So you know what I mean. We all have that problem. We just don't want to do those things we don't want to do. We can sometimes hear our voices complaining, like we did when we were children and Mom or Dad told us to do something and we said, 'I don't want to.' That's a familiar voice. But what if we decided not to listen to that voice—and decided that we would be *willing* to do what we didn't *want* to do? Like exercise, diet, study, get the work done, or do things that are unpleasant. We just decided. We were willing, and we did it."

"I've done that at times," Jennifer said. "It seemed hard to do."

"Okay, Jennifer, let's think about that. What things have you done in the past, and what things do you do now that you actually didn't want to do?"

"Well, let's see. I lost ten pounds two years ago. I just decided I had to fit into my clothes, and I didn't want to let myself go. And when I was in college I studied for exams—and a lot of times I got things done that I didn't think I'd be able to finish. And I also decided to break up with my boyfriend, although part of me really didn't want to."

"Was it useful to you to do things you didn't want to do?"

"Yeah, those things were really useful."

"It sounds like you felt better about yourself after doing what you didn't want to do."

Think of it this way. How have you made yourself willing to do anything you didn't want to do? You decided it was important enough to do. You didn't necessarily know it was going to work out, but you did it anyway. You did it even if you were tired, had a headache, or weren't prepared. You chose to do it. You put on your "mental Nikes" and Just Did It.

And what happened when you did things you didn't want to do? You made progress. You felt empowered. You realized that your lack of energy and motivation couldn't keep you from choosing to do what had to be done. You called on your self-discipline to do what you didn't want to do.

Think about some things that would be good for you to do, but that you don't really want to do. Ask yourself, *Am I willing to do this?*

Use the blanks below to finish this sentence: "I am willing to . . ."

- _____

- _____

- _____

## Constructive Discomfort

Getting better in all areas of our lives involves a certain amount of discomfort. Losing weight requires exercise, building a better relationship may require patience and tolerating frustration, making a decision requires the discomfort of the uncertainty. Facing your fears may mean you have to be anxious. Discomfort is inevitable. We just learned that it's important to do things you don't want to do, but now you can focus even more on your ability to tolerate discomfort. I think of this as the problem of "constructive discomfort."

We've just examined your willingness to do what is necessary to get better—but now let's focus on your attitude toward discomfort. Do you think of discomfort as overwhelming, exhausting, depleting, too frustrating, and ever-lasting? Or do you view discomfort as a temporary inconvenience, as challenging, as giving you a sense that you are overcoming obstacles, and as an inevitable part of your life worth living? Do you think of discomfort as destructive or constructive?

What is *constructive discomfort*? It's the ability to do what is uncomfortable to accomplish your goals. Think about discomfort as a means to an end. It's a tool.

Here are some simple exercises that you can do to build up your discomfort tolerance.

1. *Take a discomfort history:* What are some things you've done that were uncomfortable, but you did them *anyway*?

2. *Relate discomfort to pride:* What have you felt proud about? Was there some discomfort involved?

3. *Assign yourself some discomfort:* Keep track of things that you do that are uncomfortable. See if they are linked to getting things done.

4. *Recognize that discomfort is temporary:* All discomfort is temporary. It won't kill you. In fact, it will make you stronger. Dancers say, "It was a good workout. *It hurt good.*"

If you are not doing something that is uncomfortable every day, then you are not making progress.

You can use your discomfort as an investment—to do what needs to be done so you can get what you really want.

Practicing discomfort is like building mental muscle. It's called self-discipline.

Discomfort is temporary. Pride is forever.

## "I Shouldn't Have to Do This"

This is another roadblock to making progress—your rules about what you shouldn't "have" to do. For example, after a breakup in a relationship, you might think, *I shouldn't have to go through this. I shouldn't have to be lonely.* It is hard and it is often unfair. Some of the worst things at times happen to the best people. And it seems to compound the unfairness when you realize that now you have to deal with your suffering by doing extra work.

One way to look at this is to realize that you don't have a choice about the situation. The only choices you have are (1) doing something to make things better and (2) not doing something to make things better. What happened to you might be unfair—it might even have been traumatic. But that terrible thing happened before today. Today, you can ask yourself if there is anything that you can do to help yourself cope with the unfair and terrible experience that you had.

Imagine that your house has been damaged by a hurricane. You now have a choice: you can have it fixed up, or you can focus your attention on how horrible the hurricane was. Where are you going to put your energy and your resources?

We often find ourselves making wise choices to do what we really shouldn't have to do. Why do we do it?

Because it's in our interests. It's a way of making our lives better.

## What Kind of Person Do You Want to Be?

When we go through a crisis in our lives, we tend to focus on getting over the bad feelings we have right now. That's natural. But you can also think of your depression as an opportunity to decide what kind of person you would like to be. Do you want to be the kind of person who waits for things to happen to you, or do you want to be the kind of person who *makes* things happen for you? Waiting to feel better means that you will be passive. Doing what needs to be done means that you will get more done. Which kind of person do you want to be? A "waiter" or a "doer"?

Jennifer's tendency was to wait until she felt better. I suggested that she had another choice: "You can act better now and feel better later."

We can also think of this as being proactive—"I make things happen," or "I aim for my goals." Jennifer had some good examples from the past of goals that she had aimed for and accomplished. She had taken difficult courses in college, studied hard, and done well. She had lost weight in the past. She had moved to New York—without knowing anyone—and made friends. When she was proactive, she felt better. When she was passive, she felt helpless.

The ancient Greeks and Romans—going back to Aristotle and the Stoics—knew the value of this way of thinking. They emphasized habits of character that made up the "good life"—virtues such as generosity, courage, self-discipline, and integrity. You made choices based on these virtues.

The important thing about a habit is that you practice it regularly without having to feel motivated and without getting rewarded by anyone. It's just something you do—and there's something about you that makes you do it. You are the kind of person who does these things. If you develop the "habit" of getting things done, then you won't be relying on your feelings. You won't be sitting and waiting for your motivation to show up. Your habit will be to persist in the face of fatigue and difficulty. That's the kind of person you will be.

The key to Aristotle's approach was just that—to aim for *the kind of person* you wanted to be. You needed to know what your purposes were. Jennifer recognized that she wanted to be a kind, generous, honest person. But she also realized that she needed to develop the habit of *self-discipline*—to be able to take action in the face of negative moods and to do what was hard to do.

Do you want to be someone who gets things done, someone who doesn't procrastinate, someone who is able to do difficult things—even when she doesn't want to do them? Or do you want to be someone who waits to feel motivated, who is only willing to do easy things, comfortable things? Do you want to be a person who sets goals and can keep doing difficult things for a long period of time—over days and weeks, if necessary—to accomplish what he wants to accomplish? Or do you want to be someone who quits the moment it gets frustrating?

You decide.

Finish the sentence below: "I want to be the kind of person who . . ."

- _____

- _____

- _____

A young man I know graduated from West Point—the United States Military Academy. The training there is rigorous and demanding. I asked my friend to name the most important thing he got out of his training at West Point. Without hesitating, he said, "I learned I could do things I never thought I would be able to do."

Maybe you can learn the same thing. Perhaps we will make that a daily habit for you.

Let's look at the steps you can take to get where you want to go—and be the kind of person you want to be.

## PLANNING WITH PURPOSE

Imagine that you are starting a long journey. You get into your car, you have a full tank of gasoline, and then it occurs to you, *I have no idea where I want to end up.*

You may have a dozen maps, but if you don't know where you want to end up, the journey will not begin. You are stuck.

You may be focused right now on how you feel—tired, sad, helpless, and hopeless. How can you reconnect with the larger purpose of your life? One way is to identify some goals that you want to accomplish over the short term and over the long term. You need to think ahead—think about what you want to aim for.

Ask yourself what you would really like your life to look like. Jennifer wants to improve her social life, exercise more, learn new skills, and get more done. For example, you might want to find another job, travel more, or find a partner.

Keep in mind that you need to *keep your goals in front of you*—they're essential guides when you make decisions about how to use your energy and time. It's a good idea to break them down into goals for each day, each week, and the longer term—the next month and even the next year. Jennifer's daily goals were to get out of bed within ten minutes of waking up, shower, have breakfast, go to the health club (three times during the week), and get to work on time. Her weekly goals included making plans to see friends, returning phone calls that she'd been avoiding, and getting out to see a movie or go to a museum every week. Over the long term she wanted to take a film course, go on vacation with one of her friends, and go out on some dates.

Use the spaces below to write down some goals of your own. Be as specific as you can— "go to the gym twice a week" is more useful than a vague statement like "get into shape."

List some of the goals that you want to accomplish in the next day:

- _____

- _____

- _____

List some of the goals that you want to accomplish in the next week:

- _____

- _____

- _____

List some of the goals that you want to accomplish in the next month:

- _____

- _____

- _____

List some of the goals that you want to accomplish in the next year:

- _____

- _____

- _____

Now you have a purpose every day, week, month, and year. You have something to aim for at every step. You can now get your map out and start the journey.

## My Experience with Setting Goals

If you are having problems motivating yourself—if you think that nothing will work out, obstacles are everywhere, and the future is hopeless—I'd like to give you an example from my own life. I know what it's like to be told you can't do something. I know what it's like to have obstacles all around you. I know what it's like to get yourself motivated.

My parents were divorced when I was not yet two years old. My mother moved my brother and me back to New Haven, Connecticut, from Virginia where we had been living. My father was an alcoholic who never sent us a dime to live on. We were impoverished and living in a housing project; and, for a few years, we relied on welfare so we wouldn't starve to death. I remember when I was about seven years old, my mother served us cereal for dinner. I asked her why we weren't having something else. She said, "We don't have any money for food." When I was 13, I decided I didn't want to be poor when I grew up. I thought, *The only way to get out of this poverty will be to get an education.* My brother, Jim, and I would work as ushers at Yale sporting events—football and swimming—and I got myself a paper route. It was the only way to get some money. And, with that money, I bought books on how to build my vocabulary. I made up a list of books to read that would help me get into college. I kept a list of how much time I spent each day reading in various areas—history, literature, science, vocabulary.

My mother told me when I was 15, "Don't plan on going to college. I have no money to pay for tuition." I told my mother, "Don't worry about paying my tuition. I am going to get a scholarship and go to Yale." And I did.

But it all came down to having a specific goal—getting out of poverty and going to college. I was using cognitive behavioral therapy on myself back then—I just didn't know it. What was I doing?

I was . . .

- *Identifying my long-term goals:* Get out of poverty and go to college.

- *Scheduling specific behaviors every day:* Setting aside time for reading and learning vocabulary.

- *Keeping track of what I was doing:* Monitoring my reading and vocabulary building.

- *Willing to set aside other things so I could accomplish my goal:* Willing to take time away from my friends or television to get my work done.

- *Willing to delay gratification:* Being willing to do things now so that my life would be better in the future.

You may say that this won't work for you—that you're not capable of the discipline a person who's not depressed can muster. But I believe it can and will work for you. I've seen it happen.

Building the habits that create motivation worked for me. That's why I believe so strongly that it can work for you, too.

## What Did You Do When You Weren't Depressed?

One way to break out of your depression is to do what you do when you are *not* depressed. *Act as if* you are not depressed, and you might act your way out of your depression. Jennifer knew that she was a lot more active when she wasn't depressed—going to the health club, getting up on time, getting more things done at work, not distracting herself at her desk with Internet searches, seeing her friends more often, and going out to cultural events. So we decided to start with the past to help us move forward today.

We worked on taking a brief history of all the things Jennifer could remember that made her feel good in the past. She remembered that she used to like dancing, she loved having a dog, she found it very meaningful to read to the blind. She remembered how she loved traveling, loved the beach, hiking, biking, and playing with her friends when she was a kid.

Then she began to cry. "All those things are in the past. They're over and gone."

And I said, "They don't have to be. Let's think of some things that you can plan to do now."

Remember the "reward menu" we talked about in Chapter 2? Let's go back to that idea for a minute. Imagine that you are in your favorite restaurant, and you have a coupon that allows you to order whatever you want, and it's free. Let's get the menu out.

On the menu are all the things that you used to enjoy doing before you were depressed, as well as some things that you've wanted to do but never tried. Now you have to decide which ones to order. It's entirely up to you.

Jennifer decided to order two familiar rewards from her menu—going to the health club and having dinner with her friends. But she also decided that she would rent a bike and ride it along the riverside bike path around Manhattan. She had never done that before. It looked like an absolutely beautiful ride. So now she had some old goodies to look forward to and something new she had never tried.

I asked her to keep track of the new and old experiences that she was trying out. I wanted her to get a sense of what it was like to experiment with the menu. As with any menu, of course, some items would not be to her liking. That was okay. We could always add more items to the menu.

What did you do more of when you were less depressed? Write down some ideas that may become items on *your* menu:

- _____
- _____
- _____

## Plan and Predict Your Pleasure and Effectiveness

When you are depressed, your pessimism leads you to believe that whatever you do will be a waste of time—that you won't get any pleasure from it, and you won't feel effective or competent. But the only way to find out what life has in store for you is to carry out an experiment to test out your pessimism. You can use Table 6.1 on pages 126–127 to predict the pleasure and effectiveness you expect to get from an activity you've planned. Then, when the activity is done, go back and record what you actually experienced. This is much like the exercise we did in Chapter 2, where you kept track of your pleasure and effectiveness to get a sense of how you responded to different activities. The difference here is that you're going to make predictions and then compare them to the actual outcomes.

This self-help homework is good for a number of reasons. It helps you plan ahead so you have things to look forward to. It helps you realize that there are certain activities associated with low pleasure and effectiveness—for example, perhaps sitting at home watching television is unrewarding. And it helps you recognize that there are some activities—seeing friends, exercising, going out, calling people—that are rewarding and make you feel effective. You can add these to your reward menu and start assigning them to yourself. Most important, you can find out whether your negative predictions ("That will be a waste of time") are accurate. For example, Jennifer found out that she generally predicted low pleasure and effectiveness but actually experienced higher pleasure and effectiveness. This motivated her to schedule more things to do. The way to challenge your pessimism is to collect the facts.

Here's how to use the table. For each hour of the week, fill in what you _plan to do_ and how much pleasure (P) you _think you will experience_, just the way you did in Chapter 2, using a scale where 0 is no pleasure and 10 is the most pleasure that you can imagine. Note the degree of effectiveness (E) you expect to feel, using the same scale. For example, if you predict that you will derive a pleasure rating of 3 and an effectiveness rating of 4 from exercising at 8:00 A.M. on Monday, then write "exercise,

P3, E4" in the box for Monday at 8:00 A.M. Then, after you've exercised, go back and write in what you actually experienced.

If you like, you can try a variation on this experiment. Spend a few days doing the things that you used to do when you were less depressed. Rate each experience according to how much pleasure you get and how effective you feel. Then do the same for days when you do almost nothing. (This means, essentially, that you're rating the pleasure and effectiveness of doing nothing.) Now, compare the two.

For example, Jennifer thought about going to the health club. But, feeling depressed and too tired, she decided to stay home. She sat in her apartment thinking about how lonely she was. The "activity" was "sitting at home thinking about how lonely I feel," her pleasure rating was 1 and her effectiveness rating was 0. The next day, she decided to carry out the experiment of going to the health club. She found that her pleasure was 4 and her effectiveness was 5—considerably better than sitting at home.

## Examine the Costs and Benefits

If you've been passive and lying around, like Jennifer, you know that it feels like you don't really have a choice of what to do. You don't have the motivation, and you don't feel like doing it. But lying around *is* a choice. You can either choose to lie around, or you can choose to do something else.

If you are willing to make a choice linked to your purpose and the kind of person you want to be, and if you are willing to do what you don't want to do, then you are ready to examine what will happen if you actually do something. The first thing to ask yourself is, *What are the costs of doing it, and what are the benefits?* And the second thing to ask yourself is, *How long am I willing to do this before the benefits kick in?*

Let's start with the costs and benefits of doing something. Take exercise. What are the costs of exercising for 30 minutes? You might experience fatigue, sweating, and even some discomfort. You also won't be able to just lie around and watch television or Google nonsense on your computer. You have convinced yourself that these are enjoyable distractions. Okay, now think about the benefits of exercise. Possible benefits are: you might feel better simply taking action, it distracts you from your negative thinking, you might feel more energized afterward, and you might get a benefit from the endorphins that kick in when you exercise. Now, how about the longer-term benefits? What if you exercised five days each week for six months? What would the benefits be? You can immediately see that by *investing* over and over again in positive behavior that the payoffs will be greater and greater.

Use Table 6.2 to analyze the costs and benefits of a choice you're considering.

| Table 6.2 Cost-Benefit Analysis | |
|---|---|
| Costs | Benefits |
|  |  |
|  |  |
|  |  |
|  |  |

You should also consider the alternative to doing something—that is, doing nothing. What are the costs and benefits of just doing nothing? Well, the costs are that you will probably feel ineffective, you won't get anything done, and you will stay depressed. The benefits are that you won't "waste" your time and energy.

## CONCLUSION

One reason we often don't try something is that we want to feel better right away. You may get out there, do something that used to feel good when you were not depressed, and find yourself disappointed. Then you're tempted to just give up and sink back into your passivity and lethargy.

But the good feelings that you are aiming for may take a while. You should ask yourself if you are willing to do positive things over and over—for some period of time—to build up the pleasure and effectiveness that you want. The costs are up-front: tolerate difficulty now to make life easier later.

You can lie there and wait for the motivation to show up—or you can identify your purposes, invest in self-discipline as a new habit that you want to nurture, commit to choice, and see if the motivation comes after you take action. Activity creates new realities—new energy, new experiences, even new friends. And as you go along and do what you need to do you, whether or not you are motivated or feel like it, reward yourself every day with praise for doing what is hard to do. Only you know how hard it was—to overcome yourself.

## Challenging Your Lack of Motivation

- Don't wait for motivation to show up. Action creates motivation.

- When you say you're not motivated to do something, you're really saying, "I don't want to do that." Be willing to do what you don't want to do.

- Decide what kind of person you want to be. Do you want to be someone who waits for things to happen or someone who makes things happen?

- Choose your purpose. Set specific goals you want to accomplish in the next day, week, month, and year.

- What did you do when you weren't depressed? Act against your depression by doing some of those things.

- Predict how much pleasure and effectiveness you expect to feel from a given activity. Then try it, and track the results. Test your pessimism.

- Sample your reward menu. Add the activities that yield the most pleasure and effectiveness, and then put them on your schedule.

- Examine the costs and benefits of doing things—long-term and short-term.

- Don't expect an immediate payoff. Over time, your new habits will create new realities. You can start right now.

**Table 6.1**
**Weekly Activity Schedule**

| Hour | Monday | Tuesday | Wednesday |
|------|--------|---------|-----------|
| 6 A.M. | | | |
| 7 | | | |
| 8 | | | |
| 9 | | | |
| 10 | | | |
| 11 | | | |
| 12 NOON | | | |
| 1 P.M. | | | |
| 2 | | | |
| 3 | | | |
| 4 | | | |
| 5 | | | |
| 6 | | | |
| 7 | | | |
| 8 | | | |
| 9 | | | |
| 10 | | | |
| 11 | | | |
| 12 | | | |

| Thursday | Friday | Saturday | Sunday |
|----------|--------|----------|--------|
|          |        |          |        |
|          |        |          |        |
|          |        |          |        |
|          |        |          |        |
|          |        |          |        |
|          |        |          |        |
|          |        |          |        |
|          |        |          |        |
|          |        |          |        |
|          |        |          |        |
|          |        |          |        |
|          |        |          |        |
|          |        |          |        |
|          |        |          |        |
|          |        |          |        |
|          |        |          |        |
|          |        |          |        |
|          |        |          |        |
|          |        |          |        |
|          |        |          |        |
|          |        |          |        |

# CHAPTER 7

# "I Just Can't Decide":
# How to Overcome
# Your Indecision

Wendy feels paralyzed. She gets up in the morning and has a hard time deciding what to wear. She ponders different dresses, jewelry, and shoes, thinking as she considers each one, *But I'm not sure if this is the best choice*. She ends up leaving late and rushing to work. And at work she finds that it takes her a lot longer than it should to get things done. She can't decide if a report is good enough to hand in to her boss, she deliberates—sometimes for hours—about what the best course of action is going to be, and she is often pushing against deadlines. Her indecision has made it difficult for her to decide whether she should buy an apartment or keep renting. There are good arguments either way, of course—but she's been thinking about this for months. When she thinks of calling her friend Gail, she can't decide to pick up the phone: she knows that it's been too long since she last spoke to Gail, so making the call feels hard, but she also knows that Gail can be a good source of support for her. Even in restaurants it's hard for Wendy to make a decision— she keeps comparing the different entrees, and even after her food arrives, she wonders if she made the right choice.

When we are depressed, it's common for us to have a hard time making decisions. Perhaps we've had a hard time with it our whole lives. One woman described herself when she was six years old: "I remember walking across the living room and stopping in the middle and not being able to decide which way to turn." Another woman was plagued by doubts about whether she should volunteer at one place rather than another; the result was that it took her over a year to start doing volunteer work (which she eventually found very rewarding). A man who had recently lost his job knew that exercise usually made him feel better, but he couldn't decide whether or not to go to the gym. He struggled between his urge to stay in bed and his recognition that exercise—although sometimes difficult for him—might make him feel better. (And, of course, by not deciding to go to the gym, he was deciding *not* to.)

When you are depressed, you often think that any decision that you make may make things worse. You focus primarily on the downside, you feel that you won't be able to handle a bad outcome should one occur, and you know that you often blame yourself if things don't work out. As a result, you may require more and more information before deciding, freezing you in your footsteps. Or you may seek reassurance from others before you do anything. Locked in a battle between the pros and cons of making a change, you often procrastinate, delay, hedge, or simply stay put. And when you can't decide what action to take—or whether or not to take any action at all—it can make you feel helpless, convince you that you'll never be able to achieve your goals, contribute to your feelings of hopelessness, and ultimately make your depression worse.

Let's take a look at how you can break this cycle and start making easier, better decisions to move you forward, based on what's most important to you.

## WHAT DO YOU BASE DECISIONS ON?

Whether or not we're depressed, our day-to-day decisions are often based on our momentary feelings and discomforts. Wendy seems to be making decisions based on how she feels right now—or how she might feel in the next ten minutes. If she goes to the health club and is trying to decide what exercise to do, she thinks, *I might feel tired on the elliptical machine.* Or when she's considering calling a friend, she thinks, *I might feel uncomfortable talking with Jenny.* I'm sometimes the same way. I got up this morning—it's Sunday—at 6:45 A.M. I had planned to get some writing done this morning, but I was feeling lazy. Part of me wanted to go back to sleep, another part wanted to watch the news, and another part wanted to Google nonsense. I thought, *Oh, writing on indecision will be unpleasant. It's Sunday morning. Don't I deserve a break?* Ironically, I was having a hard time making a decision—but only for about ten minutes.

My longer-term goals and values included getting this book done and out, and doing a good job of telling you what I have learned over the years—so you can put it to use for yourself. I made a decision to spend a couple of hours writing, rather than loafing and avoiding. My longer-term goals (Get the book done) and values (Be effective and productive) took precedence over my immediate feelings (I'd rather go back to sleep).

## Decide with Purpose

In the last chapter, we talked about getting motivated by not waiting for motivation, but instead just doing the things that are good for us whether we "feel like it" or not. We face a similar challenge in making decisions. When we are depressed, we tend to ignore our longer-term goals and values and make decisions that will avoid discomfort in the short term. But you can change this habit just like any other, using some of the same strategies we've already discussed.

When you are feeling indecisive, you can ask yourself, *What are the longer-term goals that I want to aim for?* Are you trying to build your relationships, be more effective at work, get into shape, get more done? Then make decisions based on those goals. What are your values—do you want to feel productive, self-disciplined, reliable, and responsible? Then make decisions that will let you build these character strengths.

To clarify your values, think back to the ancient Greek model. Almost 2,400 years ago Aristotle identified effective values in living a good life: strengths of character that include honesty, kindness, self-control, and courage. The "good life," according to Aristotle, is defined by acting in accordance with these values—which he called virtue—over and above the influence of fleeting feelings and desires. Plato (who was Aristotle's teacher) used a telling phrase to describe how we feel when something bad happens. He described it as "the fluttering of the soul." We may feel this when we are emotionally "hit" by something; and, in a sense, our emotions take over. But then the next *move* for the ancient philosophers was to stand back, examine what was going on, and make a decision based on values—or, as they would say, *virtue*. Life was about purpose—not about pleasure and pain.

If your decisions are guided by your values, then your decisions can often be clearer. Aiming for the values of self-control and endurance can help you get out of bed rather than sleep in, get to the health club rather than sit on the couch, eat healthful foods rather than comforting junk, stay on task on the job rather than getting distracted, be a reliable friend rather than slip into isolation, do what needs to be done to have good relationships, and choose to move forward rather than staying mired in indecision.

It's a good idea to write out the values that you want to direct your life. These can include courage, self-discipline, honesty, kindness, generosity, patience, friendliness, and other character traits. Focusing on the values and virtues of your life gives meaning to daily activities and helps you make decisions. So, if you want to practice the virtue of self-discipline, then do things every day that require delaying gratification and doing what is difficult to do. If you want to practice the virtue of friendliness, then contact friends, praise them, support them, and show appreciation to them.

Just as your values can direct your life and your decisions, so can the important goals that you strive for. For example, your goals might be getting control over your budget, developing a larger support network, healing conflicts with friends and family, deepening your spiritual life, and cleaning your apartment or house. Goals are related to your values, but they are more specific. As we discussed in the last chapter, it's helpful to make a list of the goals that you wish to achieve in the short term and long term. Break them down as far as possible into goals for the day, the week, the month, and the year to come. When you have a decision to make, think about how it may help or hinder you in achieving one of these goals.

## Examine the Tradeoffs

Are your decisions based on feeling good *right now*? If they are, I suspect you will make near-sighted decisions that will be very costly in the future. If you want to feel better right now—right at *this moment*—then you will make decisions to avoid, procrastinate, or accomplish only trivial things. Good decision making is based on good goals and values that guide your actions and your life over the long term. If your time perspective is very short—only the next few minutes or hours—then you will not accomplish the bigger goals in your life.

Let's take getting into better physical shape. How would you do this? Would you make a decision to avoid exercise because the costs of exercise (discomfort) are greater than the benefits (losing weight) *for the next 45 minutes*? If you go to the health club and exercise for 45 minutes, you probably won't lose weight today. But you might feel uncomfortable right now. It might be that the costs of exercise are greater than the benefits for the next 45 minutes. But what if you thought of the costs and benefits of exercising for three months—going back over and over? What would be the longer-term benefits? You might get into better shape, which might positively affect your depression.

I often say to my patients, "Do you want to feel better for the next five minutes or for the next five years?" If you want to feel better for the next five minutes, then you will probably make decisions that lead you to avoid discomfort, overeat, not exercise, refuse new challenges, put off difficult tasks, and drink too much. Life is not about the next five minutes, though. If you want to feel better for the next five years, then you'll probably make quite different decisions. You'll decide to do what's hard now so it's easier in the future.

## THERE ARE NO PERFECT DECISIONS

A lot of people who are indecisive feel paralyzed by their desire to decide *right*. They want to make perfect decisions that have perfect outcomes, that have no uncertainty attached to them, and that pose no possibility of regret. I am sitting here racking my brain trying to think of what decision would meet those criteria at any point in your life. Even ordering lunch could pose the possibility of some regrets: you could get food poisoning. Or deciding to show affection toward your spouse could also lead to a bad outcome: he or she could be in a grumpy mood. Who knows? The point is, you don't.

How can you tell if perfectionism is your problem in making decisions? Well, ask yourself if you have a hard time accepting uncertainty. Is "It looks like it probably will work out, but it still could fail" a degree of risk you can't live with? Or maybe you think you need to collect as much information as humanly possible before you make a decision. But the more information you get, the more likely you are to see some downside. Or are you looking for perfection of a different kind—assurance that it will never be possible to regret this decision?

Let's look at some ways that the search for perfection can derail your decision making—and some ways you can take the pressure off.

### Reject Certainty as a Goal

I remember years ago when I decided to go into private practice. I had been a full-time academic professor, and I was doing well. But I had decided to leave the academic life to pursue clinical training and eventually set up my own practice. I had a lot of doubts. I had almost no money saved (I had used my savings to get more clinical training), and I had only a few patients at this point. I was in a store with a friend, buying a couch for my new apartment, when I suddenly sat down on the couch and began to shiver. I asked my friend, "Is it cold in here?" and he said, "No." Then I realized I was having a panic attack.

Being a freshly minted cognitive therapist, I asked myself, *What are your negative thoughts?*

Well, I was flooded with negative thoughts and images. They sounded like this: *Who are you kidding? You'll never have a successful practice. You can't afford this couch. You will end up impoverished, with no patients, and creditors hounding you. You are going to fail.* And then I had the image of myself sitting on this couch in my new apartment with the heat turned off because I couldn't afford the utilities—sitting in the dark with the wind blowing through a broken window.

So, my first patient was going to be *me*. I called on all my cognitive-behavioral therapy training. *Bob, you don't need to know for sure that you will do well. All you need is to see ten patients a week to pay your bills. You are good at what you do—and there are other people out there who see patients and make a living. You will have to work hard. You will have to use your cognitive therapy on yourself. And you can always decide to get a job somewhere—go back to academia or work in a hospital—if this doesn't work out.*

I realized I didn't need perfect certainty or perfect outcomes. I just needed to be open to giving it some time. My panic attack subsided. My doubts continued, though. In fact, like a lot of therapists going off into private practice, I would have a flood of doubts in the summer when my caseload dropped. And then I read a biography of Freud. Not that I am a Freudian—just that his life and his contributions have been fascinating. And something in his biography really helped me. Apparently Freud continued to worry about losing *his* practice every summer when he took vacations and his patients were away. Having doubts, not having perfection, living with uncertainty—all of those were the ingredients of life. *There is no certainty in an uncertain world.*

I wonder if Columbus would have embarked on his journey to North America if he'd demanded certainty. Probably not.

## How Much Information Is Enough?

When you are indecisive, you may be saying to yourself, "I need more information." But when you start collecting information, you often engage in biased and pessimistic searches.[1] For example, let's take Maria, who is ambivalent about her relationship with Larry. She thinks that she needs to collect more and more information about him to decide whether or not to continue the relationship—but she does this by focusing on his negatives. In fact, she often interrogates him to find out what his "weak points" are—and this often leads to arguments that confirm her negative bias and her belief that she will get hurt in a relationship.

When you are depressed, you are overly pessimistic, so you look for information to *confirm your pessimism*.[2] To give you another example, Wendy, whom we met at the beginning of the chapter, would inspect her face under a magnifying mirror to see if she needed more makeup. No one looks good under magnification! It's important that you weigh both the positive and negative information.

It's equally important that you know when enough information is enough. One concept that psychologists use to get around the tendency to overresearch is "satisfying"—as in, "Does this alternative satisfy the minimum requirements?"[3] Looking around you to see the choices other people make is one way to figure out where the minimum requirements really lie. By focusing on satisfying rather than perfection, you can set reasonable goals and use the "good enough" standard to meet them, much as we discussed in Chapter 5. For example, Wendy was looking for the best possible appearance—so she spent an inordinate amount of time getting dressed, trying on every possibility in clothing and jewelry before she could leave for work. We decided to try a weeklong experiment in "satisfying"—aiming for a look that was "good enough, but not the best possible." This was hard for Wendy, she said, because her fear was that if she just "settled" for satisfying, she would feel awkward, unattractive, and ordinary. But she tried it anyway. A couple of mornings she still spent more time than she wanted to, but on a couple of mornings she did settle for satisfying. This was a breakthrough for her—recognizing that "good enough" was just that. "I don't have to be the best," she realized. "I don't have to find the perfect outfit. I just have to be as good as others—*just good enough*." She only had to dress as well as others—she didn't have to be perfect. No one is.

You may also want to set a time limit on the information search. One man who was worried about his money would stay up until 2:00 A.M. to search for more and more information about stocks and investments. This resulted in a loss of sleep, increased anxiety and depression the next day, and—almost always—a biased search for the reasons that things would be bad. Setting a time limit before you begin the search can be helpful in shifting away from obsessive focus on information. For example, for Wendy, the time limit was five minutes—as opposed to "as much time as I can take."

Setting limits is also helpful if you're using an emotional rather than a rational standard for deciding how much information is enough. Your standard for searching may be something like, "Until I feel comfortable," or "Until I don't have any doubts."[4] But making decisions may mean choosing to do something that *is* uncomfortable, where there *are* doubts, no matter what you do and no matter how much information you gather. Setting limits before you search is one way of putting a stop to endless information gathering.

As I mentioned above, it can be useful to ask, *How much information is enough for most people?* or *What do reasonable people do?* For example, a woman who needed to have a biopsy was considering various doctors, and she had a list of several highly reputable practitioners to consider. "But I am not sure which is the *best*," she said, going back and forth between different names. I asked her what a reasonable person would do—what most people would feel satisfied with. She agreed that most people would be satisfied with any one of these doctors, but she had a history of trying to get as much information as possible. The problem with this mental strategy is that there is no end to it. There is always more information out there. But collecting more information only added to this woman's doubts and her inability to make a decision. We decided to set a time limit, accept imperfect information, and go forward as a reasonable person would. Incidentally, the biopsy was negative.

## Accept Doubts, but Act Anyway

You may think that you cannot make a decision because you have doubts.[5] "I can't volunteer at the community center because I don't know for sure that it will work out for me," you say, or "I can't call my friends because I don't know for sure that they will be happy to hear from me." You sit and ponder and think, "It might not work out—so I will wait until I find some activity I don't have doubts about." You think that the rule you have to follow is to avoid doubts.

But important decisions in life often involve doubts. For example, Maria really liked Larry, but she had some doubts about him. He didn't have much money, and he had never been married. On the positive side, he was warm, attentive, interesting, and smart—and he loved Maria. "But I still have my doubts," she insisted.

Perhaps so. "But, Maria," I asked her, "has there ever been anyone that you didn't have doubts about?"

"Not really," she had to admit.

Perhaps doubts are part of evaluating the complexity of relationships. We have doubts because people have mixed qualities, and we ourselves sometimes even want conflicting traits in someone. You might want someone who is decisive—but not overbearing. You might want someone who is attractive—but not so attractive that other people would flirt with him or her.

Now let's say that you think, *Yeah, but I still have my doubts!* Well, then you have two alternatives. You can either wait until there are no doubts, or you can go ahead and move forward, carrying your doubts with you, in much the same way you invited your negative thoughts to come along with you for a walk. Let's say that you think, *Maybe I will move forward even though I have these doubts.*

In this light, you can look at moving forward as a way to collect information—not excessive, overresearched, perfect information, but new facts and feelings that may emerge to put your doubts in perspective. You can make a decision—to move forward—while still being *indecisive about your doubts*. "You can decide to date Larry and see what it's like as you get to know each other," I told Maria. "Then you can see if your concerns about your doubts change in any way. You can see if you doubt your doubts more or less as time goes on. This is what I call being 'indecisive about your doubts.'" This idea appealed to Maria, since it meant she could decide to continue seeing Larry without having to put all her doubts to rest. Doubts don't have to determine a decision. You can simply decide to doubt your doubts.

## See Decisions as Experiments

My patient Ruth viewed decisions as final exams she would either pass or fail. Making decisions and taking action on those decisions carried the risk of failing, regretting, and criticizing herself. For her, failure was the likely outcome, and failure was final and fatal. She couldn't stand the idea that things would not work out. Since decisions were so fearsome, she would delay making them; instead she would obsessively review all the evidence, over and over.

But what if you looked at decision making as a process of experimentation? What if you thought, *Let me find out what happens when I try this*? When we carry out an experiment, we are simply collecting information—we're just watching to see what happens, just as if we were mixing two chemicals in a beaker.

Let's take the experiment of exercising. I just thought a little while ago, *I need to move around a little—I need an exercise break*. So I decided to try an experiment: *Let me find out how I feel if I get on the treadmill for 25 minutes while I watch the morning news program*. (I want to assure you that I had met my goal of writing already—so I could allow myself this little break.) I carried out my experiment, and I am pleased to tell you I feel better. But what if I felt worse? What if I felt more tired, more grumpy, or more discouraged because I'd wasted 25 minutes of work time? Then what would be the result? I'd have information that on this Sunday morning at 9:15 A.M., getting on the treadmill made me feel worse. I'd have to enter that information into my bank of information about all other times that I have gotten on a treadmill. I'd have to weigh that information against all the other information. (The fact is that I almost always feel better when I get on the treadmill. That's what repeated experiments have proved.)

Let's go back to Ruth, who tends to withdraw from contact with her friends, then finds it difficult to decide to get back in touch. If she doesn't contact them, she's losing a source of support, reward, and meaning in her life. If she does contact them, it may be unpleasant, since they may be angry with her for being out of touch. Well, she can *experiment* with calling her friends: *Let's see how they respond*. Now, her initial thought— let's call it her "hypothesis," since we are now experimenters—is that her friends will be annoyed with her, that they will criticize her for taking so long to get back to them or just meet her advances with coldness. Okay. Let's find out.

Right now, in her indecisive and avoidant mode, Ruth is *assuming* that her friends will be critical or cold. But, actually, we don't know. What if she's wrong—what if they are happy to hear from her? Then what? Then Ruth has gained important information—and she is back in touch with her friends, able to receive their support and to be a good friend to them in return.

But what if her experiment turns out to have a negative consequence? Isn't that possibility a good reason to remain indecisive and avoidant? Not really. Let's say that Ruth calls her friend Richard and he says, "You know you don't return calls or e-mails. I think you are unreliable." What then? Well, if Ruth wants to try to repair the friendship, she can apologize to Richard, validate him, and tell him that she is going to make it a priority to be more reliable. Richard may accept that, or he may not accept it. But what's the alternative? If Ruth just avoids Richard forever, then she won't have Richard as a friend anyway. The best decision is to try the experiment, take her chances, and learn from the results.

## Be Willing to Absorb Some Losses

When you are fearful of making the wrong decision, you may think that a mistake is something you can never recover from. In your view, a mistake is final and fatal. You can't absorb the loss.

Sometimes the "losses" you fear are really trivial when you think about them, and it's not hard to realize that you can actually absorb them. You might be deciding whether or not to exercise and think, *I could feel really exhausted*. So what? What is really going to happen if you get tired? Can't you recover from that? Or you might consider being more friendly to people, initiating conversations and reaching out. What is the potential loss there? Someone may be unfriendly back to you. What will happen then? I know that I try to be friendly to people but sometimes they are not friendly back to me. How does that make my life worse? I would rather be friendly to ten people and get one negative response than become reclusive and unfriendly. I can handle the "loss" of someone's rudeness.

Or you might fear that you could get rejected by friends. This would be a genuine loss. For example, calling up your friends after a long absence could lead to recognizing that a friend is no longer interested in being your friend. (I'd wonder what kind of friend that was, but I am sure it could happen.) But if you don't contact friends, you lose them anyway. So that loss is more likely to occur through avoiding friends than approaching them. If you lose a friend whom you otherwise would not have called—well, that's like saying I didn't get a seat at the show that I wasn't going to go to anyway. You don't lose something unless you have it and use it.

Maria was stuck in indecisiveness about Larry partly because she didn't think she could absorb the loss if her decision proved wrong.

*What if it doesn't work out?* she thought. *I'll have to go through the agony of a breakup.* As a result of her fear, she kept her distance for a while and kept looking for signs that Larry was the wrong person for her. This, of course, would eventually *guarantee* a breakup, unless she was willing to take some risk.

"If you approach every relationship like this—keeping a distance, testing the guy, looking for problems—what is the eventual outcome?" I asked Maria.

"Nothing will work out," she replied.

"Well, here is the dilemma. If you try your best to make it work, you might increase the probability that it will. But there is no guarantee. The issue is whether you think you can recover from a relationship that doesn't work out. But your testing and negative approach almost guarantees that it won't work out."

Maria recognized that she was boxing herself into a corner. In order to move forward with Larry, she would have to face the possibility that there might be a breakup. As we looked at the evidence, we saw that she had been through breakups before. They were difficult, but she survived. One reason that the breakups were so difficult was that she often blamed herself for the relationship not working. She blamed herself especially for her own negativity and complaining. I wanted to show her a way to make the potential loss easier to absorb. "Maria," I said, "you may have to take a chance that a relationship can fail even when you are on your best behavior. But at least you can say, 'I did everything I could to make it work.'" This idea appealed to her. She could accept the difficulty of a potential breakup better if she knew she had approached the relationship in a positive way.

## Don't Defeat Yourself by Demanding Reassurance

Sometimes we deal with our indecision by seeking reassurance from other people. This strategy can be valuable: you may get more information, your friends may validate you so you feel understood, and you may be able to sort out your ideas and see things in a more reasonable light. But sometimes reassurance seeking can fuel your obsessive search for certainty.[6]

It's understandable that you want to talk to friends about your decisions. That can be helpful. But if your reassurance seeking is constant, it may end up driving them away. They may begin to think, *All she ever talks about is how hard it is to make a decision*—or you may *think* that they're going to think this and turn away from you. Constantly consulting other people can also reinforce your belief that you can't make decisions on your own. Even if you actually get no new information or insight—even if you've already thought of everything that your friend has to say—you may begin to think that your friend was the decision maker, not you. And, in some cases, in seeking reassurance you may be seeking someone else to blame for a poor outcome: "I made this decision because you told me it was a good idea."

I tell patients that their decisions are their decisions. They have to be willing to weigh the alternatives, consider their long-term goals, take action, and absorb the costs. One patient would call me up in between sessions and ask me if a decision she'd made was a good one. I told her that I couldn't serve the function of affirming her decisions—she had to learn how to make these on her own. Only then would she feel empowered—and ultimately more decisive. I reminded her that the way to learn how to ride a bike is to discard the training wheels at some point.

To gauge whether your search for reassurance is problematic, ask yourself if the following statements are true of you:

- Reassurance only works for a short time—then I need more reassurance.

- I feel panicked if I can't get reassurance.

- I think that the only way to handle my anxiety at times is to get reassurance.

- I fear that I may be driving people away by seeking reassurance.

- I am disclosing too much about myself at work because of my need for reassurance.

- I don't seem to know how to reassure myself.

- If I don't get reassurance I don't think I can make a decision.

If you look at the statements above—especially the first three—you can see that reassurance seeking feeds into negative beliefs about decision making. If reassurance seeking serves you only for a short time, you need to recognize that it is *you* who has to accept the uncertainty and risk. You have to accept potentially negative outcomes in order to pursue positive outcomes. Nothing is being dropped in your lap. Your belief that you panic if you don't get reassurance arises from your habit of getting other people to tell you what to do. Only by practicing your own decisions can you let go of the panic and realize that you have made good decisions without other people. Haven't you made decisions about lots of things in your life that were your decisions?

Your belief that the only way to handle anxiety is to get reassurance feeds into more indecisiveness. In fact, you can handle your anxiety much better by using the cognitive-behavioral-therapy techniques outlined in this book. You can look at the costs and benefits, give yourself credit for progress, recognize that you can recover from potential losses, build a case for the positive, and carry out experiments to gauge the results of decisions and gather information for the future. You can practice mindful meditation to ease your anxiety (you'll find some techniques in Chapter 12). You can accept that anxiety is part of life and that it won't kill you. You can make good decisions even *while* you are anxious.

And, most important, you can ask yourself, *What advice would I give a friend?* It is this good-friend technique that allows you to give yourself the assurance you need. When you take care of yourself in these ways, you won't panic if you don't get reassurance from an outside source. You can now rely on yourself—your own best friend.

## CONSIDERING THE COSTS

I've mentioned weighing the costs and benefits of decisions. So let's look at some specific ways to assess what a decision—or indecision—is costing you.

One of the consequences of searching for information is that it takes time, and when the search is excessive and exhaustive, the time it takes is excessive, too. Psychologists call this "search cost." I remember a friend of mine who was a bit obsessive. When we met for lunch, he would spend many long minutes considering all the alternatives on the menu. The problem was that I only had a limited time for lunch.

In a different case, the search cost might be financial. In this case, it was personal. What was the real search cost here—the consequence of this need to examine and exhaust all the alternatives? We were delayed in ordering, our conversation was affected (because he spent all this time with the menu when we could have been talking), and eventually I decided it wasn't worth it to me to have lunch with him.

## Evaluate the Opportunity Costs of Indecision

If you are waiting around to feel better—and in the meantime you're avoiding the activities that you used to enjoy—then you may think you're stuck in indecision. In fact, you've made a decision: by not deciding, you're deciding. You are choosing to do nothing rather than to do something else.[7]

Now, this may sound obvious—but think about it. If you are isolating yourself in your apartment, then you are missing an opportunity to meet someone. If you are lying in bed until late in the morning, then you are missing the opportunity to get into better shape, feel more effective, and make progress in your life. We can call this your "opportunity cost." When Ruth and I looked at the opportunity costs of her inaction, she realized that she might be missing opportunities to get into shape, feel better about herself, enjoy the company of her friends, meet new people, learn new skills, and feel more effective on the job.

The same thing can be true if you are stuck in a relationship or job that feels like it's going nowhere. If you weren't stuck—if you managed to get out and move on—would new opportunities become available? Perhaps getting out of a bad relationship will be painful; perhaps you'll feel lonely and sad for a while. But is it possible that it will open the door to new opportunities?

## Reject Sunk Costs

Does this sound familiar? You purchased a coat—you paid good money for it—and then you brought it home, tried it on, felt it wasn't right for that day, put it in the closet, took it out every few weeks, and then put it back in. You've worn it once or twice, if at all. Your partner says, "Why don't you give that coat away? You never wear it." But you say, "I can't. I paid good money for it." In fact, if you didn't own the coat, you would never go out and buy it now—because you know it's not right for you. But because you own it, you can't get rid of it. It's a "sunk cost."

You've sunk time, money, energy, and reputation into something, and you feel you cannot walk away from it. You can't throw it out, leave it behind, or give it away.[8]

Think about your life right now. Begin with your possessions. Are there things that you have been keeping—maybe even hoarding—that you can't seem to throw out because you paid money for them or simply because you have them? Do you feel stuck in a relationship that you know is self-defeating, but you are unable to break it off because you've invested so much of yourself in it? Or you are stuck in a job that's wrong for you, but you're afraid that making a change means "throwing it all away"?

The irony of a sunk cost is that the more we put into it—the more it costs us—the harder it is to abandon it. Staying with a sunk cost can also make us more depressed—more helpless, less confident, and more regretful. For example, people often stay in abusive relationships for a long time because the relationships have made them feel helpless and inferior—the very traits that keep them from asserting themselves. Sunk costs can become self-fulfilling prophecies.

Diane was stuck in a no-win relationship with Paul, who was married and not very likely to leave his wife. This went on for three years as Diane became angry, anxious, and eventually depressed. She felt stuck. "I know it makes no sense for me to continue, but I can't leave," she said. "I feel stuck. I feel I've been burdening my friends with this for too long—they can't stand hearing about it. But I just can't seem to leave." Diane's relationship with Paul was a sunk cost—she had sunk time, effort, emotion, and even her reputation with her friends into this relationship. It was hard to walk away.

Sunk costs are everywhere. We have sunk costs in relationships we cannot leave, jobs we no longer find rewarding, houses we can't afford to sell for less than top dollar, clothes that fill up our closets and attics, and junk that we collect. When we say, "I can't throw that out because I paid good money for it," we are honoring a sunk cost. We are making a decision looking backward at what we paid for it, rather than looking forward to how useful it will be.

But good decisions are about looking forward, not backward. Good decisions are based on future utility—that is, what you will get out of them in the *long run*—and aimed at moving you toward your future goals. They're about the future, not about the past. Sunk costs are almost always about rescuing past mistakes and trying to make them work out. Sunk costs are about throwing good money after bad.

Why do we honor sunk costs? There are a lot of reasons. First, we don't want to admit that we made a mistake. As long as we are holding on to the sunk cost, we can also hold on to the hope of redeeming it. Perhaps, finally, Paul will leave his wife for Diane, perhaps that coat in the closet will come back into style, or perhaps your job will finally become rewarding. Second, we think that giving up on a sunk cost means admitting that we've wasted all that time and effort. "If I walk away," Diane said, "it means it was all for nothing." But that's not really true. As we examined her relationship with Paul, we saw that there were a number of good things in it for a while—communication, intimacy, good times. So it wasn't a total waste of time. And even if we granted that a sunk cost *was* a total waste of time and effort, wouldn't it still be better to cut your losses sooner than later? Third, we view walking away from a sunk cost as an admission of failure. We say, "I must have been an idiot for staying in for so long." A more rational way to look at it would be to say, "I finally made a decision to cut my losses." But depressed people don't see good decision making that way—they see a bad decision as a sign of being stupid, inferior, and unable to make any good decisions ever. The reality is that bad decisions may simply be a sign that you are making decisions in the first place. I don't know anyone who hasn't made bad decisions.

## Cost-Cutting Measures

Sunk costs are also opportunity costs. As I mentioned above, if you are stuck in a bad situation, you may be missing out on new opportunities. Diane finally did decide to break things off with Paul—and she did go through a period of sadness, loss, and self-doubt. But she began feeling better. As she felt better, she stopped therapy. A year later she came back for a checkup. She said to me that the only thing that she regretted now was that she hadn't broken up with Paul earlier. She was dating someone she had met online, who seemed nice even though he wasn't likely to be a permanent partner. Things were less confusing, and she felt more in control of her life. She had given up the sunk cost of Paul and cut out the opportunity cost of a dead end.

You can break free from sunk costs by asking yourself, *What decision would I make if I had to go back to the beginning—before I made the decision to get into this?*[9] For example, if you never bought the coat or never got into the no-win relationship, would you do it again? If the answer is no, then why hold on to it now? You can also ask yourself, *What advice would I give a friend?* If the answer is, "Get out," then give that advice to yourself. The only reason you are staying in is to try to prove that a bad decision will turn out to be a good decision. And you can recognize that giving up a sunk cost doesn't mean it was a total waste of time. You may have gotten some use out of it—some pleasure. The problem is that the costs now outweigh the benefits.

You may be stuck in a sunk cost because you don't want to feel the sudden rush of pain that giving up will bring. "I don't want to feel the sadness of a breakup," Diane said as she began to cry. "I don't want to feel lonely." But the sudden "hit" of giving up may be a temporary sadness, a shorter-lived pain, than continuing with the lasting pain of the sunk cost. In fact, giving up on a sunk cost may lead to mixed feelings—including some relief. Giving up on a sunk cost will also allow you to focus on goals and behavior within your control—new relationships, activities, and interests—that you can start pursuing almost immediately. You cannot control the past decisions that led to a sunk cost. But you can control what you do now—and in the future. Giving up on a sunk cost opens new doors.

## Conclusion

Making decisions can help you overcome your depression by enabling you to take action, achieve your goals, pursue your values, and feel empowered and effective. But your depression itself gets in the way—for a number of reasons: you want a perfect outcome, you underestimate your ability to live with difficulties should they arise, you fear change, and you demand certainty.

In this chapter we learned some rules for good decision making: Focus on the outcome that you want to achieve, accept ambivalence as a natural part of the process, give yourself the right to decide imperfectly with imperfect information, cut the costs of poor choices, weigh the costs of deciding *not* to decide, and view decisions as experiments—not make-or-break choices but opportunities to learn. Practicing decision making by weighing the short-term costs against the long-term benefits helps you decide to do what is difficult now so that your life can be easier in the future.

## Challenging Your Indecision

- Make decisions based on your goals and values, not on how you feel right now.

- Examine the longer-term and shorter-term trade-offs. Do you want to feel better for the next five minutes or the next five years?

- The search for perfection can derail your decision making. Don't aim for certainty. You don't need it.

- Know how much information is enough.

- Important decisions often involve doubts. Accept your doubts and act anyway.

- See decisions as experiments. What will happen if you try this or that?

- Realize that you can absorb some losses if your decision proves wrong.

- Don't look for too much reassurance from others. It can get in the way of making your own decisions.

- Count the "search costs" and "opportunity costs" of indecision. What else could you be doing in the time you spend researching a decision? What opportunities are you missing?

- Reject "sunk costs"—time, money, or energy you've put into a decision that no longer serves you. Decide to move on.

# CHAPTER 8

# "I Keep Thinking Over and Over . . .": How to Overcome Your Rumination

Ann and Leon broke up, and when Ann came to see me, she told me she had spent the previous few weeks sitting in her apartment just thinking over and over, *What went wrong?*

They had been dating for seven months, there were frequent arguments, Leon was often too busy with work, and she couldn't rely on him. A number of times Ann thought that he wasn't right for her; but at the time, she didn't want to be alone. After their last argument, they didn't speak for days. Then Ann got an e-mail from Leon telling her that it wasn't working out and that he wouldn't be seeing her again. "I keep thinking," Ann said, "maybe I missed something. We did have some good things together. But I just don't understand how he could break up with me through e-mail."

Ann's mind was spinning its wheels. She couldn't seem to move beyond the breakup. She kept replaying different scenes in their relationship. "I keep going back to the arguments. I wonder if I could have handled things differently." Or she searched for clues that Leon was selfish and cruel: "I keep thinking there were some signs that he was self-centered, but why didn't I see them?" Ann had a hard time accepting the idea that Leon could have had some good qualities ("He was funny and took me out to nice places") and also be selfish. "I can't put it together," she insisted.

Ann was suffering from one of the most common problems in depression—the tendency to ruminate. The word *ruminate* is derived from the Latin word *ruminari*, "to chew over," like a cow ruminating (chewing) on its cud. When we ruminate, we keep repeating a negative thought or memory. We may say to ourselves:

- I can't get this out of my mind.

- I can't understand why that happened.

- I wonder why this happened to me.

- I just feel so bad—I can't get my mind off
  of how terrible it is.

- It's just so unfair. Why me?

Research shows that people who ruminate when problems arise are far more likely to get depressed and to stay depressed. Women are more likely to ruminate than men.[1] In fact, there is some recent research showing that there may even be a "rumination gene"—so we may be predisposed toward rumination.[2] But the good news is that you can do something about it.[3]

## RUMINATION AND DEPRESSION

When you are ruminating you are focusing on yourself—especially your sadness, your negative thoughts, your aches and pains, and your past. You keep complaining to yourself—and, eventually, to others—about how badly you have been treated and how unfair life is or how worthless or inferior you feel you are. One patient would sit in my office and go from one rumination to another—complaints about her husband, her boss, her friends, her childhood, and her depression. Another would ruminate during our meetings about his physical aches and pains, going from one area of his body to another—and then he would ruminate about how unfair his wife was to him.

There are several reasons why rumination is a key element in depression.[4] First, when you ruminate you are exclusively focusing on negatives. You are dredging up every bad experience, feeling, and sensation that your mind can latch on to. Second, you are asking questions that have no answers—like "What is wrong with me?" or "Why me?" By focusing on unanswerable questions, you make yourself feel both confused and helpless—which makes you more depressed. Third, you are complaining about something that you are not taking action on, such as "I can't believe this is happening." This only makes you more frustrated and depressed. Fourth, when you ruminate you are not engaged in the real world outside of you. You are not taking action, and you are not solving problems or getting rewards. You are trapped in your head. Fifth, when you ruminate you are emphasizing your feelings of helplessness rather than your sense of empowerment. You are taking away your sense that you can actually do something that will make a difference. All of these ill effects of rumination might make you wonder, *Why am I doing this to myself if it is so bad for me?* The answer is that you actually think rumination is *helping* you.

## How Does Rumination Make Sense to You?

When we ruminate, we think that we can go over the past and finally make sense of it. We think we will figure out why something happened; and, as a result, we will feel better about whatever it was that caused us pain—and be able to avoid the same mistake again.[5] Ann thought, *If I figure out why Leon broke up with me, I can move on,* or *I can avoid this problem in another relationship.* Some of us ruminate because we don't trust our memories; we think that we may finally recognize a crucial detail we've overlooked that will make sense of what happened, and then and only then can we close the case on the past. "Maybe I'm missing something," Ann would say to me. So rumination is your strategy for figuring things out, preparing to solve problems that might arise by learning from the past, and making sense of your experiences.

What's wrong with these aims? First of all, you don't have all the information you need to achieve them. Even if you ruminate for weeks, you won't know what other people are thinking or what they have kept from you. We almost never know for sure why someone did something. And, second, ruminating doesn't help you close the case and move on—it keeps you stuck in the past. You are re-running an old film rather than creating new experiences.

How is rumination different from simply reflecting on the past? Don't we want to think about what happened, make some sense of our lives, and learn from mistakes that we—or others—may have made? Doesn't reflection help us? Of course, reflection does help, and we are wise to reflect on and learn from our experiences. Reflection helps us sharpen our judgment about the future and engage in self-correction so that we won't repeat our mistakes. But rumination goes beyond reflection. When we ruminate we are stuck, we keep repeating, we spin our wheels in our heads—and we get nowhere.

Take a look at Figure 8.1 and see if you recognize yourself in it. Do you assume that "Everything should make sense," "People should act only one way," "Life should be fair," or "I need to understand"? Then you may think that rumination is a useful mental tool to get clarity, understanding, and certainty—but it won't work.

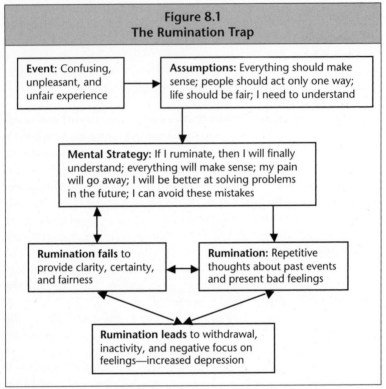

**Figure 8.1**
**The Rumination Trap**

Let's look at an example of an event that might lead you into the rumination trap. Something unpleasant—let's say, the breakup of a relationship. This event causes painful confusion, which leads you to think, *Everything should make sense—so why doesn't this?* This question arises from your assumption about how the world should work: things should make sense, things should be fair, people shouldn't feel ambivalent. How can you make things make sense again? You decide to use your mental strategy of ruminating. Maybe if you go over things often enough and carefully enough, they will fall into place and relieve your confusion and pain.

You are off and running in your head. But no matter how much you ruminate, you still don't get certainty or clarify; you are still confused. So you ruminate more and more. Now you're really stuck in your head, isolated and inactive—and finally depressed. The rumination trap is one of the biggest predictors of getting depressed and staying depressed.

## Is Rumination Working for You?

We've talked about what you hope to gain from your rumination. You can also ask yourself what the disadvantages are for you. For Ann, the disadvantages were that she was stuck in the past, she felt depressed and angry and anxious when she ruminated, and she had a hard time enjoying her life. For other people the disadvantages include increased self-criticism, regret, inability to enjoy the present moment, and irritability. To me, rumination just seems like hitting yourself in the head over and over—to no avail.

Ask yourself if the disadvantages outweigh the advantages. Next time you catch yourself ruminating, see if you feel better for it. Ask yourself, *Will this really help me? Will I be better off or worse off if I continue with this rumination?*

If you conclude you will be worse off, then you can start using the techniques in this chapter to break the cycle.

### LEARNING TO LET GO

The thing that keeps you ruminating is that you think you need certainty and clarity (and you believe those things are actually attainable). You think that you need to know for sure exactly what happened. "There are so many unanswered questions," Ann would say about Leon. "Why would he say one thing but do another?"

What's so bad about not knowing for sure why things happened—or even what happened? Stop and think about this. What good would it do Ann to know exactly why Leon did what he did? Even if she could find that out for sure, the current reality is that he is gone, it's over, and she needs to move on in her life. Getting the answer to the past is not going to help her live a better life today.

Looking in the rearview mirror doesn't help you get to where you want to go.

## Tolerate Uncertainty

Think about all the uncertainty you already accept. You accept uncertainty when you're driving down the highway—you don't know if someone will crash into you. You accept uncertainty when you have a conversation—you don't know what the other person will say. And you accept uncertainty on your job every day. You accept it because you have to live in the real world.

Most ruminators equate uncertainty with a *bad outcome*. But uncertainty is neutral. I don't know if there will be a hurricane tomorrow, but that doesn't mean I need to take shelter in the basement. And ruminators sometimes think that getting certainty is a sign of responsibility— "I need to know why things happened so I can take care of myself better." But that's not altogether true. The best way to take care of yourself is to be clear about your values and practice the habits of an empowered life— which is what this book is helping you to do.

Just as it is hard for us to tolerate uncertainty about events and their causes, we also have a hard time tolerating ambivalence. Ann would continually say, "I can't understand how he could be nice at one moment and cold at another." What she was really saying was that it was hard to accept that Leon was ambivalent—he felt different things at different times. But ambivalence is part of human nature. We are complex beings, continually changing our perspective, experiencing new motives and possibilities, and seeing things in different ways. Ann wanted to see things only one way—"Either Leon loves me or he doesn't"—but that was unrealistic. People have mixed feelings, and ruminating about it won't change the mix.

## Accept Your Own Ambivalence

The truth is that Ann herself had very mixed feelings toward Leon, throughout the relationship and after. When they were dating she felt attracted to him, enjoyed his company at times, and thought he was quite intelligent. Yet at other times, she found him unreliable, self-absorbed, and irritable. She had been ambivalent toward him for quite some time. When they broke up, her ambivalence just took a different form—she missed him, she felt confused, she was somewhat relieved that it was over, and she was angry. Ann had a hard time with the conflicting information she got from her own feelings because she thought, *I really want to feel just one way.*

The problem with this intolerance of your own ambivalence is that it tells you that you *have to get rid of a feeling*—you have to make yourself feel only one way. But you may feel conflicting feelings about someone because the relationship was more complicated than that. Think about any long-term friendship or relationship that you have. Don't you have mixed feelings toward your best friend, your parents, or your colleagues at work? Don't you have mixed feelings toward yourself—some things that you like about yourself and some things that you don't like? Perhaps mixed feelings are a sign that you appreciate the complexity of relationships and people. Perhaps mixed feelings are realistic.

What would be the problem in simply *accepting* mixed feelings? Ann began to realize that no matter how much she ruminated about Leon, she would continue to turn up mixed feelings—both in herself and in him. But if she could accept ambivalence as a sign that things were complicated and that there were pros and cons to the relationship, then she would recognize that mixed feelings can be accepted. And—since one of the reasons behind her rumination was to get rid of mixed feelings—as a consequence of accepting mixed feelings she could step away from rumination.

## Would You Be Better Off Taking Reality as a "Given"?

We often ruminate because we cannot accept reality the way it is. We are like the cow that ruminates, chews its cud, chomping on it over and over. The more you chew it over, the worse you feel and the less likely you are to do positive things. We keep chewing it over because we cannot accept it. But what would it mean to "accept it" as it is?

Let's take Ann. There were a number of things that she had a hard time accepting. She couldn't accept not knowing why the breakup of her relationship had happened, or that Leon had conflicting qualities, or that it was unfair. She couldn't accept not knowing for sure or that it seemed to "come out of the blue." Accepting these things would be hard for Ann—at least, this is what she believed. But what does it mean to accept reality?

If you accept reality, you are only saying, "I see what it is—I see the way it is." You recognize what is "given." You are not saying that it's fair, or that you like it, or that it doesn't hurt. I broke my finger last year by slamming a window on it. It hurt a lot. I could have sat around and mumbled to myself, "I can't believe what an idiot I am for slamming a window on my finger." But that wouldn't have helped. Or I could have kept repeating, "Why me?" But that wouldn't have helped either. Rather than ruminating, I had to accept that I had pain, go to the emergency room, get my finger put in a splint, and learn how to type with one hand while I worked on my book. I could ruminate or cope. I decided to cope. It was actually painful trying to write the book with a broken finger, but it gave me an opportunity to take my own "medicine" and use constructive discomfort and successful imperfection.

Now if you decide to accept reality the way it is, you have a place to start from. You can say, "Okay. I'm here. Where do I want to go?" Ann could accept that Leon had done what he did, accept that it made sense that she was hurt and sad and angry, accept that she didn't have a boyfriend right now, and accept that she had some work to do.

Think about something that you used to ruminate about in the past but you don't ruminate about now. What changed? You simply accepted that reality for what it was. And then you decided to create a new reality by living in the real world and getting on with the life you had.

## Why Does the Past Have to Make Sense?

Ann's rumination was her quest to "make sense" of what happened. "There are some things that I just don't understand," she would say. But why does everything have to make sense in our lives? Let's take a trivial example. Let's imagine that you are driving down the highway and you are late for a very important appointment. Someone passes you and is driving erratically. He is waving out the window screaming at you and everyone else. Your first thought is that he may be drunk—or insane. But at this point in time, what is more important to you—figuring out why he is acting that way or getting to your appointment? When we ruminate, we are often trying to make sense of what has happened to us.

But what would be so bad if some things that happened to you actually don't make sense? What if Ann could never figure out why Leon acted the way he did? Would this prevent her from having friends, being productive at work, or having another relationship that would be more satisfying to her? How does the fact that something in the past that made no sense have any relevance to your life?

Lots of things make no sense—and we don't stop to think about it; or, if we do, we don't care. Ruminators seem to hold an assumption that they need to make sense about things that have happened to them. They think that this will give them *closure*.

But there's another way of getting closure. You can say to yourself, *What happened doesn't make sense—and it was unfortunate—but I need to get on with my life and leave it in the past.* You can get closure by closing the chapter on the past and moving to the next stage in your life. Living life now closes the past.

In fact, the more you live your life now and focus on achieving your goals, the less relevant the past will be. I've never met anyone who has said, "I've got a wonderful relationship now, I'm really happy with my life, my work is going well—but I need to figure out why something happened ten years ago." If you are living a rewarding life now, making sense of the past is irrelevant.

## Will Rumination Solve Your Problem?

Since Ann held the belief that rumination might be a form of solving problems and getting information, I asked her, "What problem have you been solving with your rumination?" The problem, of course, was to make sense of the past. She sat in silence for a moment and then admitted, "I'm getting nowhere with it." But I suggested that making sense of the past might have no relevance to building a better life now. Were there other problems in her life right now that she *could* solve? "What would make your life better?" I asked her. "I guess if I felt better about my personal life. Maybe if I saw my friends more or met someone new."

One way of breaking free of rumination is to redefine the problem that you are trying to solve. Rather than placing the problem in the past, we can focus on the problem in front of us today. Here are some common targets to aim for today:

- See my friends more

- Meet new people to date

- Get more active—go to the health club, concerts, meetings

- Get more focused at work

The great thing about each of the goals that Ann listed is that she could actually do something about them—and she could start today. She could call up her friends, or she could go online to a dating Website and get back in the game. She could go to the health club and work out. If you focus on rumination about unsolvable problems, you feel frustrated and helpless. When you move from rumination to actual problem solving in the real world, you immediately shift from feeling helpless to being able to get things done.

"I wonder if you could do an experiment over the next week, Ann. When you find yourself ruminating, could you do a mood check and rate how you feel? And when you are engaged in the problem solving that you just listed, rate your mood. What do you think you'll find?"

Ann smiled a little and said, "You know the answer to that."

"Let's find out."

Ann decided on an action plan: She would go to the health club three times a week, starting with that very night. She would contact five of her friends and begin to make plans for dinner and other activities. And she would write up a to-do list for work and start facing her procrastination by tackling things she had been avoiding. She felt better already knowing that, instead of ruminating endlessly in her head, she was going to start taking action in the real world.


## Set a Time Limit

Of course, the ideal would be to give up rumination altogether. But that may be impossible for you right now. You may feel overwhelmed, like your intrusive thoughts about the past can't be stopped. But even if you can't shut off your ruminating mind, you can do something about it. One thing that is helpful is to set a time limit—say, five minutes. You can say to yourself, *I'll allow myself five minutes to go through this (useless) rumination—and then I will shift away from it.*

It can also be revealing to write down your rumination. You will find it is the same set of thoughts over and over again. This is a key insight for you—that you are not really coming up with anything new. Keep a list of these ruminations. Go back and ask yourself if there is anything that you have missed. (Some ruminators don't trust their memory—they think that there is something that they have missed.)[6] I am willing to bet that you will see yourself repeating the same thoughts and memories over and over. Nothing new. Just the same old thing. Spinning your wheels in your mind and acting surprised that you are not moving forward.

## SHIFTING YOUR ATTENTION

You've been focusing on your rumination and only feeling worse. Your mind can be in one place at one time—but only one place. So now I want you to think of something else beside the rumination. Shift your attention somewhere else.

But you may say, "How do I shift away from my rumination after five minutes? That's impossible!" I suggested to Ann that, since your mind will only focus on one thing at a time, she could simply refocus her attention on some other object or immediate experience. We started with the ordinary objects in my office—lots of books, some paintings, furniture, and lamps. "Ann, look around my office and try to notice all the different colors and shapes. Now tell me the different colors that you see and where you see them." Ann began describing the different objects that were green, blue, brown, and so on. I then asked her to describe the paintings in my office, which I think are quite beautiful. She described the different colors and shapes and content of the paintings. Then I asked her, "Have you noticed that for the last few minutes you didn't ruminate at all?"

You often think that your mind is literally hijacked by rumination. Once the rumination appears in your head, you can't let it go. It's trapped you. But that's not so. You can shift your attention to awareness of the sights, sounds, even the smells around you. You can even take out different objects with different fragrances and smell them and try to describe the delicacy and intricacy of odors. And deliberately shifting away from rumination helps you set a limit to it.

## What Are You Missing When You Ruminate?

Let's imagine that you spent every minute for the next two days only focused on your mind—your thoughts, ruminations, regrets, feelings. I guarantee two things—you would get very depressed and very bored. Every moment would be internally focused. You would be sitting in a chair noticing every thought that comes to your mind and asking yourself, *What does that mean?* Your task would be to make sense of every bad thing that has happened in your life. This means that you would spend all your time remembering only the bad things, focusing on them, forming images of your worst memories, and reliving the most unhappy moments—so you could "figure things out." And you would miss out on everything that was actually going on around you. Does this sound like a formula for misery? It is. And it's exactly what you are doing when you ruminate.[7]

Okay. Let's imagine that you have already been doing this—ruminating—so you don't have to suffer for the next two days. You can skip that step. Instead, let's imagine a different experiment. In this experiment you are *externally* focused. You are focused on observing everything around you. For example, right now I am sitting in my study in our home in rural Connecticut. I am looking outside and noticing the leaves changing on the trees. There is only a slight tinge of yellow; most of the leaves are still green. It is late September, early fall. As I walk out of the house, I notice that the air is crisp. I see the mums in the garden, and I look up at the sky. There's a hawk flying overhead, gliding from one side to another, probably looking for prey. There are leaves on the ground. It's a beautiful day. I am happy to be alive—and to feel alive.

Noticing, observing, and feeling the real world right now is an alternative to rumination—even if your day is not in an idyllic setting.[8] When you find yourself ruminating you can ask yourself, *What is going on right now at this moment? What do I hear, what do I see, what do I feel?* Let's take a closer look at taking a closer look—by seeing what mindfulness can teach us.

## Stand Back from Your Mind

Sit down right now and start to ruminate. Go back to an unpleasant memory or experience and dwell on it. Notice how your mind keeps spinning, keeps turning over negative thoughts and questions. Notice how you are trying to make sense of it, trying to figure it out, trying to get to the bottom of things.

Your mind struggles against the past and the present, grasping for answers. *How could my sister say that?*—and then you ruminate about it. You collect memories of other emotional injuries. You dwell on these thoughts and images—they're unacceptable, unfair, terrible. You are spinning your wheels in your mind, the wheels dig you in deeper, and you sink.

Notice what your mind has been doing. It's been very active going after those thoughts and memories. It's been active in trying to make sense. It's been judging, struggling, protesting, demanding—answers, justice. You wish you could lose your mind, but it won't let you go. And this nightmare of the mind continues for you each day. Whenever you ruminate, you are lost in your mind, controlled by it, obeying it, responding to it, acting and judging with it, and not living in the real world—at this moment in time.

Here's an alternative. It's called mindful awareness.[9] When we are mindful and aware, we simply notice and observe. We do not try to control. We do not judge. We take things in and let them out.

Let's take your breath. Allow yourself to sit quietly for this moment. Notice your breath. Let it go in and out. Notice where your breath is. Keep your awareness on your breath and let yourself stand back and observe it. Perhaps you notice that your mind is drifting away from your breath to other sensations or thoughts. Gently bring your awareness back to your breath, noticing its movement and where it is. Let go of trying to control your breath and let go of judging your breath. It is not a good or bad breath—it is just a breath. In and out. Where do you notice it, and where is it going?

Stay with your breath—in and out—for ten minutes. You are not trying to accomplish anything. You are noticing. You are standing back and observing. You are gently bringing yourself back into your breath, moment to moment, and letting go, moment to moment. Your breath is a moment—this moment—and it is gone. And the next moment—that is here and then gone. You have given up a struggle, and now you are simply aware of the moment.

When you notice yourself beginning to ruminate, stand back from your mind, let the thought go, and then begin to practice this mindful awareness of your breath. For a moment, let go of the past and the struggle to understand the past. Let it go and return to your breath. And your rumination will intrude on your awareness and distract you from your mindful breathing. Gently let go of the rumination and bring yourself back to your breath, to this moment, here and now. At some point the rumination will intrude again. Gently let it go again. Do this as many times as you need to.

As the past recedes and is gone, the present moment is here. And, then, in another moment, it too passes, like the waves on the shore gently coming and going, moment to moment.

## Accept the Intrusive Thought

When you ruminate what happens is that a negative thought about the past or present enters your mind, and you think you have to pay attention to it. For Ann, the thought *I can't understand why Leon treated me this way* appears in her mind, and she thinks that she has to put everything else aside to solve the problem. The thought is saying, "Pay attention to me. I'm here. You can't do anything until I am satisfied." She is a willing, obedient slave to the thought.

What if, instead, you simply accepted the intrusive thought as a companion? What if you accepted its presence with the same mindful awareness you just brought to your breath—not going where it wants to lead but not struggling against it either? Imagine you just say to the thought, "Okay, I know you are there, but I am busy with my life right now, so take a seat, do what you have to do, and I will get back to you—if I want to." You may not get rid of the thought, the questions may still come into your mind, but you can politely and calmly say, "I hear you, but I am busy living my life."

This was a revelation to Ann. It hadn't occurred to her that she could still make plans with friends, go to the health club, date other guys, and work productively—all the while with the negative thought swimming around in the currents of her brain. She thought she had to put her life on hold until after the rumination was finally satisfied. Instead, she learned she could take the thought with her—make room in her life for the thought—while she went about living her real life in the real world.

## CONCLUSION

A hallmark of your depression may be your tendency to focus on a negative thought or experience and dwell on it over and over. This rumination only prolongs and deepens your depression. We have been looking at what you hope to gain from your rumination and what you sacrifice in your real life by spinning around in your head. You think, *I need to know why, I can't accept this,* and *If I keep thinking, I'll come up with the answer*—but rumination won't get you to the answer. In fact, accepting uncertainty, ambivalence, and even unfairness is the best thing that you can do for yourself, a way to let go of the struggles within your mind about your life so you can actually live your life.

I've suggested a lot of ways to break the cycle of rumination. For example, you can set a time limit so your entire day is not permeated with rumination. You can consider any productive action that you can take toward solving the problem—or, if the problem can't be solved, think about productive action that you can take toward other problems you *can* solve. You can use a mindful-breathing exercise to shift your attention away from the intrusive rumination to simple awareness of your breath in the present moment. You can even expand your awareness to include the intrusive thought, without having to either struggle against it or obey its demands.

Making progress on rumination is a key to changing the self-defeating processes that fuel your depression. Catch the rumination in the act, and then shift toward what is happening now, toward action, toward accepting, and toward letting go. Stay in the moment and let the past go. And as the past recedes, take action toward goals that are real, within your grasp, and available today.

## Challenging Your Rumination

- Do you tend to ruminate—to repeat a negative thought over and over in your head?

- How does your rumination make sense to you? What do you hope to gain from ruminating?

- What are the *disadvantages* of ruminating? Do you notice that it makes you feel anxious or regretful?

- Realize that you can tolerate uncertainty and accept ambivalence—your own and other people's.

- Rumination is a quest to make sense of what's past—but why does the past have to make sense? Would you be better off accepting reality as it is?

- Will rumination solve your problem? Are there other problems you could be solving in the real world instead?

- If you can't turn off your rumination, you can limit it. Set aside five minutes for "rumination time."

- Write down your ruminating thoughts and see how they repeat themselves over and over again.

- Your mind can only be in one place at a time. Shift your attention away from your rumination and onto something else.

- Ask yourself, *When I ruminate, what am I missing in life?*

- Practice mindful awareness to stand back from your mind, observing thoughts as they come and go.

- When a thought intrudes, don't fight it, but don't follow it. Accept its presence, and go on with your life.

# CHAPTER 9

# "I'm Just a Burden": How to Make Your Friendships More Rewarding

Rosa was depressed over losing her job and she began to isolate herself. She had done this before during a previous period of depression, and it had a negative impact on one of her friendships. At work she had isolated herself in a cubicle, seldom talking with the other people there. She said, "I'm just going to bore them with my life. They have everything that they could ever have; and I have nothing, so why would they want to talk with me?" When she would get home from work, she would binge eat, sitting in front of the television watching programs she could hardly recall the next day. But now she was home all the time, ruminating about losing her job, feeling depressed, hopeless, and rejected. Her feelings were like those of a lot of people who lose their jobs, but she was isolating herself even more now. When I said, "Have you called any friends to get together?" she said, "No one wants to hear about you when you're down."

But Rosa also had a habit of focusing on the negative with her boyfriend. She would look for support, hope to get validation; but sometimes she would go off on tangents, complaining about everything in her life. Sometimes men she would date would try to be supportive, and sometimes they just got frustrated and stopped calling. This added more to her depression and rumination, and made her want to isolate herself even more.

In describing Rosa's problem I don't want you to get the idea that you should never share your feelings with people—never look for validation. You are human, and you need support. And I don't mean to blame you for being depressed in the first place. That would defeat the entire purpose of this book. Rather, once you feel depressed, you may find yourself relating to people that might backfire for you. Our goal together is to give you the best tools to overcome your depression, and part of that is to make good use of your support network. They can help you. But you may have to be honest with yourself and take a look at whether you could relate to them in a more productive way.

## RELATIONSHIPS AND DEPRESSION

Many people who are depressed have significant problems in their relationships. Depression is more common among people who live alone, who are divorced, who have relationship conflict, and who have difficulties with their friendships. One way of looking at the interpersonal issues in depression is simply that conflicts and losses may lead to depression. The loss of a relationship, such as a marriage, affects you on many levels: you have lost opportunities for rewarding experiences with your partner, your financial situation may get worse, your network of friends may decline, and you may blame yourself for the divorce. All of these are real issues that we'll address in this chapter.[1]

But another way of looking at it is that depression may lead to conflicts and losses in relationships. When you are depressed, you may be less willing to engage in activities with your friends[2]—you may avoid them, cancel plans, not return calls, or not show up. As your depression cuts down your contact and interaction, your friends may conclude that you are no longer interested in them. For example, Rosa's friends invited her to have dinner and go out, but she declined their offers. She felt she had nothing interesting to say. She did this so often that some of her friends stopped contacting her—more isolation.

Alternatively, your depression may lead you to depend *more* on your friends. Maybe you complain a lot when you're with them. Maybe you ask for help and reassurance but reject any help you get. Or maybe you seek so much reassurance from them that it's difficult for them to cope.[3] So you find yourself in a bind: you don't want to feel isolated, but you don't want to burden other people.

## Are You a Downer?

All of us want to be able to turn to our friends when we are feeling down—but sometimes we can inadvertently bring others down with our behavior. Take a look at the list of "downer" behaviors and ask yourself if any of this sounds like you:

- I continually complain about how bad I feel.

- I complain about my aches and pains.

- I complain about how others treat me unfairly.

- I take a negative view of the world in general.

- I ask for reassurance—over and over again.

- I reject the reassurance once I get it.

- I don't return calls, letters, or e-mails.

- I cancel plans with friends.

- I don't initiate contact with people.

- I don't ask my friends how they are doing.

- I don't compliment people.

- I pout and withdraw.

Now, let's be honest with ourselves. We all have done these things. We are human. But when you feel really down, you may be on a negative track that ends up bringing everyone down. You need your friends— and your friends need you—but constantly complaining and ruminating about what's wrong in your life is only going to make everyone feel worse. By saying this, I am not trying to make you feel worse about yourself. I am simply suggesting that you can change your behavior to be more rewarding to your friends.

Let's examine the kinds of thoughts and feelings that may inadvertently get in the way for you.

## "I Need My Friends to Understand"

This is a reasonable concern. Of course you need validation and support from your friends. In fact, getting validation—hearing that other people care about you and know how hard it is for you—can be one of the most important elements in getting better. When we feel that we can express our feelings and get validation, we feel that we are not alone. We feel others understand and care. And when our friends do understand and care, it has a tremendously positive effect on us. We believe that our feelings make sense, we recognize that we are not alone and that others often have gone through the same experiences that we have, and we are often better able to understand the complexity of the situation and come up with useful ideas about what to do. Expression and validation are key, and we need to keep this in mind as an important need.

But it's also important to put this in perspective. Sometimes we get caught in a "validation trap" where we repeatedly complain about how bad things are and then reject any reassurance or advice. When we do this, we run the risk of alienating our friends. We also run the risk of getting caught up in our preoccupation with how bad things are and losing sight of the possibilities of how to make things better.

The Validation Trap There are a couple of ways you can get into trouble trying to get validation.[4] First, you may think that you need to escalate your complaints—really convince people that things are absolutely terrible—so they will finally understand your pain. For example, Rosa would tell her friends that she was facing a catastrophe, the worst thing that she could imagine, when she lost her job. She would say, "I don't know how I can go on living." And she would add to this, "My boss is evil. I can't believe that someone like him is alive." Now, these were honest and heartfelt statements on Rosa's part, but they left her friends with the impression that her response to the situation was so extreme as to be hard to comprehend. Escalating the extremity of your complaints to get validation may, ironically, lead people to invalidate you. One friend said to Rosa, "You need to get a hold of yourself. Things aren't that bad." Of course, this made Rosa feel worse.

Second, you may have a very demanding sense of what validation involves. You may think your friends have to know everything about how bad you feel—every detail of your troubles—to understand you or to care about you.[5] To meet this exacting standard, you inundate your friends with complaints. Rosa would send long e-mails to friends detailing her feelings and going over past events. Imagine how her friends would feel, opening their e-mail and seeing several pages of correspondence, back and forth, between Rosa and her friends, with comments by other friends. It was like a running autobiography. Some of Rosa's friends stopped contacting her because she was flooding them with minute details of her life that they didn't have time or energy for.

But how can you get out of the validation trap? The first thing to ask yourself is if your continual escalation and preoccupation is really going to lead to validation. It might—at times—but it might also backfire on you. The second thing to ask yourself is whether your expectations for validation are excessive. For example, if you think that your friends need to know every detail in order to appreciate the intricacies of your situation or grasp that things are hard for you, then you need to think again. Why would they have to know everything? Perhaps if they know that things are hard for you—*without* every detail—they can not only validate you but also help you put things in perspective.

If your expectations for validation are excessive, you may end up frustrated, angry, and even hostile toward the very friends you need—and you may not pick up on validation even when you *are* getting it. Rather than judging how well your friends are validating you, you can focus on how you're communicating your needs and start adding more positive content to your conversations. We will look more closely at how to do this in a little while.

## The Victim Trap

Rosa would get angry at her friends if they didn't show enough interest in her problems. "You don't care about me," she would say, or "You have a charmed life. How could you understand what it is like for me?" Rosa was falling into the victim trap—feeling that the world wasn't on her side and that people always treated her unfairly. She would overwhelm her friends with complaints about her family—"My mother is a total narcissist. She only cares about herself." And about her colleagues at work—"My boss favored Lorraine. She's always telling her how well she's doing." She would feel slighted, insulted, and humiliated by the slightest thing—someone not holding the door for her, a clerk being curt with her at a store, or a friend not getting back to her immediately. Everything had the potential to hurt her feelings. Rosa was becoming an "injury collector."

Now, to be fair to Rosa, this was a symptom of her depression. She had a negative filter—she saw only negative intention and malice directed toward her. She was "mind reading" ("She doesn't like me") and focused on feeling inferior ("She thinks she's better than I am.") Rosa wasn't paranoid—she wasn't crazy—but her friends began to wonder if she was going over the edge with her complaints.

What was really going on was that Rosa's depression took the form of feeling rejected and humiliated—her depressed mind was telling her that no one cared. She felt isolated, unloved, and abandoned. She felt all alone. Rosa was crying out to her friends, hoping that they would hear; but her cries were couched as complaints, personal injuries, anger, and rejection of help. As a result, her friends began to pull away. And this only made Rosa feel more depressed.

## Getting the Support You Need

If you have been complaining too much, don't worry about it for now—that's part of your depression. It is very important for you to get support and validation—to get the love and care that you need. And it's important to feel that you can turn to your friends for that support.

I've identified a number of problematic ways of seeking support—acting like a victim, rejecting help, getting angry at people for not understanding, pouting, and escalating your complaints so they sound like reports of catastrophes.[6] These strategies are problematic because they are likely to backfire after a while and drive people away. However, you can learn to ask for help in a reasonable way.

Let's take a look at some simple, constructive steps to getting the support you need.

## Learn How to Ask for Help

One way to ask for help is to be direct. "I'm going through a difficult time right now, and I wonder if I can just talk a little bit about what I'm feeling. I would really appreciate it." This sends a message that you are not acting like you are entitled—and it also helps the other person that you are asking for a *little time,* not hours. You are building a limit into what you are asking for.

Another constructive way to ask for help is to describe your problem in a way that indicates you are also thinking about solutions. For example, Rosa was able to say, "I know I've been upset—feeling lonely, feeling unlovable—but I am also thinking of things that I can do to help myself. For example, I'm thinking of taking a class and getting out and doing more things. And I'm thinking about using some of the techniques that I am learning—for example, how to recognize that some of my negative thinking is too extreme, too illogical." This gives the listener a clear message that you are not only turning to him or her for a sympathetic ear, but also helping yourself. This is a powerful position to take, since your friends want to be supportive, but they may wonder if you are actually going to support yourself. You can balance asking for help and showing that you are willing to help yourself. This gives your friends the message that you are not relying entirely on them—they want to help but they don't want to carry the entire load. Together you might be able to make it better. But show that you are doing your part to help yourself.

## Validate the Validator

When you are depressed, you need to find a balance between sharing your pain and not being a pain to others. This is a hard balance to find. Life is falling down on you, and you don't want to feel alone. But, on the other hand, you don't want to alienate the few friends you have. What can you do?

When you are talking to a friend about how bad things are, gently but clearly indicate that you know you're asking a lot, and you value your friend's support in listening. For example, Rosa could say to her friend Betsy, "I know that I've been complaining about my job. I just wanted to talk a little bit about it because I value your support. But I don't want to burden you with my problems."

When we are feeling down, we are often so desperate to be heard that we don't recognize that our listener also needs validation. But we don't want our relationships with caring people to be one-sided. Rosa found a way to get the support moving in both directions again. "Sometimes it can be hard to listen," she told Betsy, "and I know that you go the extra mile for me. I just want you to know that I appreciate that." This was a very powerful statement for Rosa to make because it validated exactly what Betsy had been feeling. Betsy knew that Rosa had problems to talk about, but she also wanted to feel recognized for what she was doing.

It's also helpful to "take turns"—that is, yield the "floor" to your friend. "I've been going on a while about my problems," Rosa said to Betsy, "and I want you to know that I do want to hear about your life. I don't want to monopolize our conversation." This gave Rosa a chance to be heard, but also gave Betsy some room to be herself, too. Rosa went on to ask Betsy what was going on in her life. "I know that you and Ron have had ups and downs, too. Tell me, how are things going for the two of you?" This was a great invitation to ask her friend to open up and get support from Rosa in turn. It also helped Rosa take her focus off her own problems and feel that she was being helpful and supportive to someone she cared about.

I suggested to Rosa that this reciprocity—give and take—was a wonderful thing about their friendship, worth noticing and celebrating. Rosa reached over to Betsy in one of her conversations and said, "You know, it's great having you as a friend. You are always there for me, and I hope that I can always be there for you."

## Advertise Your Positives

Sometimes our relationships can get overly focused on negatives. Our interactions become complaining sessions—and you might even feel that you have nothing to say unless it's a problem to complain about. I suggested to Rosa that she discuss with her friends the positive things that she was doing to help herself. "I've decided to turn over a new leaf," Rosa told Betsy. "I'm going back to the health club—I really am determined to lose a few pounds and get back into shape. And I was thinking of taking a class on film. Not that I'm going to be a filmmaker, but I think it would be cool to learn more about what's involved in making a film."

Rosa was "advertising her positives"—telling her friends about the constructive positive things she was doing. She found that she actually felt a lot better when she was talking about positives—and her friends consistently complimented her on her new plan to take positive action. "You're beginning to sound so much better," Betsy said. "I was so happy to hear that you are going back to the health club and taking a class in film. I feel like I'm beginning to see the old Rosa—the happy one. It makes me happy to see you shine again."

As your friends hear more positives from you, you feel more encouraged to do positives. Rosa told me that she actually felt motivated to do positives so she could tell Betsy about them. It was a virtuous cycle: doing positives led to talking about positives, which led to getting validated for positives, which motivated her to do more positive things for herself.

## If You Describe a Problem, Describe a Solution

Some of us get so focused on describing the problems that we have that we fail to recognize that we can also figure out how to solve them.

You spend a lot of time telling your friend about how bad you feel, how lonely you are, and how regretful you've been, but you just leave it hanging there—a set of problems with no solutions. And, then, when your friend suggests a solution, you dismiss it.

Problem solving is an important approach to depression. According to this approach, you can view depression as a sense of helplessness about real problems in your life. Rather than thinking about constructive things to do to solve your problems, you get focused on simply your problems, ruminating and escalating in your mind how impossible everything is.

What can you do? After all, you do have real problems. Are you supposed to put on a happy face and make believe that everything is just fine? No. But let's imagine the following: every time you talk to your friends about a problem, you also talk about possible solutions. For example, Rosa was able to turn this around in her conversation with Betsy: "I've been feeling lonely since I lost my job, feeling down and feeling bad about myself. Sometimes it's been really hard. But I'm also thinking about things that I can do to make things better. I know I've been reluctant to start calling people for leads, but it might be one way of getting back into things. I'm not feeling optimistic right now about finding a job, but I know that it's something that's worked for other people. At least it's worth a try."

Now imagine that you are in Betsy's place. Your friend, about whom you care a great deal, is describing a real problem—depression. But your friend is also talking about real solutions. If you are like Betsy, this will make you feel really great about Rosa and will lead you to encourage her more. "I'm so happy to hear that you are thinking about being more proactive in your job search." Betsy said. "You have so much going for you that I am sure there's a great job out there for you. Let me know how I can be helpful."

## Don't Sound Like Your Own Worst Enemy

Some depressed people spend a lot of time describing themselves as "losers" or "failures," either because they really feel that way or because they are trying to get their friends to reassure them. Doing this is like sitting down with your friend and then telling your friend why she shouldn't be spending time with a loser like you. It's both confusing and self-defeating. First, of course, you are not a loser. You are someone who is depressed and trying to do what you can to get better. Second, criticizing yourself constantly in front of your friends will only drive them away. Eventually they will get tired of reassuring you and withdraw.

If you've been your own worst enemy around your good friends, then you need to ask yourself what you think you will accomplish. Perhaps you say, "I've got to be honest about my feelings." That may be true—but only up to a point. Saying that you are depressed is an honest statement about your feelings, but labeling yourself an idiot is a thought distortion that doesn't truly represent you, much less help you. It only makes you ruminate more about how bad things are and turns off your friends.

An alternative to sounding like your own worst enemy is to sound like your own best friend. For example, Rosa had been complaining about what an idiot she was for losing her job. Who wants to hear a friend put down your friend? Rosa's new role was to sound like Rosa's best friend— when talking to her friends. "I know losing my job was hard for me," Rosa now told Betsy, "but maybe it's for the best in the long run. I've been putting myself down, thinking that I was an idiot. But I realize that we all make mistakes and I need to be more supportive to myself."

Here's the great thing about sounding like your own best friend. You begin to realize that you can be supportive to yourself, you can find options, and your real friends will be thrilled to support you in your self-help. You never go wrong by being your best friend when talking to your best friend.

## Initiate Positive Contact with Positive Activities

Like a lot of the depressed people I have seen, Rosa was inclined to isolate herself when she was depressed. Her friends would send her e-mails and call her, but she didn't respond. "I'm a real downer to be around. I don't want to see anyone until I feel better." You may have been thinking that the only thing that you can do when you see your friends is focus on how bad you feel. So, for both you and your friends, you anticipate a really down time. It doesn't have to be that way.

I suggested to Rosa that she think about planning some positive activities with friends so their meetings wouldn't be just opportunities to complain: "Why not make a date to see a friend and do something fun together?" Rosa thought about this and decided to give it a try. She called her friend and said, "Hey, Betsy. I know I've been out of touch. Sorry about that. But I was thinking about checking out that new movie we were talking about awhile back. How about going to see it next week?"

Rosa's friendship contacts were now going to be part of her "positive activities" for her self-help. As much as she could, I suggested that Rosa plan new and fun things to do with friends. This would kill two birds with one stone. First, she would be less likely to focus excessively on her negative mood around her friends. Second, she would be engaging in pleasurable activities that would actually lift her mood. It was a win-win situation for Rosa *and* her friends. She began to develop a list of positive things to do with them—go to movies, visit museums, go for a drive, go shopping, and ride her bike around the city. Her friends began to get a different impression of Rosa—she was now someone who did fun things, so she was someone they wanted to be with.

## Respect Advice

One of the common patterns for people who are depressed is to tell friends how bad things are, turn to them for advice, and then reject the advice. Rosa was no exception. She would complain to Betsy about how bad she felt, Betsy would make suggestions for how Rosa could help herself, and then Rosa would say, "You don't understand how hard it is for me." Rosa was being truthful and authentic, but she was frustrating Betsy in the process. Eventually Betsy might give up and withdraw, and that would only deepen Rosa's isolation and depression.

I suggested to Rosa that she consider "respecting advice" even if she didn't feel ready to use it. Here's what it sounded like the next time Rosa saw Betsy: "Thanks, Betsy, for trying to be helpful to me. I really appreciate your ideas about how I can make things better. Right now it's hard for me to act on those ideas, but I know that I need to make some changes. I'm going to give some thought to what you are saying." Now, put yourself in Betsy's shoes. Even though Rosa is telling her honestly that it is hard to follow her advice right now, she feels that Rosa at least respects the advice she is giving. This makes Betsy more inclined to continue seeing Rosa and offering her support.

## Become Part of a Larger Community

One of the unfortunate developments in our society over the past 30 years is the decline of participation in organizations such as churches, synagogues, clubs, leagues, and interest groups. We are becoming a nation of individuals who are isolated from each other. Rosa was no exception to this. She would often sit alone in her apartment, brooding about how bad things were for her. As she became less depressed during the course of our work together, I suggested that Rosa look into connecting with other people through an organization or interest group.

We began to make a list of possible communities that Rosa could participate in: biking club, hiking club, animal shelter work (she was a cat person), church group, political organization, reading group, environmental activism, and college alumni organization. The advantage of community groups is that they are always there (there is always something to do), you meet people with similar interests and values, and you can even feel that your life has more purpose. I told Rosa about a friend of mine, Dan, who was prone to bouts of depression and had started to volunteer at the homeless shelter that his church ran. "This is one of the best things that I have ever done," Dan had told me. "I feel that I really matter to these people. And I realize how tough life can be for others. It makes me appreciate how lucky I am."

One way of feeling great about yourself and your life is to help other people feel great about their lives—and one way of getting beyond self-criticism is to build a world bigger than yourself. A former patient sends me a Christmas card every year and keeps me posted on his life. He has become very active in Habitat for Humanity, helping disadvantaged people get housing. He now is very active in his church and his college alumni association. His life is now much bigger and more meaningful than it could be if he were simply living as an individual.

Rosa responded to the idea that when we help other people find purpose, *we* find purpose. This was the golden rule for her. She began to tutor a young girl who was having difficulty in school. "I feel every day when I get up that I matter to someone. My life has greater meaning now," Rosa told me, tears forming in her eyes. What a turn of events in her life. She had begun by feeling like a burden to her friends, but now she felt like she could matter to someone who had been a total stranger.

## CONCLUSION

I must confess that I was a little hesitant about including a chapter in this book on being a burden to your friends. You might be criticizing yourself and isolating yourself already because you feel that way. But I also realized that giving you some powerful, useful tools to help yourself cope better with your friendships would assist you in reversing your depression.

We do need each other at times. That's part of being human. But we can also think about how to be more skilled in our dealings with our friends, be more rewarding to them, and actually engage in self-help while we are seeking help. I especially like the idea of talking about the positive things that you are doing to help yourself. It reinforces you, and it is rewarding to your friends to hear that you are taking care of yourself.

Try to think about how to balance seeking support with giving validation to your validator. Help yourself help your friends be better friends. And don't isolate yourself when you are feeling down. I know that I want to be there for my friends when they are going through a hard time. It's the best way to be a friend.

## Building More Rewarding Friendships

- How has your depression affected your friendships? Are you isolating yourself or asking too much of your friends?

- Ask yourself if you're acting like a downer and inadvertently bringing others down.

- Get out of the "validation trap" and the "victim trap."

- Learn constructive ways to ask for the help you need.

- Validate your validator: let friends know that you value their support and want to support them in turn.

- Advertise your positives—things that you are doing to help yourself.

- If you tell a friend about a problem, talk about possible solutions, too.

- Don't sound like your own worst enemy. Constantly criticizing yourself to your friends may put them off and make you feel worse.

- Plan positive activities so your get-togethers with friends aren't just chances to complain.

- Respect your friends' advice. Don't ask for help and then reject the help you get.

- Connect with a larger community.

# CHAPTER 10

# "I Can't Stand to Be Alone": How to Overcome Your Loneliness

Maria had been suffering from depression for more than two years—but lately things had gotten worse. The rather casual relationship she'd had with Rick had fallen apart, and now she was retreating even more into herself. It wasn't like the relationship with Rick was all that rewarding—she saw him twice each month. Rick was wrapped up in his work and didn't seem to have much emotional depth when he was with Maria. But now that this relationship was over, things seemed even more dismal to her.

Maria's retreat into herself is a common symptom of depression—but withdrawing from others can make your depression worse. Maria felt lonely when she was alone at home, but she also felt cut off and lonely even when she was at work. She spent most of her time in her apartment, thinking about how empty her life was. Though she had been living in the city for almost seven years, she had very few friends. At the office, she kept to herself, thinking that no one would really want to talk to her. Everyone else seemed to be having a great time—restaurants, movies, clubs, traveling, boyfriends. But Maria felt stuck in the middle of the largest city in the country unable to start a conversation, meet anyone, or find anyone to spend time with.

At home she would have a glass of wine to take away this lonely empty feeling that plagued her almost all the time. She would order in food, since cooking seemed like such an ordeal—and anyway, she said, "Why cook for just one person?" As she sat in her apartment, her mind was flooded with dark, depressive thoughts that kept reminding her of how bad her life was. "I sit there in front of the television unable to concentrate," she told me. "I keep thinking, 'I'll be alone forever' and 'I must be a loser to be so all alone.'" By the end of the evening she would have finished her third glass of wine and eaten more junk food to calm herself. More reasons, she felt, to feel bad about herself.

When we are depressed we often feel that we have nothing to offer, and so we may isolate ourselves, as we saw in Chapter 9. Maria's experience is typical of so many depressed people's—isolating herself in her apartment, ruminating about how bad things are, and feeling trapped and alone. In fact, loneliness can maintain your depression for years and, paradoxically, lead you to spend even more time alone. Solitude can sometimes be a good thing—giving you time to reflect. But when you are depressed, solitude turns to loneliness and feelings of rejection and hopelessness. These thoughts and feelings spiral into fears of more rejection. Since you become more sensitive to being rejected, you are less likely to initiate conversations with people and less likely to get together with the few friends you have.

The good news is that you can do something about this—and begin reversing your loneliness today. Let's start by looking at some of the beliefs you may hold about being alone.

## COMMON MYTHS ABOUT BEING ALONE

By now you probably have a pretty good idea of how your depression can distort your thinking, making everything seem dark and difficult. If you're feeling hopeless because you've become isolated and withdrawn, chances are you're under some distorted impressions of what it's actually like to be by yourself (and how readily you can change that if you want to). Here are a handful of powerful—but ultimately untrue—beliefs that people who are depressed often hold about what it means to be alone.

### "It's Hard to Meet People"

"It's too hard to meet people," Maria said, feeling defeated before she really began to try. How many times have you said that? You probably believe it because you haven't met many people, but that's most likely because you haven't tried in the most effective way. Maria was no exception to this self-defeating belief that it was almost impossible to meet people. "When I was in college, at least you could meet people in the dorm. But here in the city everyone is anonymous, and no one seems very friendly." Meeting people seemed to be an insurmountable obstacle—and it seemed to me the key to making Maria feel more empowered and less lonely. Our work was cut out for us.

"How many people do you think you actually see on the streets and in buildings every day?" I asked her.

"I've never thought of that," she quickly replied, a bit curious.

"Well, let's think together right now. When you walked from the bus to my office, how many people did you see on the sidewalk?"

"Maybe a hundred."

"Was there anyone in the elevator?"

"Yes, there were two men and a woman who was a little older than me."

"And if you went over to Barnes and Noble after our session, how many people do you think you could see in that store?"

"I don't know, maybe another fifty people."

"Okay, so in the course of a couple of hours, we have more than 150 people that you could actually see. Now let me suggest something that I am sure you won't believe. You could potentially meet any one of those people if you really decided to."

"What? Just walk up to a stranger and start a conversation?"

"Exactly."

"But that's impossible," she said emphatically.

"If I gave you a million dollars, would you be able to do it?"

"Of course, but you won't give me a million dollars."

"You're right. But you've already established that the impossible is possible. Now I will put a price on it. Would you be able to walk up to someone and start a conversation if your happiness depended on it?"

"But it's too hard!"

"Hard, perhaps. But not impossible. Let's start slowly. Here is your plan for the next week. Now close your eyes. What color are my eyes?"

"I don't know."

"Exactly. You're not noticing what's in front of you. What color is my tie?"

"Again, I don't know."

"Okay, you can open your eyes. My eyes are brown, and my tie is blue and gray. You need to notice what's around you so people can find an opening to connect with you. Now what I want you to do is to notice the eye color of every man you see—either walking along the street, standing in an elevator, waiting for a subway, or standing in a restaurant line."

"You mean look them right in the eye?"

"Yep. Here's why. It may come as a surprise to you, but most men are sensitive to rejection—just like you. But if they see that you are looking at them, they may think you're friendly. Okay. Here's another part of your homework assignment. Try to notice if anyone is looking at you. Look around to see. And look in their eyes."

Over the next month—to Maria's surprise—people began talking to her more. Several guys were clearly interested in her. She exchanged numbers and went out on a few dates. It turned out that one of these guys had seen her at their church weeks before but just didn't have the nerve to start a conversation. She didn't realize that a lot of guys are shy, too.

I used a similar approach with another woman, Tina, who thought, "All of these guys are just narcissists." Of course, the irony was that she was talking to me, another guy. Nonetheless, I asked her to start keeping track of any acts of kindness or politeness she observed on the part of men or women. Tina came back the following week and said that she noticed women pushing baby carriages, men and women walking their dogs, people holding the door, someone giving a homeless person some money, someone else saying "Thank you," and a number of people wishing her a nice day. Some were men, some were women. She also told me that she was at a party and was talking with a man who she just met who described some of his volunteer work with Big Brothers Big Sisters. Looking for kindness can help you find caring people—some of whom have been strangers until you find them. There is kindness all around you—just open your eyes, and your heart will find it.

"You can't approach strangers." This is a very common belief among lonely and shy people. It's as if there is a rule book somewhere that limits what you can do. Who wrote this rule book? It's probably only in your head. Well, thank God I didn't believe that rule. Twenty-three years ago I was waiting for a subway in New York, and I saw a very attractive woman standing there. I got on the subway, started a conversation, then said, "I know that this sounds awkward since you don't know me, but I'd like to talk with you more. Here's my card—or I can call you." She gave me her number, I called her. We've been married for 22 years. Lucky me—I didn't believe the "rule" that you can't approach strangers.

## "If You're Alone, You Have to Be Miserable"

"If I'm alone I'll be miserable," Maria said. This is a typical mental trap for people who are lonely—if you are by yourself then you have to be sad, ruminate, and feel miserable. Why would that be?

The answer is quite simple: because, like Maria, when you are by yourself your mind is filled with negative thoughts about yourself and your situation. You're sitting there, by yourself, with this loudmouthed self-critic screaming at you, "You're a loser. You'll always be alone. You can't do anything right. No one loves you. Life is awful."

Ironically, when you are by yourself in this way you actually *do* have someone with you—your critic. Imagine if you invited someone over to your place every night, and he stood in front of you telling you that you were a loser. How would you feel? Just like you do now. Miserable.

To change the way you look at being alone—before you find yourself sitting at home, deep in a rut of depressive thinking—it's helpful to anticipate all of the negative thoughts you're likely to have and plan how to challenge them. Table 10.1 shows what Maria came up with.

| Table 10.1 A New View of Being Alone | |
| --- | --- |
| **Negative Thought** | **Helpful Thought** |
| You're by yourself because you are a loser | You're by yourself because you haven't done the things that will help you connect with others. That's what you can start doing now. You're not a loser because you have many of the qualities that you would want in a friend. In fact, you may be the person you are looking for. |
| You'll always be alone | You're not completely alone now. There are people you work with, family, and friends. If you take the initiative you can start building your support network today. |
| You can't do anything right | That's all-or-nothing thinking. List all of the things that you have done right in your life. Everyone makes mistakes, but that doesn't mean that you can't do anything right. What would a good friend tell you? |
| Life is awful | Life can feel awful at times. But life is what you make of it. Each day is an opportunity to engage in positive behavior and to connect with others. Even if life feels terrible to you, there are positive things to do if you plan them, if you're willing to try new things and willing to take a risk. |

Another helpful thing to do is to plan activities for the time you're likely to be alone. For example, for a lot of single people, being alone on the weekend is hard. So, plan ahead. To find out what's going on that you may want to take part in, go to Websites, read magazines, and ask friends. Check out cultural events, organizations, community activities, volunteer work, and churches and synagogues. Volunteer at an animal shelter, take a class, try something new.

If you are alone at night and you are feeling down, order something from your "reward menu" just for you. For example, Maria took a wonderful bubble bath with candles, she listened to some soothing and beautiful music, and she rented a video that she wanted to see. She also sent out some e-mails and got onto some Websites where she could meet new people. Being alone can be pleasure time for you, time to pamper yourself, make yourself your own best date, your own best friend.

## Be Your Best Friend

As I mentioned, when you are by yourself, feeling lonely, you are probably barraging yourself with negative messages about being a loser, thinking you will always be alone and that you can't do anything right. I've already described some ways to handle these negative thoughts, but we need to go a step further. We need to make you into your own best friend.

Okay. You are sitting alone in your apartment, and it's Saturday night. You don't have a date, you don't have any plans, and you are feeling really down. Your self-critic is banging at the door to your brain, and you are beginning to get anxious that this is going to be another one of those terrible nights of loneliness and sadness. What can you do?

The answer is that you need to be good company to yourself. This means that you can think about what your best, warmest, and most generous friend would say to you. She certainly wouldn't sound like your self-critic. She certainly wouldn't predict the worst for you. What would she say?

Let's see what this would sound like—a conversation with your best friend. Imagine doing a role-play with yourself—and you play two roles—You and Your Best Friend.

YOU. I am feeling down. I'm so lonely that I can't stand it.

BEST FRIEND. No reason to feel down. I'm with you. In fact, you are the most interesting person in my life. I think of you all the time. I love what you love. I'm always here for you. So, count on me.

YOU. Oh, you're just part of my imagination.

BEST FRIEND. So are loneliness and self-criticism. But I am the part that cares about you and is always on your side. And I can tell you some things about you that really matter, that are really good. Do you remember the time you helped your friend Jack when he was out of work? I remember that. He really felt that you were there for him. So, now it's my turn, on behalf of all the people who you've been kind to, to be there for you.

YOU. But how can I enjoy myself when I'm alone?

BEST FRIEND. Well, let's imagine that you are talking with me—your best friend. Let's reminisce about some wonderful things that you have done and experienced. Do you remember that time that you drove out to the country to see the fall foliage? The trees were magnificent. The maples were red and orange. The sky was clear and sunny. You could smell the wood burning—the smoke coming out of the chimneys of the homes around you. Do you remember that day?

YOU. Yeah. That was beautiful.

BEST FRIEND. Oh, and let's think about the wonderful movies you want to see and the books you want to read. So many terrific things to look forward to. And isn't it great that you can download music and podcasts now and listen to the most beautiful music at any time, anywhere? It's so incredible how everything can be at your fingertips now. We're so lucky.

YOU. How did you know about these things?

BEST FRIEND. I'm always with you. I'm your best friend. You just have to pause for a moment to know that I am here inside you, always on your side. You just have to listen and I will be there for you.

## "Only Losers Are Alone"

Maria told me, "Only losers are alone." This is a common belief among lonely people—that being alone is a sign of some terrible defect. Think about the logic of this. Every married person was once alone. He or she met another person who was alone. Therefore, all married people are losers and marry losers. However, the very second that they get married they are transformed into winners. Like magic!

All of us are alone at some time—in some cases, for a period of time. I know that when I was younger, I moved around North America and lived in different cities because of my work as an academic. So, when I arrived in each new place, I was alone. That is, until I made new friends and eventually found a new girlfriend. Did that mean that when I arrived in Vancouver, Canada, and got off the plane, the Canadian Customs officer would look at my passport and say, "What's a loser like you doing in a nice place like this?" I hope not.

Being alone is a situation—sometimes a temporary one that can be reversed in the next day, sometimes it's longer lasting. Either way, it doesn't mean anything about the person. Maria, though, thought that being alone was a sign that she was somehow inferior. "It's a couple's world," she said. But as we looked at this more closely, it became clear that there are couples who are unhappy and single people who are happy. "You're right," Maria said. "My friend Valerie seems pretty content. She has her work, some friends, her interests. She doesn't feel like a loser. I certainly don't think of her as a loser."

But none of this proved that Maria herself *wasn't* a loser. What if she was? We decided to look at this one more closely. "Maria, how would you define what a loser is?"

"Someone who has absolutely nothing going for her."

"Okay. Let's say you are looking for a new friend. What qualities would you want in her?"

"I'd want someone who's intelligent, has some interest in culture, someone who is physically active, a good listener. I could go on, but just someone who isn't judgmental of other people."

"Do you have any of these qualities, Maria?"

She looked at me with a smile. "Okay. You got me. I guess I do."

"So you're looking for someone like yourself?"

"Yeah. But it's hard to find someone with all those qualities."

"How is that consistent with seeing yourself as a loser if you are the very person you would love to meet?"

"Hmmm," she said, in a moment of happy self-reflection.

Yes, there are some wonderful people who are alone. You might be one of them.

## "You Can't Do Things by Yourself"

Maria felt she couldn't do things that she liked because she didn't have a partner: "I can't do those things by myself—you have to be with someone." This is one of the most debilitating assumptions that you can have—that you are imprisoned in your apartment because you are alone. Maria told me, "I can't go out to a movie or a show by myself. That's for couples." Maria felt that she would stand out like a sore thumb in a theater: "People will look at me and think I'm pathetic." She added, "Even if no one noticed, I'd feel too awkward going out by myself." Because she assumed that she could never do these things while she was alone, Maria was "unable" to go to movies, museums, concerts, lectures, sporting events, or restaurants. Her world had become much smaller as a result of her rule.

We examined this rule together. "What's the consequence for you of thinking you can't go out alone?"

Maria paused and then said, "I can't enjoy the city, and I feel trapped and miserable."

"Are there any advantages to doing things alone?" I asked her.

"Well, if I were able to do these things I might enjoy my life more. I might feel less helpless and trapped. But it's hard to do these things when I feel so self-conscious."

"Yeah, I guess it is hard. But is there any possibility that the activity itself could be enjoyable? For example, if you went to a movie by yourself, is it possible you might enjoy the movie? Or if you went to a lecture by yourself, could you possibly meet new people?"

I recall years ago when I was single, I felt liberated when I went to movies, plays, recitals, dance performances, and lectures by myself. I shared this with Maria and she said, "Oh, it's easier because you're a guy. Women look pathetic when they go out alone."

"Really?" I said, letting it sink in that this was a fairly sexist and disempowering way to look at things. "Who made the rule that men can go to movies alone but women can't?"

"Okay," she said, "women can do anything that men can do."

"I think we have agreement there," I replied.

We set up a list of activities to do by herself. Keeping in mind that she would flood herself with negative thoughts that she couldn't do these things alone, I wanted Maria to collect information about whether there were other people by themselves. So she went to stores, decided to try a movie, and got a ticket at the last minute to a play. Most of the people at the movie and play were with someone else, but there were other people who were alone; she wasn't the only one. Second, I asked her to think about the positive qualities that someone might have who was willing to do things alone. She decided, "Maybe they have confidence, maybe the women who are doing things alone are liberated and strong, maybe they don't want to be trapped because they don't have someone to do things with." Third, we looked at the advantages to being by yourself. "It might be easier to meet someone," she said. "I can start a conversation. Maybe a man might think it would be easier to approach me." As she began doing things by herself, she did enjoy her life more, she became less depressed, and she did start conversations with strangers. They didn't seem so strange to her once they began talking.

## MAKING NEW CONNECTIONS

One of the reasons people are more anxious and depressed today than they were 50 years ago is that our connection with other people has declined. Robert Putnam in his fascinating book *Bowling Alone* traces the decline of participation in community activities over this period—less participation in church groups, PTA, local organizations, labor unions, and neighborhood organizations. We also tend to move around more, from job to job, cutting off our ties to people we grew up with or have known for a while. This decrease in connectedness leads to greater isolation, fewer opportunities to share our feelings with others, and less support during difficult times.

But the reality is that there are potential communities all around us. Let's look at some ways you can connect with them.

### The Internet Is a Community

It's amazing how many stereotypes people have about using the Internet. When I first asked Maria about using the Internet to connect with people, she said, "Are you kidding me? Only a loser would do that!" She really thought that using the Internet to find friends was a sign of failure. But our stereotypes about meeting people seem to fit a time in the past—maybe 30 years ago, before the Internet. People of all kinds find the Internet incredibly empowering and efficient. You can reach out to potentially millions of people with a keystroke. You can specify interests, ages, locations, and activities, and screen people as you go along. It certainly beats standing around a bar with a lot of drunken people shouting over the noise.

We have had great success getting our patients to use the Internet for connecting with people—finding friends and finding potential romantic partners. A number of our patients have used meetup.com, where people with similar interests can find others to pursue the activities they enjoy. For example, a woman who loved baseball joined meet-ups to watch baseball games. She was able to meet some interesting men and women this way, and it also helped her overcome her biases against on-line dating.

Facebook, MySpace, and Friendster are social networking sites where you can meet new friends, specify your interests, and share ideas. Linked-In is for professional relationships—you can specify your profession, interests, and activities and connect with lots of people very quickly. For dating, there's Match, eHarmony, Yahoo Personals, JDate, and a host of other Websites. The possibilities are almost limitless.

Although these Websites are absolutely terrific—and there are new ones coming into cyberspace every day—you don't want the Web to be another way to avoid face-to-face contact. Staying at home looking online is quite lonely for many people—so think about it as a way to initially connect, but plan to follow through with a face-to-face meeting.

You also need to be cautious about meeting people online, since you don't know their background, and you don't always know if what they are telling you is the truth. Take some time to check things out with people you meet online. Don't give them money—and don't rush into anything too intense. It can be fun and interesting spending some time getting to know someone. And you may meet people who will become lifelong friends. If you're like me, I am sure that you know people who are happily married to people they have met online.

## Build Your Own Community

The Internet is a powerful tool, but you can also find opportunities to connect with people face-to-face. You can even use the Internet to help you find them! For example, I just went to a Website called VolunteerMatch (www.volunteermatch.org) and typed in "New York City" and found 1,588 opportunities to work with volunteer organizations. Many cities have a Website and organization similar to New York Cares (www .newyorkcares.org) that provides a list of opportunities to volunteer. (You can Google "Chicago cares" or "Boston cares.") The local Red Cross, United Jewish Appeal, and other organizations can also help find the right match for you. Churches and synagogues always need volunteers and often have study groups and support groups. The great thing about volunteering is that you know that someone is relying on you. Someone needs you.

You can also connect with people through hiking clubs, nature groups, cultural groups, local museums, study groups, book clubs, and other organizations. I remember years ago, when I was somewhat obsessed with sailing and windsurfing, a patient of mine, Olivia, was feeling down after finally divorcing her husband. She was an "outdoors" type of person, and she felt that New York City was not the right place for someone like her. I suggested that she take sailing lessons. "It's a great way to be outside for a good part of the year, and you are likely to meet people like yourself who are adventuresome and love the ocean." She tried it, and she really got into it. A few months into her sailing lessons, she signed on to crew on a boat in the Caribbean. While she was there, she started a romance with the man who captained the boat. A year after that, she had quit her job and was sailing to Europe with him. I thought that this was simply a "flight" into fun, but a couple of years later she was married to him. Now, I am not guaranteeing that taking up a new sport or activity will lead to such a romantic adventure, but who knows?

One of my patients was quite inventive in finding a volunteer group. Her beloved cat had died, and she was grief-stricken. A few months later, when she was feeling especially lonely and sad, I told her how my wife and I had eased our way forward when our dog had died. We had volunteered in the country at a rescue shelter to take dogs for walks in the woods. This was quite healing for us both, since we missed our dog but felt a sense of love and warmth from walking a shelter dog. Sandra decided to take the plunge herself. She walked over to the local animal shelter and asked if she could volunteer for a few hours each week. It was an experiment—and it turned out to be a huge success for Sandra. She volunteered to "socialize" the cats in the cat room, which meant that she petted them and played with them. Since she was a talkative and charming person, she met other volunteers and started new friendships. That Thanksgiving, she spent the day with a couple of friends from the shelter, having dinner at their place.

Loneliness is unnecessary—especially when there are other people who can benefit from your care and kindness. It's hard to feel lonely and miserable when you are making someone else happier. It's hard to feel your life has no meaning when there is a child who looks forward to your tutoring her. We weren't meant to live in isolation. We were meant to mean something to each other.

## There's a Pet That Needs You

Jenny had been feeling down since her husband, Eduardo, had died. Although she had friends and family who loved her, she missed the companionship—she missed Eduardo. As we talked about the wonderful times that she and Eduardo had, I could see she really needed someone to love—and someone who would love her. We both wondered where this love could be found. As she talked about her daughter, Elena, who loved her, it seemed that there was someone in Elena's life that Jenny also loved.

Elena had a cat and dog and Jenny would pet-sit for her when she traveled. "I really like her cat. It's like having family again." Then it occurred to Jenny that she could get her own cat. "But I wouldn't know where to look," she said. So Elena and Jenny went to a local animal shelter and found Sheeba. Sheeba had her own story—she had been adopted before by another family, but apparently she was too "talkative," meowing her demands all the time. That's exactly what Jenny needed—someone like Sheeba who would demand a lot from her so she would always feel needed. And Sheeba needed Jenny. For one thing, Sheeba was on "death row" at the shelter: she only had three more days there before they would put her down. As Sheeba reached her paw through the bars in the cage, it was love at first sight for them both. Nine years later they keep each other company—but Jenny also has been involved in volunteer work, she has loads of friends, and she just loves that cat. You might say that Sheeba is a "rescue cat" but I wonder who rescued whom.

## CONCLUSION

Loneliness is an epidemic that many of us have experienced at sometime in our lives. I know that when I first moved back to New York City, I was feeling lonesome. That's when I decided to use cognitive therapy on myself. I made a point of scheduling activities by myself, as well as some with other people. I continually looked for opportunities to start conversations. (As I mentioned earlier in the chapter, I met my wife on the subway!) The great thing about using cognitive therapy on your loneliness is that you can begin feeling better immediately.

Being alone can also create opportunities for you. For one thing, you can have more freedom of action. You can go to any movie, museum, restaurant, or activity without relying on someone else. It's also sometimes easier to meet people when you are alone. You have more freedom to initiate conversations—especially if there is someone else who is alone.

## Challenging Your Loneliness

- If you're feeling lonely, it may be that your depression is distorting your thinking and making it seem as if being alone is all bad. Take a look at your assumptions about being alone.

- Do you think it's too hard to meet people? It's much easier than you imagine.

- Do you think that if you're alone, you have to be sad? You can challenge those thoughts and transform your time to yourself.

- Do you think only losers are alone? Being alone is just a situation; it doesn't mean anything about the person. There are wonderful people who are alone. You may be one of them.

- Do you imagine that you can't do things that you want to do if you're alone—like going to a restaurant or a movie? Try it. You can do anything you want, even if you are by yourself.

- Shed your stereotypes about the Internet—it's a great way to reach out to people who share your interests and want to connect.

- You can build your own community. Connect with a cultural organization, a hiking group, or a book club; a church or synagogue; or a volunteer organization that needs your help.

- Animals are great companions (and getting involved with a shelter can be very rewarding). There's a pet out there that needs you!

## CHAPTER 11

# "My Relationship Is Falling Apart": How to Empower Your Intimate Relationship

Phyllis and Ralph had been married for six years when their daughter, Linda, was born. Phyllis became depressed after she quit her job to stay home and take care of Linda. Ralph tried to be supportive of her, but he was busy with his work and usually came home too late to have dinner with them. As Phyllis got more depressed, she would sulk, usually with a grim look on her face, and show little interest in Ralph when he came home. Phyllis was feeling less attractive, more pessimistic, and unmotivated to do anything. She was irritable, and she directed many of her feelings toward Ralph. If Ralph was reading the paper instead of talking to her or showing her affection, she thought, *He's not interested in me,* or *He doesn't find me attractive.* She began paying less attention to the way she looked. "Why bother?" she told me. "He's lost interest anyway."

Phyllis's continual negativity and lack of interest in things began to wear on Ralph. He began to think, *She's lost interest in me since we had Linda. She doesn't want to do anything. She's always negative.* He began to withdraw into himself. It was only when I had a chance to talk with Ralph individually that I got his interpretation and put both sides of the story together. Phyllis was thinking he had lost interest in her, while he thought she had lost interest in him. Ironically, both were partly right and partly wrong. Phyllis was depressed—and withdrawal is part of depression. But Ralph felt it was a no-win situation, since showing interest in Phyllis often resulted in more negativity from her.

## INTIMACY AND DEPRESSION

As you know, there are many different causes of depression—and your relationship can be one of them. Relationship conflict is highly correlated with depression for both women and men.[1] For one thing, relationship conflict can lead to depression: if you are dissatisfied in your relationship or if your partner is, then there is a good chance that one or both of you will get depressed at some point. In fact, women who experience relationship distress are 25 times more likely to be depressed than women without marital distress.[2] Conversely, depression can be the *cause* of marital conflict. In fact, 50 percent of couples who are in conflict have at least one depressed spouse.[3]

I am using "marital" here in a very general way—these issues apply to intimate, committed relationships, not just to married people. Even if you are currently not involved with anyone, you may get involved with someone in the future, and now might be the best time to learn how to build a better intimate relationship. By learning how to avoid the pitfalls we all are prone to, the next time you get involved with someone you will be better prepared to make it work better. In the meantime, the ideas in this chapter will not only guide you past the pitfalls of intimate relations—they can even help you become a better *friend*.

## A Vicious Cycle

Relationship conflict can add to your sense of hopelessness—feeling trapped and feeling that there is nothing that you can do about it. If your partner is critical, it may lower your self-esteem. You experience fewer rewarding experiences, you feel more lonely within your relationship, and you feel more irritable. You don't feel that your emotions are cared for. You may even feel unsafe.

As I've said, your depression can contribute to relationship problems, and your relationships can contribute to your depression.[4] So here's the other side of the coin: when you are depressed, you may see your relationship in the most negative light. You may engage in mind-reading negatives ("He doesn't find me attractive"), personalizing ("He's working late because he doesn't love me"), shoulds ("She should always be affectionate toward me"), and catastrophic thinking ("It's awful that we are having these arguments"). In addition, you may tend to think your partner is intentionally making you unhappy, you may generalize negatives beyond a single example ("She's always nagging me"), and you may blame yourself for problems when they arise.[5]

Along with affecting the way you see things, your depression may bring with it a particular style of interacting. Sometimes when we are depressed, we complain a lot to our partner, often repeating over and over the negative feelings and thoughts we have. When we are depressed, we often don't make eye contact, we pause for a long time when we speak, and we may sigh a lot. We may withdraw, pout, and refuse to engage in pleasurable activities with our partner. When our partner offers suggestions, we may reject them and even complain, "You just don't understand." We may even try to elicit negative feedback—"You don't find me attractive, do you?" Or engage in excessive reassurance seeking—"Do you still love me?"[6]

When we are depressed, we may misinterpret our partner's suggestions as criticisms.[7] But relationship problems may be the result of this criticism. It's hard to feel good if you are being criticized a lot of the time. I have found that my depressed patients often believe that they are being criticized or that they aren't loved—and I don't know what the truth is until I get a chance to talk with the spouse privately and then watch the two of them interact. There are three stories, I've found: the husband's, the wife's, and the truth. Much of the time, both partners are partly right and partly wrong. But it's not the truth that ultimately counts. It's whether they are willing to change what they do and what they say. That's what this chapter is all about.

Changing your relationship can have a significant effect on your depression. In fact, for couples whose conflict is associated with depression, couples therapy (following the ideas outlined in this chapter) can be as effective as individual psychotherapy for both partners in overcoming their depression. Couples therapy changes both the depression and the problems in the relationship that make you depressed.[8] It's like getting two for one—less depression and a better relationship. And if your partner is the one who's struggling with depression, the ideas in this chapter will help you understand what's happening and how you can help him or her get through.

## Locating the Problem

There are a lot of reasons why your intimate relationship can have difficulties. In this chapter, we will cover the major difficulties many people experience. Both you and your partner can benefit from reading it and discussing it together. The key thing is to recognize that your depression can be made worse if your relationship is getting worse. The good news is that you can actually start doing something about it today.

We all have our "theories" about our relationships, but these theories can contribute to the problem. Many distressed people subscribe to the theory that their partner's personality is the problem. "He's unemotional and rigid" or "She's demanding" are frequent complaints that I hear from distressed couples. The belief that these unhappy couples share is that their partner would have to undergo a complete personality change in order to make the relationship better. Since this is next to impossible, they feel trapped and hopeless.

Cognitive-behavioral therapists have a much different approach. We believe that distressed couples have problems because they interact in distressing ways. For example, what would it be like if you could do the following in your relationship?

- Be more rewarding toward each other.

- Show appreciation more.

- Focus more on the positives than the negatives.

- Stop bringing up the past and focus on what you can do better today.

- Accept your differences.

- Be more patient.

- Be more affectionate.

- Feel that your emotions are cared for.

- Get validation and understanding from your partner.

- Be better at solving problems together.

I could go on with a list five times this length, but if you were to get the things I listed above, wouldn't you feel better in your relationship? Wouldn't your partner? And if that happened, what would happen to your depression or your partner's depression?

Isn't it worth it to try and find out?

If you look for the common thread in the list, you'll see that each one is a behavior or a thought. You can change the way you act, and you can change the way you think about things—sometimes almost immediately. If you change the way you act and think, you will ultimately change the way you feel. And if you practice these new behaviors and ways of thinking about things, you are very likely to see improvement in both your relationship and your depression. You don't have to go back to your childhood and dig up every injury, every problem that you had. You can change your relationship today.

## WORKING WITH FEELINGS

Let's start by looking at how you and your partner respond to each other's feelings. Take a look at the following and ask yourself if either of you has ever said:

- You're always so negative.

- Get your mind off of it.

- Stop complaining. You are lucky to have what you have.

- You're just depressed. Can't you be happy for a change?

If you've heard these things, you know how ineffective they are. They make you feel worse. You feel that your partner doesn't want to hear about your feelings, doesn't think that you have a right to be down, and just wants you to snap out of it. You feel invalidated and dismissed. But we all need to feel that our partner really cares about the way we feel and is willing to put some time into sharing emotions. We don't necessarily need our partner to solve every problem, but we sure would like to know that he or she cares enough to care that the problem is bothering us.

Now, what if you or your partner were to say any of the following when the other is feeling down?

- I know it must be hard for you feeling this way.

- I can see that it makes sense that you would feel down, given the way that you are seeing things.

- A lot of times you may feel people don't understand how hard it is for you.

- You must be thinking that this really down feeling is going to last a long time. It must be hard to feel that way.

- I want you to know I am always here for you.

- I don't want to sound like I don't want to hear about your feelings. I do. But if there is anything that I can do to help you feel better, please let me know. Your feelings are really important to me.

As simple as these statements are, they powerfully convey that you care about each other and respect each other's feelings.


## Share, Don't Solve

Sometimes when our partner comes to us with a problem, we want to be supportive, so we jump in with solutions. We say, "Here's what you can do," or "Here's where your thinking is wrong." In fact, these solutions and perspectives can help—at times. But when used at the wrong time they send the message "I don't want to hear about your feelings," "Enough already!" or "You're irrational." That may not be what you mean to say, but it may be what your partner hears.

Vinnie did this with his wife, Cynthia. She had been telling him of the difficulties she was having at work with her boss (who was demanding and inconsistent) and her coworker who was moody, and he kept telling her that there were lots of ways to solve the problem. Much to his surprise, his well-intentioned advice only made things worse. Cynthia felt that Vinnie was constantly telling her what to do rather than hearing her feelings, so she got more angry with him. "You don't understand," Cynthia complained, thinking that he was a "typical man" trying to take control and tell her what to do and how to feel. And, to some extent, she was right. He was Mr. Fix-it where she wanted Mr. Feel-it.

When we are feeling down, we want to feel that our partner cares enough to hear about what is bothering us. We want to feel that we will not be dismissed or ridiculed. We want to know that our partner cares. I said to Vinnie, "Sometimes when you *share* a problem, it doesn't need to be *solved*. Maybe Cynthia wants to be heard rather than helped." The next day this method worked like a charm. Vinnie decided to go into "validation mode"—asking Cynthia how she felt, affirming the truth in her feelings, and asking her if she felt he was really connecting. Whatever problems Cynthia had to discuss seemed insignificant to her after the discussion, because she felt that Vinnie was being a real "partner."

Sometimes if you listen to the problem, it no longer feels like a problem.

In the research that my colleagues and I have done, we find that people who are depressed believe that other people don't validate them, don't care about their emotions, have never felt as bad as they do, and think their feelings don't make sense. So if your partner is depressed, you can make a real difference. You can connect with your partner's feelings.

But how do you connect with someone who is depressed? The most profound way is to help your partner understand that you care about his or her sad and depressing feelings—that you actually understand emotion.

Here's what you can do.

- *Invite your partner to share feelings:* "I know this is a hard time right now. Tell me how you are feeling about things."

- *Empathize:* Identify and label the emotions that your partner is having. "It sounds like you are feeling sad and bad about yourself. I get the sense that there are times that you feel hopeless about things."

- *Validate:* Find some truth in the perspective and feelings your partner is sharing. "I can understand why you would feel sad and helpless if you blamed yourself for this." When we validate we show that we can see that the other person's feelings make sense. We make sense of what she feels.

- *Inquire:* Ask for more information about feelings, thoughts, and needs. For example, don't just nod and say, "I understand." Show some curiosity about his feelings: "It sounds like you are feeling sad and trapped at times. What other feelings have you been having?"

- *Ask about your role in the problem:* When we are having difficulty with our partner, we don't want to feel that only one of us is the source of the problem. For example, Vinnie recognized that Cynthia was upset with him when he told her what to do to feel better. After empathizing, validating, and asking about other feelings, it was time to go the next step: "It sounds like you sometimes feel like your feelings are not as important to me as they should be. Can you tell me what I am doing that makes you feel that way?"

- *Ask for direction:* After you have identified your role in the problem, it's quite natural to go the next step and ask what you can do to make things better. Ask your partner to be specific. Don't accept "Be nicer to me." Ask, "Can you give me some examples of things that I can say or do that would help you feel I care about you?"

## Help Your Partner Feel Cared For

Once you've connected in this way, you can go even further to help your partner feel cared for and understood on an emotional level. Try these approaches:

1. *Help make sense of feelings:* Tell your partner how you understand that her emotions make sense given what has happened and how she is thinking. "Others have these feelings." "Your feelings make sense given the way you are looking at things." "You are not alone."

2. *Expand the range of feelings:* Help your partner understand that there are many feelings—not just the current one. Feelings come and go, there are mixed feelings, and feelings vary in intensity. "You have so many different emotions—some feel positive and some seem negative." "I know you are feeling sad, but are there other feelings that you are having as well?" "Are you having mixed feelings?"

3. *Reduce shame and guilt:* Help your partner understand that feelings are not a sign of being weak, but rather a sign of being human. "We all have difficult feelings at times. Your

emotions are a sign that you feel things intensely, because things matter to you. You are most human when you have feelings."

4. *Accept your partner's pain:* When you love someone it's natural that you want to jump in and make that person feel better. Sometimes that can be helpful, but at other times it may convey the message that your partner's pain is too much for you to hear. You can communicate acceptance by saying, "I know that you are having a hard time and I accept that you will not always feel upbeat." Acceptance and validation go hand in hand.

5. *Link emotions to higher values:* Sometimes your emotions can reflect the things you value—competence, love, belonging, or responsibility. You can support your partner emotionally by saying, "I know that these things bother you because you truly value _____."

## Let Go of Being Right

One of the most difficult things in doing couples therapy is to help my patients recognize that even if they are right about their complaints, it won't help them have a better relationship. "She is too emotional," one man said, explaining why he and his wife were having problems. Even if he were right (which I actually don't agree with), being right about the "facts" wasn't going to bring them any closer. No one says, "I have a better sex life now because I have the facts on my side."

But you may be highly invested in proving that you are right, even if it's the wrong thing to do. You and your partner may be locked in little trials that you play out. One day he's the prosecutor, and the next day you prosecute him. When you are the defendant you always lose, because the prosecutor doubles as a judge. These little trials go on, and each time you lose. You recognize that even if you are the prosecutor today, you may win the battle but lose any happiness. It's continually "lose-lose."

Is it better to fix the blame or fix the problem? I find that people who are unhappy are more focused on blaming than on building a better relationship. The choice, though, is yours. You can give up on being right and get on to getting better together.

## WORKING WITH NEGATIVE THOUGHTS

When we are unhappy in our relationships we typically see things in a biased and negative way—we fall prey to certain thought distortions that make a bad situation worse or, in some cases, make what might be a good situation into a terrible mess. In earlier chapters, we've talked about automatic thoughts and the part they play in your depression—these are ideas in certain recognizable patterns that come spontaneously when you're depressed, seem plausible to you, and are associated with negative feelings. Automatic thoughts, however, are just that—thoughts—and they may or may not be true. Let's take a closer look at how these familiar automatic thoughts—what I call the Dirty Dozen—play out in the minds of distressed couples and see some examples of ways to counter them.

1. *Labeling:* You attribute a negative personality trait to your partner, leading you to believe that he or she can never change: "He's passive-aggressive." "She's neurotic." As an alternative, rather than label your partner, you can look for "variability" in his behavior. "Sometimes he withdraws, and sometimes he interacts with me. Let me ask him what might lead him to withdraw."

2. *Fortune-telling:* You forecast the future and predict that things will never get better, leaving you feeling helpless and hopeless: "He'll never change." "I'll always be unhappy in my marriage." An alternative to this is to focus on specific things that you can say or do now—such as the exercises described in this chapter. Another good option is to look back at positive experiences that you have to challenge your idea that nothing will improve. You'll find more on this a little later on in an exercise called "Catch Your Partner Being Good."

3. *Mind reading:* You interpret your partner's motivations as hostile or selfish on the basis of very little evidence: "You don't care how I feel." "You're saying that because you're trying to get back at me." Rather than engaging in mind reading, you can ask your partner what he meant or how she is feeling. Sometimes it's beneficial to give your partner the benefit of the doubt: "She's simply taking a little time

to unwind" is a better interpretation than "He doesn't find me interesting."

4.  *Catastrophic thinking:* You treat conflict or problems as if they indicate that the world has ended or that your marriage is a disaster: "I can't stand her nagging." "It's awful that we haven't had sex recently." A better way of looking at this is that all couples face problems—some of them quite upsetting. Rather than look at an obstacle or a problem as "terrible," you might validate that it is difficult for both of you but that it is also an opportunity to learn new skills in communicating and interacting. Problems can be learning experiences and can provide some new ways to grow.

5.  *Emotional reasoning:* You feel depressed and anxious, and you conclude that your emotions indicate that your marriage is a failure. "We must have a terrible marriage because I'm unhappy." "I don't have the same feelings toward him that I used to; therefore, we're no longer in love." A better way of looking at your emotions is that your feelings may go up and down, depending on what you and your partner are doing. Cynthia felt very depressed about her marriage, but there were times that she really felt great around Vinnie. Emotions are changeable and don't always tell you about how good things can be. It's also important to ask yourself, *What are we doing when we feel better together?*

6.  *Negative filter:* You focus on the few negative experiences in your relationship and fail to recognize or recall the positives. You probably bring up past in a series of complaints that sounds like you're putting your partner on trial: "You were rude to me last week." "You talked to that other person and ignored me entirely." This is where "Catch Your Partner Doing Good" is so helpful—it allows you to look at things without the dark lens on. You can also keep a list of positives about your partner to remind you to put the "negatives" in perspective. We all do dumb

things at times, but it's useful to take off the negative filter and remind ourselves of the positives.

7.  *All-or-nothing thinking:* You describe your interactions as being all good or all bad without examining the possibility that some experiences with your partner are positive: "You're never kind toward me." "You never show affection." "You're always negative." Whenever you use the words "always" and "never," try assuming that you are wrong. For example, when Phyllis began looking for positives from Ralph, she realized that he was affectionate at times and that he was rewarding to her as well. The best way to test out your distorted and biased negative thinking is to look at the facts. Maybe the facts aren't as terrible as they seem to be.

8.  *Discounting the positive:* You may recognize the positive things in your relationship but disregard them: "That's what a wife or husband should do." "Well, so what that he did that? It means nothing." or "These are trivial things that you're talking about." Every positive should be counted—it's the only way to build up good will. In fact, if you start counting the positives rather than discounting them, they will no longer seem trivial to both of you. Vinnie was happy to learn that the very little things that he was doing, like complimenting Cynthia, made a big difference to her. This in turn made him less critical. And Vinnie began keeping track of Cynthia's positives, which helped him recognize that an occasional negative—which was probably due to depression—was outweighed by the many good things in their relationship.

9.  *Shoulds:* You have a list of "commandments" about your relationship and condemn yourself (when you're depressed) or your partner (when you're angry) for not living up to your "should." There is no end to these nagging negative thoughts. Here are a few typical examples:

    *My partner should always know what I want without my asking.*

    *If my partner doesn't do what I want her to do, I should punish her.*

*I shouldn't ever be unhappy (bored, angry, etc.) with my partner.*

*I shouldn't have to work at a relationship—it should come naturally.*

*I shouldn't have to wait for change—it should come immediately.*

*My partner should change first.*

*It's all his fault, so why should I change?*

*If I don't get my way, I should complain (pout, withdraw, give up).*

*Our sex life should always be fantastic.*

*If I'm attracted to other people, it means that I shouldn't stay in this marriage.*

*I should try to win in all of our conflicts.*

*My partner should accept me just the way I am.*

*If we're having problems, it means we have an awful relationship.*

Now, be honest with yourself. Are these "shoulds" helping or hurting you and your relationship? I guarantee that if you have a lot of them, you are pretty unhappy. Rather than talk about the way things "should" be, you might consider how you can make things better. Replace your shoulds with "how to" and "let's try." Rather than "We should have a better sex life," you might try action statements such as "We can give each other a massage," or "We can set up a time to be affectionate." You won't make progress by "shoulding" on each other. But you can make progress by acting differently and communicating in a caring way.

10. *Personalizing:* You attribute your partner's moods and behavior to something about yourself, or you take all the blame for the problems: "He's in a bad mood because of me." "If it weren't for me, we wouldn't have any of these problems." It's almost never all about one person—it takes two to tango and two to be miserable. Phyllis was doing

a lot of personalizing, thinking that Ralph wanted to be alone was because he found her boring. But really Ralph was so burned out at the end of the day that he needed a little while to cool down. It wasn't about Phyllis, it was about Ralph's day.

11. *Perfectionism:* You hold up a standard for a relationship that is unrealistically high and then measure your relationship by this standard. "It's not like it was in the first year—so it's not worth it." "We have problems, so our relationship can't work out." The problem with perfectionism is that it is bound to make you miserable. You may think that you are holding up your ideals, but you are really putting you and your partner down. No relationship is perfect—and no relationship needs to be perfect. Once Vinnie and Cynthia recognized how futile and depressing perfectionism was, they were able to work constructively on their relationship. "I realized that we would never have exactly what we wanted from each other, but we could still get a lot of our needs met," Vinnie finally said. It was a breakthrough to give up on having to be perfect and demanding the same from Cynthia.

12. *Blaming:* You believe that all the problems in the relationship are caused by your partner: "If it weren't for her, we wouldn't have these problems," or "He argues with me, that's why we can't get along." Again, there is a grain of truth in almost any negative thought, but blaming your partner will make you feel helpless and trapped. A better way of approaching this is to take a "Let's fix it together" approach using all of the techniques outlined here. You can validate each other, share responsibility for the problems, plan to catch each other being good, reward each other, plan positives together, and accept some differences. It sure beats blaming each other and becoming victims.

## WORKING WITH BEHAVIOR

It's often helpful to be honest with yourself and look in the mirror (with your partner) and ask yourself what you've been doing—and then ask if it has been working. Would either of you agree with any of the following?

- My partner is always criticizing me.

- My partner looks down on me.

- My partner doesn't give me any credit.

- My partner doesn't appreciate what I do.

- My partner always wants his or her way.

- We don't seem to be able to work on problems together.

- I try to win.

- If I'm upset, I just withdraw.

- My partner is the problem.

The complaints in the list above often ring true in relationships where partners don't attend to any of each other's positives, praise each other, or make each other feel appreciated. Sometimes we aren't that rewarding to our partners, but we still expect them to be rewarding and kind to us. But it's a two-way thing: if you don't reward your partner, then you won't get any rewards back.

Rewards can be praise, attention, appreciation, affection, or anything that makes your partner feel better. Often distressed couples will decrease their rewarding behavior toward their partner because they feel that they are not receiving rewards from their partner. This follows the *rule of reciprocity* in relationships—you give what you get. Thus, if you get rewarded, you will probably reward your partner. Similarly, if you get punished, you will probably punish your partner through either withdrawal or criticism. Often when a couple is in distress, as one partner decreases rewards, the other partner does so too, thereby confirming each partner's belief that the relationship is unrewarding. We saw this with Ralph and Phyllis. As Phyllis withdrew because she was depressed, Ralph withdrew as well. They both loved each other and wanted things to work out, but they disengaged. This added to their mutual despair.

## Examine Your Resistance to Rewards

You may object to rewarding your partner. You have your "good reasons." Let's take a look at them. "Why should I reward my partner? He isn't rewarding me!" Right now you may feel that your partner is not rewarding—you may be right or wrong on this. But what will make things better and who will make the first move? Someone has to take the first step. You may have to engage in positive behavior for a while before you see the results you want. Don't forget—you and your partner have been teaching each other not to reward each other for a long time. It may take some time before you teach each other more positive behavior.

But you may object, "How can I know what she likes? Nothing seems to please her!" This is a good point. Distressed couples often spend too much time complaining about what they don't get and very little time articulating what they do have. So the first step will be to help each other learn what you do that is rewarding. You can both write out a list of positive behaviors that will make you feel good, even if it's just for the moment. Be specific. For example, Phyllis's list for Ralph was "Listen to my feelings, validate me, be more affectionate, help with the chores, spend some time reading to the kids, tell me I'm attractive, compliment me on things that I do, go for a bike ride, and take me out to a nice restaurant—just the two of us."

But you may also complain, "Why should I have to tell him what I like? He should know what I like without my saying it." This is an assumption that we often make that our partners should be mind-readers. It would be a lot better if they were, but—unfortunately—they're not. Imagine if you went into a restaurant and the waiter said, "Have you decided what you want?" and you responded, "You should know. You've been working here for a while." Be specific about your needs and you might get your needs met.

Or you might say, "Why should I listen to her? She doesn't listen to me." This is part of that losing strategy of waiting for your partner to change before you take constructive action. I have a different idea. If you want to be heard, learn how to listen.

## Catch Your Partner Being Good

Let's assume that you have decided that it makes good sense to reward your partner. Rule number one in psychology is this: "If you want to see more of a behavior, then reward it." And the sooner the reward, the better. You can teach your partner what you need by rewarding her when she does what you want. Don't waste time on theories about your partner's motivation. As one clever wife said, "You mean I should train my husband like I train my dog?"

Well, as a husband I know that we can learn. We just need a little direction.

I suggest you start with the idea of "catching your partner being good." Whenever your partner shows any positive behavior, jump in as soon as possible and reward it. Here's how.

- *Be specific about the behavior:* Don't say, "You've been nice."
  It's hard to know what behavior your partner is being
  praised for. Be specific: "I really appreciated the fact that
  you made dinner." "I really felt good that you spent time
  talking to me about my work." You are teaching your
  partner what works for you. Specify the behavior so your
  partner will know how to please you in the future.

- *Ask your partner what you have done that is rewarding:* If you
  want to improve your relationship, ask your partner to
  teach you what he needs. Don't assume that you know. If
  you did, you would have been doing all the right things
  already. Again, ask your partner to be specific. "When
  you say you want me to be nicer, can you specify some
  examples of things I can say or do that you would like?"

- *Don't argue at this stage—you are only trying to gather
  information:* You may be like a lot of us and want to try to
  defend yourself. Put the defense up on the shelf for now.
  Don't respond with defenses like, "But I already do those
  things." Even if you are already doing "those things," it
  will help if your partner can specify them and then both of
  you can play "catch."

- *Can you think of anything that your partner did or said during
  the last week that gave you any pleasure at all?* This is a great
  opportunity for you to do some "positive tracking." Make
  a list of positives that your partner does every day, put
  the list up on the refrigerator or bulletin board, and look
  at it daily. Be sure to include even the smallest positives,

since you can build a lot of goodwill with consistent notice of small things. In fact, small positives may be the most powerful. By noticing them you send a loud and clear message that you are really attending to anything that is positive. This will make your partner feel appreciated. After all, would you only want appreciation for an expensive gift?

This self-help homework assignment was very instructive for Phyllis and Ralph. Because Phyllis "caught" Ralph being good by listening to her feelings and complimenting her, he learned how powerful some simple emotional techniques can be. He had thought that the only thing that mattered was solving problems and providing a good living. Phyllis did appreciate his problem solving and his hard work, but she wanted an emotional partner as well.

Another advantage to playing "catch" is that you feel appreciated when you're the one who gets caught. We all want to know that what we are doing is working. I know that my dog agrees with me that we want to know what you want. We are trainable.

## Don't Undermine Your Success

Have you ever said anything like this: "You never do anything for me"? This is *all-or-nothing thinking*—you take one example and expand it to everything. So your partner then feels that no matter what he does, you won't see it.

"You helped me tonight. But you almost never help me." The Zap Treatment gives a compliment with one hand and then slams you over the head with the other. The only thing your partner will remember is the zap.

"Why can't you be more affectionate/considerate/helpful?" Many of your "why" questions sound like accusations. Your partner may feel that the only logical answer is a self-critical comment: "Why? Because I'm an idiot." Replace your "why" questions with "I like it when you do (a specific behavior)."

Or do you withdraw and pout? You may think that by withdrawing you can send a message that you are upset. But withdrawal seldom accomplishes anything constructive and will probably make both of you feel like your relationship isn't working. Can you imagine someone saying, "My relationship got a lot better when I began pouting more"? In contrast, I can definitely imagine someone saying, "Our relationship got a lot better when I began rewarding and appreciating my partner and telling him how he was good at meeting some of my needs."

## Rules of Engagement

Vinnie and Cynthia seemed to be arguing all the time. When they weren't in mortal combat, they were withdrawing from each other. There was an uneasy truce between them.

We are going to have our differences with others, but wouldn't things be better if we had some rules to guide us when discussing things? Most arguments are disruptive and unproductive. That doesn't mean that you should never disagree with your partner. However, if you and your partner are going to get the most out of your disagreements, it would be useful to develop some ground rules.

If you and your partner are explosive in your arguing, or if you have experienced violence in your relationship, use a time-out when you feel very angry. Tell your partner that you need time-out and go to another room for at least 15 minutes. If your partner asks for time-out, don't follow him or her. Use the time to challenge your angry thoughts and to plan a more adaptive way to express your needs. Then use the following simple rules for your discussions. Keep a cool head. It will be difficult at first to stay with these rules, because you will want to win, you will want to defend yourself, and you will want to be right. It's more important to build your relationship than to be right.

Look at the following list to give you ideas of what to do and what not to do. All of us make mistakes in arguing and discussing things. Now is a good opportunity to learn from your mistakes. Practice these new "rules of engagement" with your partner.

1. *Present the difficulty as a problem to be solved by both of you.*
   "I think we have a problem when you get home from work.
   We seem to be tense. I wonder if we can work together to
   figure out how to make it better at that time."

2. *Stick to one topic.* Rather than bring up everything,
   including the kitchen sink, you should stay with one

specific problem. "Let's try to figure out how we can divide up some of the housework."

3.  *Stay in the present.* Don't be a historian of misery for the relationship. Stay in the here and now. "I wonder if we could spend a little more time talking to each other. It would mean a lot to me since I value your input on things."

4.  *Accept some responsibility.* Help your partner under-stand that it's not about blaming; it's about making communication better. Own your role. "I know that we have had a number of arguments, and I know part of it is me. I'm sometimes too sensitive. I wonder if we could work at finding some better ways to communicate."

5.  *Invite your partner to solve the problem with you.* Make it about the two of you working together. "It would be great if we could work together on finding ways to be more rewarding to each other."

6.  *Ask for some ideas about solutions.* Turn your partner into a problem solver who collaborates with you. "Do you have some ideas about how we could be more rewarding to each other? What can I do to help?"

7.  *Find points of agreement.* Don't focus on the disagreements right now. Find common ground. "I'm glad to hear that you and I agree that things can be better and that we could try being more rewarding. That's a great place for us to start working together."

8.  *Try one solution that both of you agree on.* Turn good intentions and plans into actions. "Let's try to keep track of each other's positives. What do you think about doing that for this week and seeing what happens?"

## What Not to Do—Self-Defeating Mistakes We All Make

You have a lot of tools right now to make your relationship more rewarding. You've learned ways to show that you respect each other's feelings, solve problems together, and build a stronger partnership. But, to be realistic, you are likely to fall back into some old bad habits. Don't get demoralized about that. It's part of getting better. You have to build the positives and continually reverse the negatives. Here are some things to watch out for—and to avoid:

1. Bringing up past wrongs

2. Bringing up irrelevant material

3. Labeling your partner

4. Asking, "Why do you always . . . ?"

5. Pouting

6. Threatening

7. Raising your voice

8. Being sarcastic

9. Whining

10. Interpreting your partner's motives

11. Trying to win

Just as you are trying to catch your partner being good, you need to catch yourself and try to eliminate these self-defeating behaviors. We all make these mistakes at one time or another, but ask yourself if anything has ever gotten better when you went down that path.

## Accepting Differences

Imagine that you take a rope with one end in your left hand and the other in your right hand. You pull with both hands, with all of your strength, and finally realize that you are struggling against yourself—and defeating yourself in the process.

All through your relationship you have been struggling and protesting and trying to control your partner. You pull on the rope; she pulls on the other end. You fight against the differences. Then one day, it occurs to both of you to drop the rope and get together. You have given up on one thing to get on with the big thing. Drop the rope.

Ralph was interested in business, and Phyllis was interested in psychology. But they still loved each other, and they had a child they cherished together. Many of their differences were points of struggle—"All you care about is business and money," versus "All you want to do is talk about what makes people tick."

Then it occurred to them that the struggle was only one way of dealing with things. They could also accept the differences. They could say, "Let's agree that you have certain interests, and I have some different interests. You do your thing at times, and I can do my thing at times. We don't have to agree on everything."

Phyllis preferred talking about feelings, and Ralph preferred focusing on facts. Each was trying to get the other to change and become "more like me." But what had attracted them to each other was the difference. Ralph said, "I was attracted to her warmth and depth and the fact that I could really talk to her." Phyllis said, "Initially I really liked the fact that he was so focused on his goals. My parents were scattered and always living in chaos." So these differences, at first, were the qualities that made them appealing. Why not accept the differences and recognize that there is something really appealing in there?

Another way of moving forward with each other is to see your differences as opportunities. Perhaps you can learn something from each other. Phyllis and Ralph were able to use this idea quite effectively by recognizing that they could offer each other some valuable skills. Phyllis could teach Ralph about the emotional part of life, help him explore some of his own roadblocks. As she talked to him more about emotions, it came out that Ralph's father was "super-rational" to the point where Ralph's feelings were never validated. "I never felt he understood me; although, I knew he loved me." Ralph could also understand where Phyllis's sense of chaos came from. Her father was an alcoholic, who might fly into a rage at any time and attack her and her mom. This made Phyllis feel very sensitive to any criticism or control from Ralph.

Because they were now listening to each other rather than trying to change each other, they could key into the emotional part of their relationship in a new way. Phyllis could understand that Ralph actually needed a lot of the validation and listening that *she* felt was missing—it's just that Ralph didn't realize that he needed this, and he didn't know how to ask for it. I recall what Ralph said as tears formed in his eyes: "I always felt alone when I was a kid. I would go to my room and read and hope that my feelings would go away." As he talked, he realized that Phyllis was a "feeling person," just the kind of person he wished he had near him growing up. The difference was that now he was married to her. He could accept their differences and see them as the opportunity of a lifetime.

## CONCLUSION

I usually ask my patients who are depressed to tell me about how their marriages could be better. But I realize that I am only hearing one person's story. It's always informative to hear the other person's story. I don't see myself as the judge. I think about how each person could learn how to make it better. If my patient is the wife—but the husband is dissatisfied with the relationship—it's going to help her if I help him make it better for both of them. There are no winners and losers—no right and wrong to be judged. It's all about making it better for both of you.

We've seen how your relationship can make you depressed and how your depression can affect your relationship. Whether it's you or your partner suffering from depression—or both of you—I hope that both of you are able to go over this chapter together and start working every day at making both of you happy. After all, you loved each other enough to get married, live together, and perhaps have children together. Even if you think your loving feelings have decreased—even disappeared— things can change. I've seen people whose marriages looked like they had no hope—but they managed to work hard to get back together. Just last month I got an e-mail from a former patient of mine who had been separated from his wife for several years. That was 12 years ago. They are back together—in love, connected, and knowing that they mean the world to each other.

Rather than fighting each other, you can fight together for your relationship. You have some good tools to work with now. Don't fight to be right. Fight to make each other feel cared for, fight to make each other feel loved, fight for what will make your lives happier—and fight to make it work for both of you.

## How to Empower Your Intimate Relationship

- Is your relationship connected with depression—yours or your partner's? What are you doing to make each other miserable?

- Connect with your partner's feelings. Instead of trying to solve her problem, listen and empathize. Ask about your role in the problem and what you can do to make things better.

- Make your partner feel cared for by accepting his feelings and helping him make sense of them.

- Let go of your need to be right. It's more important to fix the problem than to fix the blame.

- Watch out for negative automatic thoughts and the ways they can distort your view of your relationship and make your situation worse.

- Reward your partner. This makes it more likely that you'll get rewards back.

- Examine your resistance. What is keeping you from doing rewarding things?

- Catch your partner being good. Be specific about what she's done that pleases you, and ask her what she needs from you.

- Don't undermine your success with Zap Treatments, pouting, or questions that start, "Why can't you . . . ?"

- Learn the rules of engagement for working together effectively.

- Avoid the self-defeating mistakes that we all tend to make, such as trying to interpret your partner's motives and bringing up past wrongs.

- Accept your differences. They may be what drew you together in the first place. See if you can stop trying to change each other and learn from each other instead.

# CHAPTER 12

# "Now That I'm Better, How Do I Stay Well?": How to Prevent Relapse

I would like to tell you that once your depression has lifted and you are feeling good again, you will stay this way forever. And you might— but you might not. We realize now that depression for many people is a lifelong vulnerability. Some people are just more likely to have relapses. Some people may never have a relapse. But if you do, the average number of episodes is seven—so if you have had one episode of depression, there is some likelihood that you will have more. Getting ready to prevent that is an important part of staying well.

Who is more likely to have a relapse of depression? There are a number of factors that make you more vulnerable. These include the number of prior episodes you have had, early onset of depression, alcohol abuse, early childhood abuse, and the particular features of your depression: style of rumination, negative life events (such as job loss or personal conflicts), relationship conflict, dysfunctional attitudes, and thought distortions such as all-or-nothing thinking and a negative style of explaining events.[1] In this chapter, we'll talk about watching for early signs of depression's return so you can catch it early and reverse it as soon as possible.

The good news is that we now have several very effective ways of preventing relapse. They include practicing your self-help techniques, continuing to improve your relationships, continuing your treatment with cognitive therapy or medication, and using new mindfulness techniques when you are feeling better. You can substantially reduce your risk of a relapse in the next few years—and if you do get depressed again, you'll have tools to help yourself that have already worked. A primary rule in medical practice is that what worked before is likely to work again. So this is reason for hope.

## KEEP UP YOUR SELF-HELP

Cognitive-behavioral therapy is more effective than medication in preventing relapse for patients who get better and then discontinue their treatment.[2] And patients in cognitive-behavioral therapy who do their self-help homework are the most likely to stay well after they discontinue treatment.[3] They have the skills to continue to help themselves. So keeping up your self-help is an important part of staying well.

If you have found the techniques in this book helpful, then you might consider making a list of *specific interventions* that have helped you. I have tried to make this easy. Each chapter in this book ends with a summary of that chapter's self-help techniques. Look at the lists to pick out the techniques that have worked for you, or make a copy of the table at the end of any chapter that is especially relevant to you. This will give you some 10 or 20 techniques that you can use to become your own cognitive therapist. Many of my patients find it helpful to make self-talk/ self-help cards that remind them of their negative habits and how to reverse them. Your self-talk can include how to change your behavior, your thinking, and your relationships. You can easily refer to these self-help cards—keep them in your wallet or on your computer or your BlackBerry or Palm Pilot. This way, you'll be ready to confront the depressive demons when they pop up.

The key to self-help is helping yourself stay better by doing what worked when you felt down—and then got better. Feeling better is the first goal. Staying better requires practicing the habits that work—and knowing the signs to watch for so you can stop a relapse before it gains momentum.

## What Has Triggered Your Past Depression?

Sometimes there is a pattern to your depression. Is it set off by conflicts in your relationships, difficulty achieving your goals, or a feeling of loneliness? It's important to know your vulnerability so you can prepare for it. For example, Dan's trigger was loneliness. We put together a plan to track loneliness when it began to arise and take steps to counteract it, such as making plans with friends, getting involved in volunteer activities, and planning things to do by himself. We also identified his typical negative thoughts when he felt lonely (for example, *I will always be alone*, and *I'm alone because I am a loser*). We then developed rational responses that he could readily use when he had these negative thoughts and feelings.

What triggers your depression? What can you do the next time the trigger sets things off? What negative thoughts come up when it does, and how can you respond to them?

## What Are the Early Signs of Your Depression?

It's also important to know the early symptoms of your depression. These may include insomnia, loss of interest, loss of pleasure, or sadness. Some people have symptoms of self-criticism and discouragement early on. Try to remember what your early signs are so you can catch depression early and reverse it. You can look back at the Quick Inventory of Depressive Symptomatology in Chapter 1 to see what your pattern is and what feelings may be the forerunners of a relapse. It's a good idea to take this simple self-test every week to make sure you catch any problem early.

## How Does Your Behavior Change?

What are you doing differently when you are depressed? Do you sleep more or engage in fewer challenging and interesting activities? Do you spend a lot of time passively watching television or browsing the Internet? Are you preoccupied with pornography? Some people notice that they begin drinking more or overeating—or eating less—when they get depressed. If you know the changes depression makes in your behavior, you can spot them in their early stages and reverse them as soon as possible. For example, if your early sign of depression is decreased activity, then get out your schedule and plan a week ahead of time. Go to the health club, take walks, go to movies, set up time with friends, or go to museums. Get *super-active*. Or if your early signs are health behaviors such as drinking or overeating, then become a health fanatic for a month. Cut down on drinking, exercise, plan nutritious meals, and get enough sleep. Do the opposite of the symptom. Act *against* so you can move forward.

## Use Your Reward Menu

One of the easiest ways to stay on track in your antidepressant life-style is to have an easy reference for rewarding activities that you do daily. Don't wait to feel ready to do them—plan them ahead of time and carry them out. For example, my reward menu includes exercise, walk-ing to work, listening to my iPod, reading, and taking enough time to enjoy my lunch. Build your reward menu, and keep adding to it. Also, plan longer-term rewards such as trips, special treats for yourself, and acquiring new skills and interests. Reward menus—both short-term and long-term—give you something to do and something to look forward to.

## How Does Your Thinking Change?

When you get depressed, there is a typical pattern to your thinking. Go back over the exercises in this book, and see if you can catch your-self trying to be perfect, needing approval, fearing failure, or needing certainty. See if you are engaging in typical negative thought distortions such as mind reading (*She thinks I'm boring*), labeling (*I am boring*), all-or-nothing thinking (*Nothing works for me*), or discounting the positives (*Just because he finds me interesting doesn't mean anything, because he's my friend*). When you get depressed, do you tend to predict negatives and think that events are simply awful? Write yourself some self-talk/self-help cards that tell you how to challenge these negative thoughts. For example, your cards might say, "What's the advantage to thinking this way?" or "What does the evidence say?" or "What advice would I give a friend?" or "I can act against the way I think."

## Avoid Ruminating

It's important to recognize that your tendency to ruminate can be an early sign of your depression coming back. If you find yourself getting stuck on a negative thought and repeating it until your mind-set gets worse and worse, go back to Chapter 8 and see if you can begin using the techniques there. For example, this might include catching your rumina-tion, examining the costs and benefits of the rumination, setting aside a limited rumination time, or practicing acceptance of things as they are.

Write out a short self-talk/self-help card to quickly activate your antirumination program. Think about what has worked in the past for you so you can reverse the rumination as soon as possible.

## Inoculate Yourself Against Depression

The best way to avoid a relapse is to inoculate yourself with the negative behaviors and thoughts that characterize your depression. I like to do this as a role play with patients who have recovered: "Let's make believe that you are getting depressed again. I'll be your negative thoughts. Let's see how you would challenge them." Or I might take the role of the negative behavioral patterns: "You're just too tired. You should lie in bed for hours so you can conserve energy. Challenge me." Eliciting your negative patterns and practicing challenging them can inoculate you against a relapse.

### BUILD YOUR RELATIONSHIPS

We've already seen that your relationships can have a powerful effect on your depression. Many people notice that when they become depressed, they lose interest in people or think that they are a burden to others. Your depression may begin with isolating yourself from other people; if so, act against this tendency and make plans to get together with people. Or you may be complaining more and focusing on negatives when you are with people. Use the techniques that we discussed in Chapter 9 for building better friendships. Or if your intimate relationship gets bumpy when you start getting depressed, go back to Chapter 11 and see how you and your partner can improve rewards, decrease negatives, accept your differences, and solve problems together.

Here are a few things to keep in mind.

## Choose to Be with Rewarding People

One way to ensure a relapse is to choose to be with people who treat you badly, people who are judgmental and negative, or people who are just downers. Sarah decided to avoid seeing Karen, who was drinking heavily and did nothing to help herself. Sharon developed a checklist of qualities to avoid in men—narcissism, disloyalty, and unreliability. Manuel made a list of the people in his life and divided it into two columns—rewarding people and unrewarding people. He decided to pursue the former and avoid the latter. If you are with rewarding people, life feels better to you.

## Don't Sound Like a Downer

As we discussed in Chapter 9, you should try to catch yourself complaining, being judgmental, or rejecting support. Don't be a downer with your friends. Mark kept a list of any complaints that he made to his girlfriend so he could catch himself when he was stressing the negative too heavily. Then he gave himself an alternative: "Describe some positive things that you are going to do." Advertising your positives rather than just your negatives helps keep your friends engaged, and that can keep you from isolating yourself and slipping into depression.

## Reward Your Friends

Friends are the medicine that keeps you sane. You need to reward them. Karen made a point of thanking her friends for support, praising them when they told her about positive things that they did, and empathizing and validating them when they had problems of their own. Reminding your friends that you are also on their side keeps them in your corner.

## Build Your Community

Don't isolate yourself. Jill reversed her isolation by volunteering at an animal shelter once or twice each week. Irene joined a synagogue, made new friends, and felt more connected. You can also look into online communities, professional groups, and other resources. Keeping connected helps keep you well.

## Empower Your Intimate Relationships

Love and intimacy are great antidotes to depression. Marriages need continual work—it's like staying in shape forever. But the work can be wonderful. Set up weekly short discussions—"What can we do that will make things better for you?" Practice the skills of active listening—rephrase, validate, inquire. Use acceptance to learn from your differences rather than struggle against them. You get the love you give—but giving is an active process. It's not just how you feel; it's what you do.

### CONTINUE YOUR TREATMENT

If you have gotten better in cognitive-behavioral therapy and you've already had a couple of prior episodes of depression, it may be helpful to consider "continuation treatment." This is a good idea if you have a pattern of rumination, relationship difficulties, self-esteem problems that keep coming back, or recurrent episodes of depression or intense anxiety. Getting better and staying better are two phases of self-help. Continuation treatment can help keep you on track. This can involve seeing your therapist once every month or six weeks to stay on top of your depression. Continuation treatment dramatically reduces the likelihood of relapse.[4]

## Using Medication to Prevent Relapse

If you have had two or more episodes of depression and you are being treated with medication, you and your doctor should consider continuing the medication even after you get better. You might continue for six months after recovery, perhaps at a lower dose, and then consider tapering off.

Some patients are able to go off their medication months after their depression has lifted. Others, especially those who have had several episodes of depression, do best with "maintenance treatment" to block future episodes. You should never discontinue medication without consulting your doctor.

## Augmentation

Even if you are on medication, you might experience "break-through" episodes of depression. Nothing works 100 percent of the time, but maintenance medication reduces your risk of relapse considerably. If you do experience a relapse, your doctor can consider augmenting your treatment by increasing the dosage, adding a medication, or using other forms of treatment. You can find more information about all these biological treatments for depression in Appendix A.

Some people who have had several prior episodes of depression say, "I don't need medication—I feel fine." But the reason that you feel fine may be that you are on medication. So don't assume that feeling better means that you are no longer vulnerable. Having said this, we do know that the behavioral, cognitive, and interpersonal approaches to preventing relapse are very powerful. You and your doctor can make this decision together.

## PRACTICE MINDFULNESS

From time to time in this book, I've given you exercises that draw on the techniques of mindfulness meditation—such as observing the clouds or imagining yourself falling with the snow. Mindfulness—a practice of nonjudgmental awareness of the present moment—has been found to be useful in preventing future episodes of depression as well. Professors Zindel Segal, Mark Williams, and John Teasdale recognized that patients most prone to relapse are those who tend to get sucked into their negative thinking and have a hard time just letting go of their negative thoughts and feelings.[5] They developed a form of treatment that borrows extensively from Buddhist practice of mindful awareness and meditation, inspired by the brilliant work of Jon Kabat-Zinn in Boston, who had been using mindfulness to help patients cope with physical pain.[6] Initially, they called their model "attentional training" because the goal was to help you train your attention on experiencing the present moment in a nonjudgmental way—to be "completely awake," as the Buddha once said of himself. The more popular label today is Mindfulness-Based Cognitive Therapy (MBCT).

MBCT, which is based on an eight-week stress-reduction program, significantly reduces relapse of depression when used in conjunction with other therapies. Discuss your options with your doctor, but according to a recent study, MBCT is more effective than keeping patients on just antidepressant medication over a 15-month period.[7] However, MBCT may not prevent relapse in all formerly depressed patients. We recommend practicing mindfulness on a regular basis, in addition to MBCT.[8]

You can find useful exercises for practicing mindfulness in books such as *Full Catastrophe Living* by Jon Kabat-Zinn, *A Path with Heart* by Jack Kornfield, and *The Mindful Way Through Depression* by Williams, Teasdale, Segal, and Kabat-Zinn. We will also look at a few exercises that you can do in the pages ahead. But mindfulness will require practice. Don't try to control, don't try to excel, and give yourself and your mind the time and space to grow. Buddha means "awakened one"; practicing mindfulness is a gradual awakening to your awareness, accepting and observing your breathing, your sensations, and your mind as it is in this moment.

If the exercises here work for you, you might consider making mindfulness a consistent presence in your life. Classes and workshops that provide basic meditation instruction are given almost everywhere in the country, while long-term retreats are available for those who wish to go deeper. Basic principles and techniques are universal; differences in approach are less important than what the approaches have in common.

## Mindful Awareness of the Breath

Sitting in a comfortable position, breathe naturally. While breathing, notice your breath, in and out. Each breath is a moment that comes and now is gone. Attend to your breath and notice how your mind may drift to other thoughts, sounds, and sensations. Gently bring your mind back to your breath. Center yourself on your breath as you notice the moment it is in and that this moment also passes. And another moment comes, and you let go of that moment as it passes with the breath—in and out, moment to moment.

You will notice that your mind is very busy. It is judging, thinking, anticipating, remembering. It keeps inviting you to follow it, obey it. When I first tried this exercise, my mind kept drifting off to other thoughts—*Will I have enough time to get my work done? What is that sound from the street? Am I doing this correctly?* I realized that my mind was going 100 miles an hour, completely escaping from the present moment. In mindfulness, you practice standing back and noticing, saying gently to yourself, "There's that thought again," while you simply bring your attention back to the present moment, back to your breath.

So, with mindful awareness of breathing, you gently come back to the breath, the breath centers you, and you de-center from all the other thoughts. This helps you train your attention on what is immediately at hand—your breathing. You are developing a *different relationship to your thoughts*. Your thoughts have been controlling you and distracting you. Now they are just thoughts, and the breath is the center.

## Body Scan

While lying or sitting in a comfortable position, begin your breathing practice, gently noticing the breath in and out. Then notice your stomach and how it feels and what the sensations are there. Watch as your breath goes into your stomach and through and then comes back— slowly watch your breath into and out of the stomach. Then, directing your attention to your left shoulder, breathe into the shoulder and out. Notice whatever sensations, warmth, or tension there is in your shoulder, breathing in and out to that feeling and sensation. And then do the same down your left arm. Continue to the other parts of your body, your hands, both right and left, your legs, your feet. Spend a few minutes noticing the sensations that are there and breathe into that feeling in every part of your body. Be in the moment, aware of what is there, and aware that this moment comes and goes.

## Expand Your Awareness

With your eyes closed, once you have been aware of your breath for a while, allow your mind to notice what is around you in the room. Shifting attention gently from your breath to the room—the sounds you hear and the sights you remember—bring your mind back to your breath. Then allow your mind to be aware of the buildings and spaces around your room and then around the building where you are. Eyes closed, you are aware of the larger space around you. And then allow your mind to drift to the clouds above, and look down and around at the larger space that is beyond. And then allow your mind to drift above Earth so that

Earth is a small planet below and you are watching. And moving your mind ever farther into space and into the stars of the galaxy, be aware of all that is around you.

Perhaps you have disappeared for a moment.

## Mindful Awareness of Thoughts and Emotions

As you have been practicing your mindful meditation, you have noticed sensations, thoughts, and emotions. Sometimes you get sucked into them, sometimes you are afraid of them. You either obey or avoid. But in your mindful breathing, you can now observe your thoughts and feelings, stand back, and take the position of the observer who sees without judging. You stand back and say, "There is that thought," or "There is that sadness," or "There is that pain." You are not challenging these thoughts, because now you are only an observer. You can watch the thought—it comes and goes and another thought comes. Your mind comes back to your breath. Every thought and feeling is a moment that is here now and then gone, like waves that lap against the shore and then recede into the ocean to disappear until another wave comes.

## Loving Kindness

You may have noticed that you have been angry or sad or afraid of your thoughts, feelings, and sensations. You want to make them run away, to leave forever, so you can have things the way you want them. But now, with mindful awareness and acceptance of all that is in the moment, you observe your sadness, you notice that you feel it in your heart, in your eyes. Now, you call upon your feelings of love and kindness and acceptance and direct them toward your sadness, toward the heavy feeling. You say, "I am here to love you and the sadness, here to accept you, to make a home where we live together." You can imagine your feeling of love going directly into the cells of your sadness to caress it with your mind and your heart. And you feel kindness toward this part of your sadness. You have made room for the feeling, and it is here and now and then it is gone. And your kindness and love flow in and out, breath by breath, moment by moment.

## CONCLUSION

There is bad news and good news. For many people depression is a recurring problem—many people have several episodes of depression during their lives. But you can dramatically reduce the recurrence of your depression by using any or all of the ideas outlined in this chapter. And you can use the ideas in this book as a guide to living an antidepressant life.

You are not helpless when it comes to depression. One of my patients who got better—and who stayed better—said to me, "I notice that my rational responses are more automatic than my negative automatic thoughts now." A former patient of mine called me for a referral for a friend. I hadn't seen him in 12 years. He said, "I'm still using the techniques you taught me." He hasn't been depressed since. Another former patient returned to treatment years after I had last seen him. This time he had lost his job, and he was feeling depressed again. We got him back on medication and began developing plans to get him active and proactive and strongly modify his negative thinking. This time he got better more quickly than the first time.

What got you better can keep you better. But you have to use it. It's like exercise. Keep doing it—make it part of your lifestyle.

## Preventing Relapse

- Keep using the self-help that helped you get better. Pick out the techniques in this book that were most useful for you and make a list, or create self-help cards you can refer to anytime.

- Be alert for a possible relapse. It helps to know what to look for. What has triggered your depression in the past? What are the early signs of your depression?

- How does your behavior change when you get depressed? Watch for these changes, and stop them in their tracks. Build a reward menu and use it.

- How does your thinking change when you get depressed? Write some self-talk/self-help cards to challenge your negative thoughts should they arise.

- Ruminating is a common warning sign of depression. If you find yourself slipping into a pattern of repetitive negative thoughts, go back to the techniques in Chapter 8 that helped you overcome it.

- Inoculate yourself against depression by practicing how to challenge the thoughts and behaviors that characterize it for you. I like to do this as a role-play with my patients—I play the "voice" of depression, and they talk back.

- How do your relationships change when you get depressed? Notice if you're starting to isolate yourself or complain more, and take steps to act against these changes.

- Choose to be with rewarding people. People who judge you, treat you badly, or just bring you down can prime you for relapse.

- Be a rewarding friend to your friends. Thank them for supporting you, help them when they need it, and don't act like a downer.

- Build your community. Stay connected through online groups, professional organizations, or volunteer work.

- Your intimate relationship can be a great antidote to depression. Do the work it takes to keep it working for you.

- If formal cognitive-behavioral therapy has helped you get better, consider continuing it, seeing your therapist once every month or six weeks to stay on top of things—especially if you have had a couple of prior episodes of depression.

- If you've been treated with medication, consult your doctor to see if you should continue it—perhaps at a lower dosage—once you are better.

- If you do experience a relapse while on medication, ask your doctor about augmenting your treatment with additional medication or another biological approach.

- Use mindfulness practice to cultivate an awareness of the present moment, free from judging or controlling, and stand back to observe your thoughts as thoughts—nothing more.

# CHAPTER 13

# Final Thoughts

In writing this book, I had to think through my experiences with the thousands of people whose lives have been affected by depression. In looking through my files, I was reminded of the names of people I haven't seen in years. There is the woman who felt that, after her divorce, her life had lost meaning—but who gradually rebuilt a meaningful personal and professional life. Then there was the man in his mid-50s who had been abusing alcohol and drugs and leading a life that seemed self-defeating. He felt hopeless. Every Christmas I receive a card from him. He has been sober, non-depressed, and—most important for him—helping other people overcome addiction and find a life filled with meaning. His story warms my heart because I know that he inspires many other people. He is the "multiplier effect"—I helped him, and now he helps so many other people.

I also think about the marriages that have been repaired because of our work together. Sometimes it's a struggle. Couples come in with one or both partners feeling hopeless. Perhaps they haven't had sex in months, one partner is depressed (or both are), and they're always arguing or avoiding each other. But then they learn how to communicate, compromise, and persevere. They learn how to forgive. And they learn, once again, how to have fun. After all, they loved each other enough to have made the commitment to get married. Working hard at something that is valuable—working hard to make your relationship better—is often the best thing that you can do for your depression.

And I recall Linda, who improved in therapy and then, years later, faced some of the most horrible events one can imagine. One daughter was disabled, another daughter died, and her husband's business nearly collapsed. Yet, despite the overwhelming events that befell her and her family, she was able to endure. I realize that human beings are capable of handling almost anything given the tools, willingness, and support they need.

And I recall my own neighbor—an elderly woman who was in the hospital and whose leg needed to be amputated. She was 72 years old and had been depressed her entire adult life. Her doctor said that if she did not allow the amputation, she would die from the infection. From her point of view, life wasn't worth living to begin with and having an amputation was just one more nail in her coffin. Why live? But I thought she deserved a chance. She had been in talk therapy for years, on and off, focusing on her childhood and her many disappointments. Traditional therapy hadn't worked for her. But she had never tried medication. I said to her, "You've never tried antidepressants. You don't really know how you might respond. Why not try this experiment: Have the amputation, start antidepressant medication, and see how you feel? You can always kill yourself later."

She thanked me for my support but said it was hopeless. Yet in the next week she had the surgery and began to take her medication. Much to her surprise, her mood improved within a few weeks. Her partner visited her daily and talked to her, and they played backgammon as she regaled him with stories. Her life had gotten better—even after a leg amputation. She had a new chance in life.

Their stories could be your story.

Depression is a difficult obstacle in your life. It keeps you from enjoying the simple pleasures that are available to all of us. It sometimes makes you your own worst enemy as you criticize yourself for every imperfection. It hangs in gloomy darkness over you as you struggle to find meaning and hope. But depression can be beaten.

I mentioned before that I don't get depressed seeing depressed people. It's because the chances are so good that people will get better. If you are depressed, you know how hard it is to get through a day. You may have no energy, you don't enjoy anything, you see no hope, and you don't know what to do. When people tell you to snap out of it, you feel angry—even humiliated. You feel all alone; no one can really appreciate what is going on for you. Your life feels empty, the day drags on, and you are lonely even around other people. Your sadness seems unending. Why go on?

Yet it's just this kind of story I hear every day. Facing the darkness that seems to envelop you, I reach out with my tools of healing. I suggest that we might look at the way you think, consider some alternatives, try to change some behavior or the way you communicate your feelings. I suggest we work on short-term plans—even plans for the next day, the next week. Maybe we can consider, at some point, plans for the next month or year. Gently, firmly, directly I nudge you toward new "experiments" with living your life, always recognizing that it is hard for you—but also recognizing that it is harder for you to stay stuck.

Perhaps my suggestions might seem naïve at times. You say, "He makes it sound so easy. What does he know?" Yes, these are reasonable doubts, reasonable complaints. I know it's not easy. It's like physical therapy for back pain. It may be hard now—but it becomes easier in the future. It's like building new habits that don't come easily. I have been nudging you to increase your activity level, and you say, "I don't have any energy." I say, "Perhaps the energy will come later. Perhaps you need to take action before the motivation comes." You may look at me like I am from another planet, but I repeat to you, "How will it hurt if you try this?"

Remember what we discussed at the beginning of this book? I realize you may be saying, "I can't do this because I'm depressed. I can't exercise, I can't call my friends, and I can't work. My depression keeps me from doing anything." But then I suggest, "Why not act *against* your depression anyway? Take small steps. Try keeping track of how you actually feel when you do these things. Try it. You never know."

Or maybe you're saying, "My depression is realistic. I have good reason to feel this way." Yes, there are reasons to feel sad. All of us will suffer terrible losses. But think about the mother with the disabled child, think about the alcoholic who had 35 years of drinking behind him, and think about the older lady who had her leg amputated. They had good reasons to feel confident about their depression and certain about their hopelessness. Yet they recovered. I know. I saw it.

As you climb into your life again, sometimes you will slip back. Sometimes you will have dark and gloomy days. Sometimes life will not seem like it is worth living. But moods change, events change, and you can make a difference. In this book you were introduced to many of the tools to help you climb back to the place you belong.

At the darkest moment in the dead of night, there is hope. There is a way out, a door to walk through, a time when the dark night comes to an end. Something can awaken in you as your depression lifts. You have been sleeping and have now awoken from a nightmare.

The sun rises.

# Biological Treatments for Your Depression

The good news is that today there is a wide range of biological treatments that can be helpful with controlling depression. In this section, we will look at the advantages and disadvantages of antidepressant medication and the various classes of medications available. In addition to medications that are classified as antidepressants, there are also medications that can be added to your regimen to help you handle your anxiety, help with your sleep, and help increase the effectiveness of the other medications that you are on. Finally, we'll look at other biological treatments, such as electroconvulsive treatment, that may help in certain cases.

## ANTIDEPRESSANT MEDICATION

Sometimes you can feel overwhelmed with the many options available for the treatment of your depression. That is a sign of the tremendous progress that we have made in the last 20 years in providing consumers with choices that fit their individual needs. Your doctor will want to consider your current general health in prescribing medication. You should also tell your doctor about any other medications—both prescribed and over-the-counter—that you are taking. Alternative medications or natural cures can be helpful for some people, but they may also interact with medications to produce unwanted side effects. For example, one woman who was taking St. John's wort (a plant-based alternative substance) had a full-blown manic episode because it reacted with her other medications. Discuss your interest in alternative or natural cures with your health-care professional before taking anything.

Try to get as complete a history as you can of your prior experiences with medication. If you have had very unpleasant side effects from a past medication, let your doctor know. You have the right to access your medical records from your prior doctors, so get those records. Moreover, if a medication has been effective in the past for your depression, you should tell your doctor that, too. What worked in the past will likely work again. In some cases, medications that have worked for close relatives (if they were being treated for depression) may be more likely to work for you. Before you see your doctor, write out a list of information that you want to present (as well as a list of questions you may have). You may forget some important information if you simply rely on your memory at the time.

Keep in mind that antidepressant medications take two to eight weeks to become effective—and sometimes they take longer. Your doctor may start you off at a low dosage, see how you tolerate side effects, and gradually increase the dosage. In many cases, side effects wear off as you become habituated to the medication. Side effects can also be related to the dosage, so your doctor may be able to minimize these effects by reducing the dosage and combining your medication with another medication to improve the antidepressant effectiveness of the first drug. Your doctor may also combine two classes of antidepressant medications. You should never increase or decrease your dosage or combine medications without your doctor's approval. Never self-medicate.

We can group antidepressants into categories that reflect their chemical composition and the brain activity that they affect. Some of the newer antidepressants may target more than one process. One very common class of medications is selective serotonin reuptake inhibitors (SSRIs), which includes Prozac, Zoloft, Paxil, Luvox, Celexa, and Lexapro. You should not take an SSRI if you're already taking a monoamine oxidase inhibitor (MAOI), such as Nardil or Parnate.

Tricyclic antidepressants (TCAs), an older class of medications, include doxepin, clomipramine, nortriptyline, amitriptyline, desipramine, and trimipramine. These medications are used less often because the side effects tend to be more difficult for patients to tolerate. However, they are effective and can be considered when other classes of medication do not work for you. Other antidepressants include trazodone (Desyrel), bupropion (Wellbutrin), venlafaxine (Effexor), milnacipran (Ixel) and duloxetine (Cymbalta); norepinephrine (also called noradrenaline) and reboxetine (Edronax). You can also consider mirtazapine (Remeron).

Your doctor may augment your antidepressant medications with amphetamine substances such as Adderall and Ritalin to increase your energy level. Tryptophan, an amino acid, can be used to augment treatment, although one should be cautioned about possible side effects of this drug. Serious side effects of tryptophan supplements have been eosinophilia-myalgia syndrome (also called EMS, consisting of pain or a rash) and serotonin syndrome (confusion, agitation). In some cases, your doctor may prescribe a low dosage of an antipsychotic to reduce the rigidity of your negative thinking. Antipsychotics include quetiapine (Seroquel), risperidone (Risperdal), and olanzapine (Zyprexa). Usually they are prescribed for a shorter period of time, just until your depression has lessened somewhat. Lithium, although best known as a treatment for bipolar disorder, is also an effective antidepressant, especially for patients with higher suicide risk. However, lithium requires blood monitoring and careful supervision and should only be prescribed after other alternatives have failed to work. Finally, thyroid medication can be used for patients with depression when other treatments are not sufficient. A common medication for this is triiodothyronine (T3).

Why bring up all of these possible alternatives? Some depressed patients—looking at their illness from the perspective of hopelessness—become discouraged if their first medication is not effective. A recent large-scale, multisite study called STAR*D (Sequenced Treatment Alternatives to Relieve Depression) suggests that augmenting a treatment or changing to a new treatment can have significant beneficial results. Switching or augmenting medications and/or adding therapy generally increased the likelihood that patients would get a positive response. It's important to keep this in mind: there are many alternatives that you and your doctor can try, and you won't know if any of them work until you try them.[1]

## What about Side Effects?

Some medications can produce unpleasant side effects, so your doctor will want to gauge how acceptable these are. A medication won't be effective in reducing your depression if the side effects are unacceptable. Some antidepressant medications, for example, may reduce your sexual drive and arousal or make it difficult to achieve orgasm. Of course, you'll want to consider whether the problem may be due to the use of medications that you are taking other than antidepressants—for example, medications that are taken for high blood pressure can also have this effect. If sexual side effects are a problem for you, tell your doctor. He or she can recommend a number of alternatives that may help, including lowering the dosage; taking "drug holidays" (discontinuing the medication for a day or so); replacing your medication with one not known for sexual side effects, such as bupropion (Wellbutrin) or mirtazapine (Remeron); or supplementing your medication with bupropion, gingko biloba (a natural remedy), yohimbine (Procomil), or sildenafil (Viagra). Never take any of these other drugs (prescribed or over-the-counter) or reduce your medications without first consulting with your doctor.

## Stages of Medication

Your doctor will start you on a medication and, depending on your response, increase the dosage and/or add another class of medication. This initial phase of treatment is known as the "acute" phase; it's the phase during which you assess whether you are getting significant benefit from the medication. This can take from 6 to 12 weeks (or longer), depending on your response. The important thing at this point is to decrease your symptoms. Once your symptoms have abated, you will enter the "continuation" phase of treatment, during which you will continue on the medication (sometimes at a lower dose, sometimes not) to ensure that your depression does not rebound. This phase can last between four months and a year. If you have not had a recurrence of depression during that time, you and your doctor will consider if you should be maintained on antidepressant medication for more than a year to avoid future episodes. This "maintenance" phase is best used for patients who have had several prior episodes of depression.

## What about Anxiety?

Many people who are depressed also have significant anxiety. Your doctor may want to start you on both an antianxiety medication and an antidepressant. The most common antianxiety medications—and the fastest-acting—are benzodiazepines such as Xanax, Klonopin, Ativan, and Valium. They can start working almost immediately—usually within 30 minutes. Your doctor may want to start your treatment with a benzodiazepine to give you some short-term relief. However, most patients will want to taper off after a couple of weeks in order to avoid side effects or even addiction. Some patients will continue using benzodiazepines for a few months, along with cognitive-behavioral therapy and other antidepressant medications. Side effects include lethargy, sedation, and difficulty concentrating. You should avoid alcohol while using benzodiazepines.

## Do You Have Bipolar Disorder?

Even though your doctor will ask you questions about any prior manic episodes, you may need to be proactive in exploring for yourself whether you've had any experiences that might indicate a bipolar tendency. You can think back—and ask a close family member—to see if you ever have had a period of a week or more when you have had inflated or grandiose self-esteem (thinking *I'm the smartest person I know*), decreased need for sleep (such as getting by on three to four hours and not feeling tired), rapid speech (speaking so quickly people have a hard time following you), "flight of ideas" (your ideas are all over the place), increased goal-directed activity (you take on numerous tasks), increased sexual drive, and risky behavior (you take unusual chances that you normally would not take). Manic episodes are often characterized by irritability, as well, and they can be combined with depression in what is called a "mixed state." Some episodes are not as severe—they are called "hypomanic episodes."

Many people who have mania or hypomania are not aware of their episodes. For example, patients don't come to see me because they are feeling "overly sexy" or "too brilliant" or "too productive." Many people seem to enjoy their mania—they think it gives them energy and creativity. And many lack insight—they don't know that they are talking so fast that no one can follow them or that they are taking risks they may regret later. These factors may make a patient a poor historian about his or her past or present condition. This is why it's a good idea to consult with close family members about whether you have had manic episodes.

If you have had a prior episode of mania or hypomania (not related to the use of a drug such as amphetamine, cocaine, or steroids), then you may have bipolar disorder. Bipolar disorder is an illness that is strongly genetically linked and requires lifelong treatment. Many very successful people with good family lives have bipolar disorder. The key is to make sure that you get the right diagnosis and the right medication. Bipolar illness is like diabetes—it is a lifelong vulnerability that needs continual medical treatment, but it can be managed and controlled in most cases.

The reason it is important to assess mania or hypomania is that if you rely on antidepressant medication alone you are likely to cycle further into mania in the future. A drug qualifies as a "mood stabilizer" if it is effective in reducing the likelihood of manic and depressive episodes. Patients who have bipolar disorder can be helped by being placed on a mood-stabilizing medication such as lithium or certain anticonvulsant medications that have been found to be effective in stabilizing mood, such as valproate (Depakote) and lamotrigine (Lamictal).

If you have a manic episode in the course of your treatment, your doctor may initially treat you with an antipsychotic medication that can help reduce the agitation. (Antipsychotics used to be called "major tranquilizers"—they actually calm you down quite a bit.) Mood stabilizers may be added to or substituted for the antipsychotic medication once the acute episode has been relieved.

## More Information about Medication

Your doctor will want to work with you to determine which antidepressant to start with. Like any approach in medication, finding the drug that works for you is a matter of trial and error—you start a medication; assess the side effects should they occur; see if it is effective over the course of several weeks; and then determine if you need to increase your dosage, decrease it, add an additional medication, or discontinue the medication. Some patients respond better to one class of medication rather than another. You won't know until you try. It can be frustrating for you—and the side effects may be unpleasant. There is nothing more rewarding at this point than finding something that can help reverse your depression.

Updated information on a wide range of medications can be found on at the National Institutes of Health Website (http://www.nlm.nih.gov/medlineplus/druginformation.html) and Physicians' Desk Reference Website (http://www.pdrhealth.com/home/home.aspx).

### ALTERNATIVES TO MEDICATION

A small percentage of patients may not benefit from therapy or medication. When depression is severe, unremitting, or unresponsive to treatment and there is a risk of suicide, you and your doctor may consider another form of treatment. The most common next step is electroconvulsive treatment (ECT), or shock therapy. In the minds of many people, ECT seems barbaric. It sounds horrible to consider passing a shock through your brain. Some people assume that it is dangerous, permanently damaging, or even unethical. But let's consider the facts.

## Electroconvulsive Treatment (ECT)

Electroconvulsive treatment (ECT), in which an electrical current is passed through the brain to induce a seizure, was in the past more widely used for severe depression than it is today. Since the advent of medication for depression—and unfavorable depictions of ECT in the media—it has been used less often. The patient undergoing ECT (usually in a hospital) is first given a sedative to put him to sleep, then given a medication that paralyzes his muscles so there are no fractures during the seizure. Electrodes are placed on his forehead and one temple (or both temples if he is receiving bilateral ECT) to monitor seizure activity. An electric current is administered, inducing a seizure that lasts between 30 and 60 seconds. The patient wakes in about 15 minutes. Patients usually undergo between 3 and 12 ECT sessions over several weeks to complete the course of treatment.

As with any biological intervention, there are advantages and disadvantages. But before you reject ECT as an alternative, you might consider the positives. There is no more effective treatment for severe depression than ECT.[2] Indeed, a review of the research in this area has led some to conclude that ECT is more effective than medication and that bilateral ECT is more effective than unilateral ECT.[3] It often works quite rapidly, and it can dramatically reverse profound depression. Someone with severe vegetative symptoms—fatigue, slurred speech, immobility, incapacitation—or someone with severe suicide risk can sometimes achieve remarkable change in a short time. Unlike the horrifying images of shock treatment that are depicted in the movie *One Flew over the Cuckoo's Nest* and in the popular media today, shock treatment is actually quite controlled in its application and highly effective.[4]

The disadvantages also need to be considered. For many people there is short-term memory loss—often memories of events that occur right around the time of the treatment. Most—if not all—memories of longer-term events is eventually recovered. However, in some cases, people permanently lose some longer-term memory of life events. You also need a complete physical examination to rule out any risk of cardiac problems. Despite these disadvantages, most patients who have had ECT say that they would do it again.

I have seen a number of patients in therapy who have had dramatic positive responses to ECT. In some cases, it's almost night and day. (Of course, it's also important for these patients to continue taking their antidepressant medication.) Some patients at risk for recurrent episodes of depression have maintenance ECT—they go in for brief sessions every month or so to maintain their improvement. A friend of mine is an example of this. In her 60s now, she spent 35 years getting the wrong diagnosis (unipolar depression—she was actually bipolar). Even though she was eventually placed on lithium, she was still not completely stabilized. She now gets monthly ECT, takes her medication, and is doing the best she has been able to in 40 years. Her story is an inspiration to anyone who has given up hope. She stuck with it and finally found the right treatment.

## Other Electrical Treatments

In a treatment called transcranial magnetic stimulation (TMS), which has recently been approved for the treatment of depression, an electrical coil is placed over the scalp and an electrical current stimulates the cortex. The patient is not under anesthesia, and many of the side effects associated with ECT (such as memory loss) do not arise. Recent reviews of the research indicate that this is an effective treatment for treatment-resistant depression;[5] although some have warned that it may not be as effective as suggested.[6]

Another electrical stimulation technique that has received attention—but still needs more research to support it—is vagus nerve stimulation (VNS). This involves placing an electrode in the chest of the patient that stimulates the vagus nerve (think of this as a kind of pacemaker for this cranial nerve). Again, this intervention is still in its beginning phase, but anecdotal reports suggest some efficacy with some patients, and it has recently been approved for treatment-resistant depression.[7]

## Seasonal Affective Disorder Therapy

A common variation of depression is seasonal affective disorder (SAD). People with this particular illness show increased depressive mood during the winter months when the hours of sunlight are decreased. Their moods often improve during the summer. (In a smaller percentage of patients, depression is more common in summer.) The symptoms of seasonal affective disorder include increased need for sleep, craving for carbohydrates, and overeating. Up to 38 percent of patients seeking treatment for depression have a seasonal component to their disorder[8] and 5 percent of the general public has SAD.[9] Women are more likely than men to suffer from SAD.

Light therapy is often prescribed for patients with SAD, and research indicates that it can be quite effective.[10] In fact, recent research shows that combined cognitive-behavioral therapy with light therapy for SAD is the most effective treatment.[11] It works on a simple principle: Bright light helps wake you up in the morning and jump-start your circadian rhythms. You can get bright light for 15 to 30 minutes from sunlight, from a high-intensity lamp, or by purchasing a commercially produced bright light specifically designed for this purpose. Commercially produced bright lights are available from Apollo Light (www.apollolight.com), Sunbox (www.sunbox.com), and other manufacturers. Some patients with SAD also benefit from melatonin supplements. Finally, negative air ionization can also be effective in reducing SAD.[12]

## CONCLUSION

Perhaps the options for medication seem so vast that they are overwhelming. There are many different classes of medications; possibilities for augmenting medications; ways to treat side effects; and specific medications for your sleep, anxiety, and other problems. But the very fact that there are so many options should give you hope. The use of electrical stimulation (ECT, VNS, TMS) may appear controversial in some circles. You will hear strong opinions on both sides. However, in the case of severe depression that may have a dangerous suicidal component, you should consider all options that are available. Experienced clinicians—especially those who have worked in hospital environments—will often attest to the dramatic effects of these electrical treatments. As with any treatment, you should carefully weigh the costs and benefits, with your doctor's help. The good news is that we are moving forward all the time with more and more sophisticated and effective treatments.

# Resources for Further Treatment

## HOW TO FIND A GOOD COGNITIVE-BEHAVIORAL THERAPIST

Finding the right therapist is an important part of your self-help program. I have listed several Websites that you can use to locate someone in your area. However, you should also be organized and assertive in what you are looking for. When you speak to your prospective therapist, you can ask about his or her training and experience in using cognitive-behavioral therapy is. After you meet with the therapist, ask for a description of the plan of treatment, how your will progress be measured, and what techniques will likely be used. Most people who do cognitive-behavioral therapy will have you fill out some self-report forms—and you should keep copies for yourself so you can measure your own progress.

Here are some Websites to locate referrals:

- The Academy of Cognitive Therapy: www.academyofct.org

- The Association of Behavioral and Cognitive Therapies: www.abct.org

If you live in the United Kingdom you can find certified cognitive-behavioral therapists by going to the Website of the British Association for Behavioural and Cognitive Psychotherapies at: www.babcp.org. You can also access up-to-date information on medications at:

- The National Institutes of Health: http://www.nlm.nih.gov/ medlineplus/druginformation.html

- The Physicians' Desk Reference: http://www.pdrhealth .com/home/home.aspx

- WebMD: http://www.webmd.com/depression/default.htm

More information on depression, anxiety, and cognitive-behavioral therapy is also available on our Website at the American Institute for Cognitive Therapy in New York City: www.cognitivetherapynyc.com.


## THE MULTIDIMENSIONAL PERFECTIONISM SCALE

As we read in Chapter 5, depression can be the result of your perfectionistic thinking. The Multidimensional Perfectionism Scale was developed to assess different aspects of perfectionism. The listing below identifies these different subscales for perfectionism. Add up your scores to see which subscales most characterize you. There are no cut-off points; examine your perfectionism across these different subscales.

- **The Concern over Mistakes** subscale includes items 9, 10, 13, 14, 18, 21, 23, 25, and 34. This subscale reflects your negative reactions to mistakes, a tendency to interpret mistakes as equivalent to failures, and a concern that you will lose the respect of others if you fail.

- **Personal Standards** subscale includes items 4, 6, 12, 16, 19, 24, and 30 and reflects your tendency to set very high standards and the excessive importance placed on these high standards for evaluating yourself.

- **Parental Expectations** subscale includes items 1, 11, 15, 20, and 26 and reflects your belief that your parents set very high goals for you.

- **Parental Criticism** subscale refers to items 3, 5, 22, and 35 and reflects your view that your parents are (or were) overly critical.

- **Doubting of Actions** subscale refers to items 17, 28, 32, and 33 and reflects the extent to which you doubt your ability to accomplish tasks.

- **The Organization** subscale includes items 2, 7, 8, 27, 29, and 31 and its subscale is somewhat separate but related to certain dimensions. It measures the tendency to be orderly or organized and reflects an overemphasis on order and orderliness which has often been associated with perfectionism.[13]

| Scale | Score |
|-------|-------|
| The Concern over Mistakes | |
| Personal Standards | |
| Parental Expectations | |
| Parental Criticism | |
| Doubting of Actions | |
| Total of above Scales | Total Score |
| Organization* | |
| * The Organization subscale is scored separately and is not included in your overall score. | |

Look over your responses on the different subscales and try to evaluate if you are more or less concerned with different kinds of perfectionism. There are no absolute "norms" for these scales or subscales, but you can get some idea whether you are prone to perfectionism. You might want to take this test over again after you complete the different chapters in this book and after your depression decreases. Do you think that your perfectionism might be related to your depression, your self-esteem, your indecisiveness, or your fear of making mistakes? Does your perfectionism make you more prone to regret?

# ACKNOWLEDGMENTS

Let me begin by thanking the many people who have honored me by trusting me with their problems and having the courage to work on their depression. My patients have taught me how people can have courage in the face of what seems like hopeless suffering. Much of what I know I owe to them. Thank you for letting me take part in your lives.

I owe a great deal to my mentor and friend, the father of cognitive-behavioral therapy, Aaron T. Beck, whose work has inspired so many of us in the treatment of depression. In addition, I owe much of my understanding about depression and its treatment to the many researchers throughout the world who continue to add to our ability to help people. My gratitude goes to the outstanding researchers whose work has informed this book: Brad Alford, David D. Burns, David A. Clark, Rob DeRubeis, Norm Epstein, Connie Hammen, Allison Harvey, Susan Nolen-Hoeksema, Steve Hollon, Sheri Johnson, Thomas Joiner, Jon Kabat-Zinn, Warren Mansell, Cory Newman, Costas Papageorgiou, John Riskind, Zindel Segal, Marty Seligman, Roz Shafran, Jean Twenge, and Adrian Wells.

My good friend Paul Gilbert from the United Kingdom has been a major source of support—he is truly a combination of wisdom, compassion, and humor. Frank Dattilio, Philip Tata, Dennis Tirch, and Lata McGinn have been friends and colleagues throughout. I also want to thank my colleagues at The American Institute for Cognitive Therapy who have been patient enough to listen to me rehearse and review most of the ideas in this book. My editorial assistant, Poonam Melwani, has been magnificent in making this—and other projects—possible. Thanks also go to Patty Gift and Sally Mason from Hay House for their support of this project. My agent, Bob Diforio, has been a constant in my life for several years. He is a true bulldog

And, of course, to my wife, Helen, I owe the most gratitude. I am at a loss for words to find the right expression to thank her.

# ENDNOTES

## Chapter 1: What Is Depression?

1. S. B. Patten, "Accumulation of Major Depressive Episodes over Time in a Prospective Study Indicates That Retrospectively Assessed Lifetime Prevalence Estimates Are Too Low," *BMC Psychiatry* 8, no. 9 (May 2009): 19; A. J. Rush, M. H. Trivedi, H. M. Ibrahim, et al. "The 16-item Quick Inventory of Depressive Symptomatology (QIDS), Clinician Rating (QIDS-C), and Self-report (QIDS-SR): A Psychometric Evaluation in Patients with Chronic Major Depression," Biological Psychiatry 54, no. 5 (2003): 573–583.

2. Ronald C. Kessler et al., "Mood Disorders in Children and Adolescents: An Epidemiologic Perspective," *Biological Psychiatry* 49, no. 12 (15 June 2001): 1002.

3. Jean M. Twenge, "Birth Cohort, Social Change, and Personality: The Interplay of Dysphoria and Individualism in the 20th Century," *Advances in Personality Science*, ed. Daniel Cervone and Walter Mischel (New York: Guilford, 2002), 196–218.

4. Jean M. Twenge and W. Keith Campbell, *The Narcissism Epidemic: Living in the Age of Entitlement* (New York: Free Press, 2009).

5. P. F. Sullivan, M. C. Neale, and K. S. Kendler, "Genetic Epidemiology of Major Depression: Review and Meta-analysis," *The American Journal of Psychiatry* 157 (2000): 1552; Armen K. Goenjian et al., "Heritabilities of Symptoms of Posttraumatic Stress Disorder, Anxiety, and Depression in Earthquake Exposed Armenian Families," *Psychiatric Genetics* 18 (2008): 261.

6. Edward Shorter, "The History of Lithium Therapy," *Bipolar Disorders* 11, suppl. 2 (June 2009): 4–9.

7. JoEllen Patterson et al., *The Therapist's Guide to Psychopharmacology: Working with Patients, Families and Physicians to Optimize Care* (New York: Guilford, 2006).

8. Jennifer L. Warner-Schmidt and Ronald S. Duman, "Vascular Endothelial Growth Factor Is an Essential Mediator of the Neurogenic and Behavioral Actions of Antidepressants," *Proceedings of the National Academy of Sciences* 104, no. 11 (13 March 2007): 4647; Ronald S. Duman, "Depression: A Case of Neuronal Life and Death?" *Biological Psychiatry* 56, no. 3 (1 August 2004): 140.

9. Eva M. Pomerantz, "Parent x Child Socialization: Implications for the Development of Depressive Symptoms," *Journal of Family Psychology* 15, no. 3 (September 2001): 510; Valerie E. Whiffen and Teresa M. Sasseville, "Dependency, Self-criticism, and Recollections of Parenting: Sex Differences and the Role of Depressive Affect," *Journal of Social and Clinical Psychology* 10 (1991): 121; Jenny Firth-Cozens, "The Role of Early Family Experiences in

the Perception of Organizational Stress: Fusing Clinical and Organizational Perspectives," *Journal of Occupational and Organizational Psychology* 65, no.1 (March 1992): 61.

10. A. Bifulco, G.W. Brown, and Z. Adler, "Early Sexual Abuse and Clinical Depression in Adult Life," *British Journal of Psychiatry* 159 (1991): 115.

11. Sidney J. Blatt and Erika Homann, "Parent-child Interaction in the Etiology of Dependent and Self-critical Depression," *Clinical Psychology Review* 12 (1992): 47.

12. T. Harris, G.W. Brown, and A. Bifulco, "Loss of Parent in Childhood and Adult Psychiatric Disorder: The Role of Lack of Adequate Parental Care," *Psychological Medicine* 16 (1986): 641.

13. Chris R. Brewin, Bernice Andrews, and Ian H. Gotlib, "Psychopathology and Early Experience: A Reappraisal of Retrospective Reports," *Psychological Bulletin* 113, no. 1 (January 1993): 82.

14. Constance Hammen, "Depression in Women: The Family Context and Risk for Recurrence," *The Economics of Neuroscience* 6 (2004): 41; M. M. Weissman, "Advances in Psychiatric Epidemiology: Rates and Risks for Major Depression," *American Journal of Public Health* 77 (1987): 44.

15. Dave E. Marcotte, Virginia Wilcox-Gök, and D. Patrick Redmon, "Prevalence and Patterns of Major Depressive Disorder in the United States Labor Force," *The Journal of Mental Health Policy and Economics* 2 (1999): 123.

16. Kenneth S. Kendler et al., "The Structure of the Genetic and Environmental Risk Factors for Six Major Psychiatric Disorders in Women: Phobia, Generalized Anxiety Disorder, Panic Disorder, Bulimia, Major Depression, and Alcoholism," *Archives of General Psychiatry* 52, no. 5 (May 1995): 374; Kenneth S. Kendler et al., "Stressful Life Events, Genetic Liability, and Onset of an Episode of Major Depression in Women," *American Journal of Psychiatry* 152, no. 6 (June 1995): 833.

17. Laura A. Pratt and Debra J. Brody, *Depression in the United States Household Population, 2005–2006*, NCHS Data Brief Number (2008).

18. Walter F. Stewart et al., "Cost of Lost Productive Work Time among US Workers with Depression," *Journal of the American Medical Association* 289 (2003): 3135.

19. F. Bonnet et al., "Anxiety and Depression Are Associated with Unhealthy Lifestyle in Patients at Risk of Cardiovascular Disease," *Atherosclerosis* 178, no. 2 (February 2005): 339.

20. K. Andersen et al., "Depression and the Risk of Alzheimer Disease," *Epidemiology* 16, no. 2 (March 2005): 233.

21. M. J. Bos et al., "Depressive Symptoms and Risk of Stroke: The Rotterdam Study," *Journal of Neurology, Neurosurgery, and Psychiatry* 79, no. 9 (September 2008): 977.

22. Jane Leserman, "HIV Disease Progression: Depression, Stress, and Possible Mechanisms," *Biological Psychiatry* 54, no. 3 (1 August 2003): 295.

23. J. G. E. Janzing et al., "The Relationship between Depression and Mortality in Elderly Subjects with Less Severe Dementia," *Psychological Medicine* 29, no. 4 (July 1999): 979.

24. Keith Hawton, "Suicide and Attempted Suicide," *Handbook of Affective Disorders*, ed. Eugene S. Paykel (New York: Guilford Press, 1992), 635–650.

25. A. J. Rush, M. H. Trivedi, H. M. Ibrahim, et al. "The 16-item Quick Inventory of Depressive Symptomatology (QIDS), Clinician Rating (QIDS-C), and Self-report (QIDS-SR): A Psychometric Evaluation in Patients with Chronic Major Depression," Biological Psychiatry 54, no. 5 (2003): 573–583.

26. Laura A. Pratt and Debra J. Brody, *Depression in the United States Household Population, 2005-2006*, NCHS Data Brief Number (2008).

27. Ronald C. Kessler et al., "Mood Disorders in Children and Adolescents: An Epidemiologic Perspective," *Biological Psychiatry* 49, no. 12 (15 June 2001): 1002.

28. Ronald C. Kessler and E. E. Walters, "Epidemiology of DSM-III-R Major Depression and Minor Depression among Adolescents and Young Adults in the National Comorbidity Survey," *Depression and Anxiety* 7 (1998): 3.

29. M. B. Keller et al., "Recovery in Major Depressive Disorder: Analysis with the Life Table Regression Models," *Archives of General Psychiatry* 39, no. 8 (August 1982): 905.

30. K. Mikael Holma et al., "Long-term Outcome of Major Depressive Disorder in Psychiatric Patients Is Variable," *Journal of Clinical Psychiatry* 69 (2008): 196.

31. Walter F. Stewart et al., "Cost of Lost Productive Work Time among US Workers with Depression," *Journal of the American Medical Association* 289 (2003): 3135.

32. Laura A. Pratt and Debra J. Brody, *Depression in the United States Household Population, 2005–2006*, NCHS Data Brief Number (2008).

33. Paul E. Greenberg et al., "The Economic Burden of Depression in the United States: How Did It Change between 1990 and 2000?" *Journal of Clinical Psychiatry* 64, no. 12 (December 2003): 1465.

34. Keith Hawton, "Suicide and Attempted Suicide," in *Handbook of Affective Disorders*, ed. Eugene S. Paykel (New York: Guilford Press, 1992), 635–650.

## Chapter 2: The Depressed Mind

1. Ronald C. Kessler et al., "Lifetime and 12-month Prevalence of DSM-III-R Psychiatric Disorders in the United States. Results from the National Comorbidity Survey," *Archives of General Psychiatry* 51 (1994): 8.

2. Paul Gilbert, "Evolution and Depression: Issues and Implications," *Psychological Medicine* 36, no. 3 (March 2006): 287; Robert L. Leahy, "Pessimism and the Evolution of Negativity," *Journal of Cognitive Psychotherapy* 16, no. 3 (Summer 2002): 295.

3. Robert L. Leahy, "Pessimism and the Evolution of Negativity," *Evolutionary Theory and Cognitive Therapy*, ed. Paul Gilbert (New York: Springer, 2004): 91–118; Robert L. Leahy, "An Investment Model of Depressive Resistance," *Journal of Cognitive Psychotherapy: An International Quarterly* 11 (1997): 3.

4. Robert L. Leahy, "Pessimism and the Evolution of Negativity," *Journal of Cognitive Psychotherapy* 16, no. 3 (Summer 2002): 295; Randolph M. Nesse, "Is Depression an Adaptation?" *Archives of General Psychiatry* 57 (2000): 14; Leon Sloman, Paul Gilbert, and G. Hasey, "Evolved Mechanisms in Depression: The Role and Interaction of Attachment and Social Rank in Depression," *Journal of Affective Disorders* 74, no. 2 (April 2003): 107.

5. J. M. Eagles, "Seasonal Affective Disorder: A Vestigial Evolutionary Advantage?" *Medical Hypotheses* 63 (2004): 767.

6. Nicholas Allen and Paul B. T. Badcock, "The Social Risk Hypothesis of Depressed Mood: Evolutionary, Psychosocial, and Neurobiological Perspectives," *Psychological Bulletin* 129, no. 6 (November 2003): 887; Robert L. Leahy, "Pessimism and the Evolution of Negativity," *Evolutionary Theory and Cognitive Therapy*, ed. Paul Gilbert (New York: Springer, 2004), 91–118.

7. Anthony Stevens and John Price, *Evolutionary Psychiatry: A New Beginning*, 2nd ed. (London: Routledge/Taylor and Francis Group, 2000).

8. Nicholas Allen and Paul B. T. Badcock, "The Social Risk Hypothesis of Depressed Mood: Evolutionary, Psychosocial, and Neurobiological Perspectives," *Psychological Bulletin* 129, no. 6 (November 2003): 887.

9. Aaron T. Beck et al., *Cognitive Therapy of Depression* (New York: Guilford, 1979); Robert L. Leahy, *Cognitive Therapy: Basic Principles and Applications* (Northvale, NJ: Jason Aronson, 1996).

10. From *Treatment Plans and Interventions for Depression and Anxiety Disorders* by Robert L. Leahy and Stephen J. Holland. Copyright 2000 by Robert L. Leahy and Stephen J. Holland. Used by permission.

11. Zindel V. Segal et al., "Cognitive Reactivity to Sad Mood Provocation and the Prediction of Depressive Relapse," *Archives of General Psychiatry* 63, no. 7 (July 2006): 749; Sheri L. Johnson and Randy Fingerhut, "Negative Cognitions Predict the Course of Bipolar Depression, Not Mania," *Journal of Cognitive Psychotherapy: An International Quarterly* 18 (2004): 149.

12. Gary P. Brown and Aaron T. Beck, "Dysfunctional Attitudes, Perfectionism, and Models of Vulnerability to Depression," *Perfectionism: Theory, Research, and Treatment*, ed. Gordon L. Flett and Paul L. Hewitt (Washington, D.C.: American Psychological Association, 2002), 231–251.

13. Robert J. DeRubeis et al., "How Does Cognitive Therapy Work? Cognitive Change and Symptom Change in Cognitive Therapy and Pharmacotherapy for Depression," *Journal of Consulting and Clinical Psychology* 58, no. 6 (December 1990): 862.

14. Tony Z. Tang et al., "Cognitive Changes, Critical Sessions, and Sudden Gains in Cognitive–Behavioral Therapy for Depression," *Journal of Consulting and Clinical Psychology* 73, no. 1 (February 2005): 168.

15. Susan Nolen-Hoeksema, "The Role of Rumination in Depressive Disorders and Mixed Anxiety/Depressive Symptoms," *Journal of Abnormal Psychology* 109 (2000): 504.

16. Susan Nolen-Hoeksema, "Gender Differences in Depression," in *Handbook of Depression*, ed. Ian H. Gotlib and Constance Hammen (New York: Guilford, 2002), 492–509.

17. Gemille Cribb, Michelle L. Moulds, and Sally Carter, "Rumination and Experiential Avoidance in Depression," *Behaviour Change* 23, no. 3 (2006): 165.

## Chapter 3: "Nothing Works Out"

1. Robert L. Leahy, "Decision Making Processes and Psychopathology," *Contemporary Cognitive Therapy: Theory, Research, and Practice*, ed. Robert L. Leahy (New York: Guilford Press, 2004), 116–138.

2. Robert L. Leahy, "Pessimism and the Evolution of Negativity," *Journal of Cognitive Psychotherapy* 16, no. 3 (Summer 2002): 295.

## Chapter 4: "I'm a Loser"

1. Committee on Quality of Health Care in America et al., *To Err Is Human: Building a Safer Health System* (Washington, DC: National Academic Press, 2000).

## Chapter 5: "I Can't Stand Making Mistakes"

1. Randy O. Frost et al., "A Comparison of Two Measures of Perfectionism," *Personality and Individual Differences* 14 (1993): 119; Robert B. Slaney, Jeffrey S. Ashby, and Joseph Trippi, "Perfectionism: Its Measurement and Career Relevance," *Journal of Career Assessment* 3 (1995): 279.

2.   Don E. Hamachek, "Psychodynamics of Normal and Neurotic Perfectionism," *Psychology* 15 (1978): 27.

3.   Paul L. Hewitt and Gordon L. Flett, "Perfectionism in the Self and Social Contexts: Conceptualization, Assessment, and Association with Psychopathology," *Journal of Personality and Social Psychology* 60 (1991): 456; Tsui-Feng Wu and Meifen Wei, "Perfectionism and Negative Mood: The Mediating Roles of Validation from Others versus Self," *Journal of Counseling Psychology* 55, no. 2 (April 2008): 276.

4.   Randy O. Frost et al., "The Dimensions of Perfectionism," *Cognitive Therapy & Research* 14 (1990): 449; Paul L. Hewitt, Gordon L. Flett, and Norman S. Endler, "Perfectionism, Coping and Depression Symptomatology in a Clinical Sample," *Clinical Psychology and Psychotherapy* 2 (1995): 47.

5.   Randy O. Frost et al., "The Dimensions of Perfectionism," *Cognitive Therapy & Research* 14 (1990): 449; Randy O. Frost and Patricia A. Marten, "Perfectionism and Evaluative Threat," *Cognitive Therapy & Research* 14 (1990): 559.

6.   Roz Shafran and Warren Mansell, "Perfectionism and Psychopathology: A Review of Research and Treatment," *Clinical Psychology Review* 21, no. 6 (August 2001): 879.

7.   Edward C. Chang, "Perfectionism as a Predictor of Positive and Negative Psychological Outcomes: Examining a Mediation Model in Younger and Older Adults," *Journal of Counseling Psychology* 47 (2000): 18.

8.   Lars-Gunnar Lundh et al., "Alexithymia, Memory of Emotion, Emotional Awareness, and Perfectionism," *Emotion* 2, no. 4 (December 2002): 361.

9.   Barry Schwartz et al., "Maximizing versus Satisficing: Happiness Is a Matter of Choice," *Journal of Personality and Social Psychology* 83, no. 5 (November 2002): 1178.

10.  A. Marie Habke, Paul L. Hewitt, and Gordon L. Flett, "Perfectionism and Sexual Satisfaction in Intimate Relationships," *Journal of Psychopathology and Behavioral Assessment* 21, no. 4 (December 1999): 307.

11.  Lance L. Hawley et al., "The Relationship of Perfectionism, Depression, and Therapeutic Alliance during Treatment for Depression: Latent Difference Score Analysis," *Journal of Consulting and Clinical Psychology* 74, no. 5 (October 2006): 930.

12.  Neil R. Bockian, "Depression in Obsessive-Compulsive Personality Disorder," in *Personality-Guided Therapy for Depression*, ed. Neil R. Bockian (Washington, D.C.: American Psychological Association, 2006), 247–265.

13.  Paul L. Hewitt et al., "Trait Perfectionism Dimensions and Suicidal Behavior," *Cognition and Suicide: Theory, Research, and Therapy*, ed. Thomas E. Ellis (Washington, D.C.: American Psychological Association, 2006), 215–235.

14. Robert L. Leahy, *The Worry Cure: Seven Steps to Stop Worry from Stopping You* (New York: Harmony/Random House, 2005).

## Chapter 7: "I Just Can't Decide"

1.  Michel J. Dugas, Kristin Buhr, and Robert Ladouceur, "The Role of Intolerance of Uncertainty in the Etiology and Maintenance of Generalized Anxiety Disorder," *Generalized Anxiety Disorder: Advances in Research and Practice*, ed. Richard G. Heimberg, Cynthia L. Turk, and Douglas S. Mennin (New York: Guilford, 2004), 143–163.

2.  David A. Clark, Aaron T. Beck, and Brad A. Alford, *Scientific Foundations of Cognitive Theory and Therapy of Depression* (New York: Wiley, 1999).

3.  Robyn M. Dawes and Jerome Kagan, *Rational Choice in an Uncertain World* (Stamford, Conn.: International Thomson Publishing, 1988); Paul Slovic, ed., *The Perception of Risk* (Sterling, Va.: Earthscan Publications, 2000).

4.  Adrian Wells, *Metacognitive Therapy for Anxiety and Depression* (New York: Guilford, 2008).

5.  Steven C. Hayes, Kirk D. Strosahl, and Kelly G. Wilson, *Acceptance and Commitment Therapy: An Experiential Approach to Behavior Change* (New York: Guilford, 1999); Marsha M. Linehan, *Cognitive-Behavioral Treatment of Borderline Personality Disorder* (New York: Guilford, 1993).

6.  Adrian Wells, "A Cognitive Model of GAD: Metacognitions and Pathological Worry," *Generalized Anxiety Disorder: Advances in Research and Practice*, ed. Richard G. Heimberg, Cynthia L. Turk, and Douglas S. Mennin (New York: Guilford, 2004), 164; Adrian Wells, *Metacognitive Therapy for Anxiety and Depression* (New York: Guilford, 2008).

7.  Robert L. Leahy, *Overcoming Resistance in Cognitive Therapy* (New York: Guilford, 2001).

8.  Robert L. Leahy, "Sunk Costs and Resistance to Change," *Journal of Cognitive Psychotherapy: An International Quarterly* 14, no. 4 (Fall 2000): 355.

9.  Robert L. Leahy, *Overcoming Resistance in Cognitive Therapy* (New York: Guilford, 2001).

## Chapter 8: "I Keep Thinking Over and Over . . ."

1.  Susan Nolen-Hoeksema, "The Role of Rumination in Depressive Disorders and Mixed Anxiety/Depressive Symptoms," *Journal of Abnormal Psychology* 109 (2000): 504.

2.     Lori M. Hilt et al., "The BDNF Val66Met Polymorphism Predicts Rumination and Depression Differently in Young Adolescent Girls and Their Mothers," *Neuroscience Letters* 429 (2007): 12.

3.     Adrian Wells, *Metacognitive Therapy for Anxiety and Depression* (New York: Guilford, 2008).

4.     Susan Nolen-Hoeksema, "The Role of Rumination in Depressive Disorders and Mixed Anxiety/Depressive Symptoms," *Journal of Abnormal Psychology* 109 (2000): 504.

5.     Costas Papageorgiou and Adrian Wells, "Metacognitive Beliefs about Rumination in Major Depression," *Cognitive and Behavioral Practice* 8 (2001): 160.

6.     Costas Papageorgiou and Adrian Wells, "Positive Beliefs about Depressive Rumination: Development and Preliminary Validation of a Self-report scale," *Behavior Therapy* 32, no. 1 (Winter 2001): 13.

7.     Costas Papageorgiou and Adrian Wells, "Treatment of Recurrent Major Depression with Attention Training," *Cognitive and Behavioral Practice* 7, no. 4 (Autumn 2000): 407; Zindel V. Segal, Mark J. G. Williams, and John D. Teasdale, *Mindfulness-Based Cognitive Therapy for Depression: A New Approach to Preventing Relapse* (New York: Guilford, 2002).

8.     Zindel V. Segal, Mark J. G. Williams, and John D. Teasdale, *Mindfulness-Based Cognitive Therapy for Depression: A New Approach to Preventing Relapse* (New York: Guilford, 2002).

9.     John D. Teasdale, et al., "Prevention of Relapse/Recurrence in Major Depression by Mindfulness-Based Cognitive Therapy," *Journal of Consulting and Clinical Psychology* 68 (2000): 615.

## Chapter 9: "I'm Just a Burden"

1.     Kathryn L. Bleiberg and John C. Markowitz, "Interpersonal Psychotherapy for Depression," in *Clinical Handbook of Psychological Disorders: A Step-by-Step Treatment Manual*, 4th ed., ed. David H. Barlow (New York: Guilford Press, 2008), 306–327; Chris Segrin, *Interpersonal Processes in Psychological Problems* (New York: Guilford Press, 2001).

2.     James C. Coyne et al., "Living with a Depressed Person," *Journal of Consulting and Clinical Psychology* 55 (1987): 347.

3.     Thomas E. Joiner, Jr. et al., "Depression and Excessive Reassurance-Seeking," *Psychological Inquiry* 10, no. 4 (1999): 269; Joanne Davila, "Refining the Association between Excessive Reassurance Seeking and Depressive Symptoms: The Role of Related Interpersonal Constructs," *Journal of Social and Clinical Psychology* 20, no. 4 (Winter 2001): 538.

4.   Robert L. Leahy, "A Social Cognitive Model of Validation," *Compassion: Conceptualisations, Research and Use in Psychotherapy*, ed. Paul Gilbert (London: Brunner-Routledge, 2005), 195–217.

5.   Robert L. Leahy, *Overcoming Resistance in Cognitive Therapy* (New York: Guilford, 2001).

6.   Robert L. Leahy, *Overcoming Resistance in Cognitive Therapy* (New York: Guilford, 2001).

## Chapter 11: "My Relationship is Falling Apart"

1.   Mark A. Whisman, "The Association between Depression and Marital Dissatisfaction," *Marital and Family Processes in Depression: A Scientific Foundation for Clinical Practice*, ed. Steven R. H. Beach (Washington, D.C.: American Psychological Association, 2001), 3–24.

2.   Mark A. Whisman and Martha L. Bruce, "Marital Dissatisfaction and Incidence of Major Depressive Episode in Community Sample," *Journal of Abnormal Psychology* 108 (1999): 674; Steven R. H. Beach et al., "Prospective Effects of Marital Satisfaction on Depressive Symptoms in Established Marriages: A Dyadic Model," *Journal of Social and Personal Relationships* 20 (2003): 355.

3.   Steven R. H. Beach, Ernest N. Jouriles, and K. Daniel O'Leary, "Extramarital Sex: Impact on Depression and Commitment in Couples Seeking Marital Therapy," *Journal of Sex and Marital Therapy* 11 (1985): 99.

4.   Joanne Davila et al., "Marital Functioning and Depressive Symptoms: Evidence for a Stress Generation Model," *Journal of Personality and Social Psychology* 73 (1997): 849.

5.   Frank D. Fincham and Thomas N. Bradbury, "Marital Satisfaction, Depression, and Attributions: A Longitudinal Analysis," *Journal of Personality and Social Psychology* 64, no. 3 (March 1993): 442.

6.   Thomas E. Joiner, "Depression's Vicious Scree: Self-propagating and Erosive Processes in Depression Chronicity," *Clinical Psychology: Science and Practice* 7 (2000): 203; Thomas E. Joiner, Jessica S. Brown, and Janet Kistner, *The Interpersonal, Cognitive, and Social Nature of Depression* (Mahwah, N.J.: Erlbaum, 2006).

7.   David A. Smith and Kristina M. Peterson, "Overperception of Spousal Criticism in Dysphoria and Marital Discord," *Behavior Therapy* 39, no. 3 (September 2008): 300.

8.   Steven R. H. Beach et al., "Couple Therapy and the Treatment of Depression," in *Clinical Handbook of Couple Therapy*, 4th edition, ed. Alan S. Gurman and Neil S. Jacobson (New York: Guilford, 2008), 545–566.

## Chapter 12: "Now That I'm Better, How Do I Stay Well?"

1. Peter M. Lewinsohn et al., "First Onset versus Recurrence of Depression: Differential Processes of Psychosocial Risk," *Journal of Abnormal Psychology* 108, no. 3 (August 1999): 483; Robert M. Post, "Developmental Psychobiology of Cyclic Affective Illness: Implications for Early Therapeutic Intervention," *Development and Psychopathology* 8 (1996): 273; Jill Hooley and John D. Teasdale, "Predictors of Relapse in Unipolar Depressives: Expressed Emotion, Marital Distress, and Perceived Criticism," *Journal of Abnormal Psychology* 98, no. 3 (August 1989): 229; John D. Teasdale et al., "How Does Cognitive Therapy Prevent Relapse in Residual Depression? Evidence from a Controlled Trial," *Journal of Consulting and Clinical Psychology* 69, no. 3 (June 2001): 347.

2. Keith S. Dobson et al., "Randomized Trial of Behavioral Activation, Cognitive Therapy, and Antidepressant Medication in the Prevention of Relapse and Recurrence in Major Depression," *Journal of Consulting and Clinical Psychology* 76, no. 3 (June 2008): 468.

3. Daniel R. Strunk et al., "Patients' Competence in and Performance of Cognitive Therapy Skills: Relation to the Reduction of Relapse Risk Following Treatment for Depression," *Journal of Consulting and Clinical Psychology* 75, no. 4 (August 2007): 523.

4. R. B. Jarrett et al., "Preventing Recurrent Depression Using Cognitive Therapy with and without a Continuation Phase: A Randomized Clinical Trial," *Archives of General Psychiatry* 58 (2001): 381.

5. Zindel V. Segal, Mark J. G. Williams, and John D. Teasdale, *Mindfulness-Based Cognitive Therapy for Depression: A New Approach to Preventing Relapse* (New York: Guilford Press, 2002).

6. Jon Kabat-Zinn, *Full Catastrophe Living: The Program of the Stress Reduction Clinic at the University of Massachusetts Medical Center* (New York: Delta, 1990).

7. Willem Kuyken et al., "Mindfulness-Based Cognitive Therapy to Prevent Relapse in Recurrent Depression," *Journal of Consulting and Clinical Psychology* 76, no. 6 (December 2008): 966.

8. Johannes Michalak et al., "Mindfulness Predicts Relapse/Recurrence in Major Depressive Disorder after Mindfulness-Based Cognitive Therapy," *Journal of Nervous and Mental Disease* 196, no. 8 (August 2008): 630.

## Appendix A: Biological Treatments for Your Depression

1. Andrew A. Nierenberg et al., "A Comparison of Lithium and T3 Augmentation Following Two Failed Medication Treatments for Depression: A STAR*D Report," *American Journal of Psychiatry* 163, no. 9 (September

2006): 1519; Patrick J. McGrath et al., "Tranylcypromine versus Venlafaxine Plus Mirtazapine Following Three Failed Antidepressant Medication Trials for Depression: A STAR*D Report," *American Journal of Psychiatry* 163, no. 9 (September 2006): 1531.

2.  Allan L. Scott and Tracy Fraser, "Decreased Usage of Electroconvulsive Therapy: Implications," *British Journal of Psychiatry* 192, no. 6 (June 2008): 476.

3.  Stuart Carney et al., "Efficacy and Safety of Electroconvulsive Therapy in Depressive Disorders: A Systematic Review and Meta-Analysis," *Lancet* 361, no. 9360 (8 March 2003): 799.

4.  Claire Hilton, "An Exploration of the Patient's Experience of Electro-Convulsive Therapy in Mid-Twentieth Century Creative Literature: A Historical Study with Implications for Practice Today," *Journal of Affective Disorders* 97, no. 1–3 (January 2007): 5; Edward Shorter and David Healy, *Shock Therapy: A History of Electroconvulsive Treatment in Mental Illness* (New Brunswick, N.J.: Rutgers University Press, 2007).

5.  Lucie L. Herrmann and Klaus P. Ebmeier, "Factors Modifying the Efficacy of Transcranial Magnetic Stimulation in the Treatment of Depression: A Review," *Journal of Clinical Psychiatry* 67, no. 12 (December 2006): 1870.

6.  A. Mogg et al., "A Randomized Controlled Trial with 4-month Follow-up of Adjunctive Repetitive Transcranial Magnetic Stimulation of the Left Prefrontal Cortex for Depression," *Psychological Medicine* 38, no. 3 (March 2008): 323.

7.  Claire Daban et al., "Safety and Efficacy of Vagus Nerve Stimulation in Treatment-Resistant Depression. A Systematic Review," *Journal of Affective Disorders* 110, no. 1–2 (September 2008): 1.

8.  Michael J. Garvey, Robert Wesner, and Michael Godes, "Comparison of Seasonal and Non-Seasonal Affective Disorders," *American Journal of Psychiatry* 145 (1988): 100.

9.  Siegfried Kasper et al., "Epidemiological Findings of Seasonal Changes in Mood and Behavior: A Telephone Survey of Montgomery County, Maryland," *Archives of General Psychiatry* 46 (1989): 823.

10. Robert N. Golden, "The Efficacy of Light Therapy in the Treatment of Mood Disorders: A Meta-analysis of the Evidence," *American Journal of Psychiatry* 162 (2005): 656.

11. Kelly J. Rohan et al., "A Randomized Controlled Trial of Cognitive-Behavioral Therapy, Light Therapy, and Their Combination for Seasonal Affective Disorder," *Journal of Consulting and Clinical Psychology* 75, no. 3 (June 2007): 489.

12. Michael Terman and Jiuan Su Terman, "Controlled Trial of Naturalistic Dawn Simulation and Negative Air Ionization for Seasonal Affective Disorder," *American Journal of Psychiatry* 163, no. 12 (December 2006): 2126.

## Appendix B: Resources for Further Treatment

1. Randy O. Frost et al., "The Dimensions of Perfectionism," *Cognitive Therapy and Research* 14 (1990): 449; Randy O. Frost and Patricia A. Marten, "Perfectionism and Evaluative Threat," *Cognitive Therapy and Research* 14 (1990): 559.

# INDEX

# ABOUT THE AUTHOR

**Robert L. Leahy** (BA, PhD, Yale University) is the Director of the American Institute for Cognitive Therapy in New York City and Clinical Professor of Psychology in Psychiatry at Weill-Cornell Medical School. He has served as Past President of the Association for Behavioral and Cognitive Therapy, the International Association for Cognitive Psychotherapy and the Academy of Cognitive Therapy. He received the Aaron T. Beck Award for Outstanding Contributions in Cognitive-Behavioral Therapy.

He has authored and edited 17 books, including *The Worry Cure: Seven Steps to Stop Worry from Stopping You* and *Anxiety Free: Unravel Your Fears Before they Unravel You.* His work has been translated into 14 languages; and he has lectured worldwide on cognitive therapy, depression, anxiety, and other issues. He is known throughout the international media as an expert on mental health.

www.cognitivetherapynyc.com

## Hay House Titles of Related Interest

**BE HAPPY! *Release the Power of Happiness in YOU,***
by Robert Holden, Ph.D.

**THE END OF FEAR: *A Spiritual Path for Realists,***
by Richard Schaub, Ph.D., and Bonney Gulino Schaub, R.N.

**IT'S NOT THE END OF THE WORLD:**
***Developing Resilience in Times of Change,*** by Joan Borysenko, Ph.D.

**IT'S THE THOUGHT THAT COUNTS:**
***Why Mind Over Matter Really Works,*** by David R. Hamilton, Ph.D.

**UNSTUCK: *Your Guide to the Seven-Stage Journey out of Depression,***
by James S. Gordon, M.D.

**UP! *A Pragmatic Look at the Direction of Life:***
***365 Ways Today Is the Best Time to Be Alive,*** by David Niven, Ph.D.

All of the above are available at your local bookstore,
or may be ordered by contacting Hay House (see next page).

We hope you enjoyed this Hay House book.
If you would like to receive a free catalogue featuring additional
Hay House books and products, or if you would like information
about the Hay Foundation, please contact:

Hay House UK Ltd
292B Kensal Road • London W10 5BE
Tel: (44) 20 8962 1230; Fax: (44) 20 8962 1239
www.hayhouse.co.uk

\*\*\*

*Published and distributed in the United States of America by:*
Hay House, Inc. • PO Box 5100 • Carlsbad, CA 92018-5100
Tel: (1) 760 431 7695 or (1) 800 654 5126;
Fax: (1) 760 431 6948 or (1) 800 650 5115
www.hayhouse.com

\*\*\*

*Published and distributed in Australia by:*
Hay House Australia Ltd • 18/36 Ralph Street • Alexandria, NSW 2015
Tel: (61) 2 9669 4299, Fax: (61) 2 9669 4144
www.hayhouse.com.au

\*\*\*

*Published and distributed in the Republic of South Africa by:*
Hay House SA (Pty) Ltd • PO Box 990 • Witkoppen 2068
Tel/Fax: (27) 11 467 8904
www.hayhouse.co.za

\*\*\*

*Published and distributed in India by:*
Hay House Publishers India • Muskaan Complex • Plot No.3
B-2• Vasant Kunj • New Delhi - 110 070
Tel: (91) 11 41761620; Fax: (91) 11 41761630
www.hayhouse.co.in

\*\*\*

*Distributed in Canada by:*
Raincoast • 9050 Shaughnessy St • Vancouver, BC V6P 6E5
Tel: (1) 604 323 7100
Fax: (1) 604 323 2600

\*\*\*

Sign up via the Hay House UK website to receive the Hay House
online newsletter and stay informed about what's going on with your
favourite authors. You'll receive bimonthly announcements
about discounts and offers, special events, product highlights,
free excerpts, giveaways, and more!
**www.hayhouse.co.uk**

# JOIN THE HAY HOUSE FAMILY

As the leading self-help, mind, body and spirit publisher in the UK, we'd like to welcome you to our family so that you can enjoy all the benefits our website has to offer.

 **EXTRACTS** from a selection of your favourite author titles

 **COMPETITIONS, PRIZES & SPECIAL OFFERS** Win extracts, money off, downloads and so much more

 **LISTEN** to a range of radio interviews and our latest audio publications

 **CELEBRATE YOUR BIRTHDAY** An inspiring gift will be sent your way

 **LATEST NEWS** Keep up with the latest news from and about our authors

 **ATTEND OUR AUTHOR EVENTS** Be the first to hear about our author events

 **iPHONE APPS** Download your favourite app for your iPhone

 **HAY HOUSE INFORMATION** Ask us anything, all enquiries answered

join us online at **www.hayhouse.co.uk**

 292B Kensal Road, London W10 5BE
T: 020 8962 1230 E: info@hayhouse.co.uk